CANADIAN LIVING'S

DESSERTS

CANADIAN LIVING'S
DESSERTS

By Elizabeth Baird and the Food Writers
of Canadian Living Magazine

A RANDOM HOUSE / MADISON PRESS BOOK

Copyright © 1992 by Telemedia Publishing Inc.
and The Madison Press Limited.

Random House of Canada Limited
1265 Aerowood Drive
Mississauga, Ontario
Canada
L4W 1B9

Canadian Cataloguing in Publication Data

Baird, Elizabeth
Canadian living's desserts

Includes index.
ISBN 0-394-22290-3

1. Desserts.   I. Title.   II. Title: Desserts.

TX773.B35 1992   641.8'6   C92-093677-6

On our cover (clockwise from right): Prizewinning Sour Cherry
Pie (p. 73); (on plate) Four-Layer Chocolate Cake with Amaretto
Cream Sauce (p. 17); fruit cup with Citrus Curd Sauce (p. 149);
(in background) Four-Layer Chocolate Cake awaiting garnish

Produced by
Madison Press Books
40 Madison Avenue
Toronto, Ontario
Canada
M5R 2S1

Printed in Canada

Contents

Introduction 6

*Cakes for Every
Occasion* 8

*Pies, Tarts
and Pastries* 68

Cool Desserts 104

*Puddings, Crumbles,
Crisps and Soufflés* 128

Wonderful Fruit 142

*Cookies, Squares
and Tiny Delights* 152

Credits 180

Index 182

Introduction

Dessert is the sweet finale, the part of the meal we always save room for — a simultaneously teasing and soothing satisfaction. At special dinners, memories of the main course fade after the frozen lemon torte has made its impression. And at a birthday party, it's all preamble until the candle-lit cake is sung to the table.

Simply put, desserts are the best-loved part of any meal. And the making of desserts is both an exacting skill and a well-loved art. Over the years, learning how to roll out a perfect tender-crusted pie, whip up a delicate angel cake or make a silky-smooth custard have been rights of passage and keys to impressive entertaining. Even today, when exercising is a way of life and the emphasis is on eating less fat and fewer calories, desserts are still one of life's little pleasures. In smaller portions, a slice of Coffee Toffee Fudge Cake or a dish of Summer Peach Ice Cream remains a well-deserved treat.

Now, for dessert lovers everywhere, we've created *Canadian Living's* DESSERTS. With over 200 of our very best recipes, this glorious full-color cookbook shows just how to make all those favorite sweet endings — everything from a wickedly rich Mocha Marble Cheesecake to lighter but equally delicious Chocolate Crêpes with a lower-in-fat creamy filling. Included are impressive but easy desserts like Tiramisu, summer fruit flans, semifreddo and frozen ice cream cakes. And we haven't forgotten the old favorites, the kind of desserts nobody wants changed except to make better or lighter, desserts that bring back memories of home and childhood — old-fashioned crisps, creamy Banana Layer Cake, cinnamon-swirled Blueberry Coffee Cake and comforting bread pudding. Make-ahead has been another important feature in selecting the most delicious recipes to appear in DESSERTS. Having a dessert in the freezer or fridge or cooling on the counter is like having dessert insurance — and helps make entertaining friends and family that much easier, and that much more enjoyable.

For everyone with a sweet tooth, here's a generous helping of DESSERTS!

Elizabeth Baird

Elizabeth Baird

Cakes for Every Occasion

For most of us, cakes are the big-moment celebration desserts. Iced and decorated, they mark the milestones of life — birthdays, weddings, anniversaries and graduations. But there are lots of other delicious reasons to get together over a slice of cake, and you'll find them all here. Welcome friends for an informal weekend brunch with delectable Cranberry Coffee Cake, dazzle a dinner party with extra-rich and creamy Mocha Marble Cheesecake, carry a Lemon Raisin Bundt Cake or Chocolate Icebox Cake to the potluck — or crown a family Sunday dinner with our irresistible Chocolate Banana Layer Cake.

Mocha Marble Cheesecake

Cheesecake is always a star-studded crowd pleaser. Dazzle everyone with this mocha marble version that's garnished with white chocolate curls (to make these large curls, see p. 27).

❏ **TIP: Cracks may appear in the cake if it is exposed to sudden temperature change or bakes in too hot an oven for too long. For the required steady oven temperature, resist opening the oven door during baking, and don't neglect the water bath in the shallow pan. It ensures even, slow, moist cooking.**

2	pkg (each 250 g) cream cheese	2
3/4 cup	granulated sugar	175 mL
3	eggs	3
1 tbsp	lemon juice	15 mL
2 tsp	vanilla	10 mL
Pinch	salt	Pinch
3 cups	sour cream	750 mL
2 tsp	instant coffee granules	10 mL
1 tbsp	hot water	15 mL
1/2 lb	semisweet chocolate, melted and cooled	250 g
	CRUST	
1 cup	chocolate wafer crumbs	250 mL
2 tbsp	butter, melted	25 mL

● CRUST: In bowl, stir together crumbs and butter until well moistened. With back of spoon or hands, press onto bottom of lightly greased 8- or 8-1/2-inch (2 or 2.25 L) springform pan. Center pan on foil square; press to side of pan to keep out water when baking cheesecake. Bake in 325°F (160°C) oven for 8 to 10 minutes or until set. Let cool.

● Meanwhile, in large bowl, beat cheese until softened. Gradually beat in sugar; beat for 3 minutes or until smooth and light, scraping down bowl twice. Using low speed, beat in eggs, one at a time, beating well after each addition and scraping down bowl often. Blend in lemon juice, vanilla and salt. Blend in sour cream.

● Dissolve coffee granules in hot water. Divide batter in half. Whisk chocolate into one half; whisk coffee into chocolate mixture. By cupfuls, alternately pour chocolate batter and plain batter over crust. Swirl handle of spoon through both batches, without disturbing crust, to create marbled effect throughout.

● Set pan in larger pan; pour in enough hot water to come 1 inch (2.5 cm) up sides. Bake in 325°F (160°C) oven for 1-1/4 hours or until shine disappears and edge is set yet center still jiggles slightly.

● Turn off oven. Quickly run knife around edge of cake. Let cake cool in oven for 1 hour. Remove from water bath onto rack and remove foil; let cool completely. Cover and refrigerate overnight or for up to 2 days. Just before serving, remove from pan; garnish with chocolate curls.

Light Cranberry Cheesecake

This cheesecake is so creamy and luscious you'll find it hard to believe that it has only half the calories and fat of regular cheesecake.

1/4 cup	graham wafer crumbs	50 mL
1 lb	low-fat cream cheese or ricotta	500 g
1-3/4 cups	1% cottage cheese	425 mL
2/3 cup	granulated sugar	150 mL
2	eggs	2
1/2 cup	light sour cream	125 mL
1 tsp	cornstarch	5 mL
1 tsp	grated lemon rind	5 mL
1 tsp	vanilla	5 mL
	SAUCE	
2 cups	cranberries	500 mL
1/2 cup	orange juice	125 mL
1/3 cup	granulated sugar	75 mL
2 tsp	cornstarch	10 mL
1 tbsp	water	15 mL

● Sprinkle crumbs over greased 9-inch (2.5 L) square cake pan; set aside.

● In food processor, blend cream cheese, cottage cheese and sugar. Blend in eggs, one at a time. Blend in sour cream, cornstarch, lemon rind and vanilla.

● Pour batter over crumbs in pan. Set pan in larger shallow pan; pour in enough hot water to come 1 inch (2.5 cm) up sides of pan. Bake in 325°F (160°C) oven for 50 to 55 minutes or until tester inserted into center comes out clean. Let cool in pan on rack. Cover and refrigerate for at least 8 hours or up to 2 days.

● SAUCE: In saucepan, bring cranberries, orange juice and sugar to boil over medium-high heat, stirring; cook for 3 to 5 minutes or until berries pop, stirring often. Dissolve cornstarch in water and whisk into sauce; cook, whisking, for 2 minutes or until thickened. *(Sauce can be refrigerated for up to 5 days.)* Top each serving of cheesecake with spoonful of sauce.

Tiny Tangerine Cheesecakes

If tangerines are unavailable, use drained canned mandarin orange segments.

2 tbsp	butter, melted	25 mL
1 tbsp	granulated sugar	15 mL
2/3 cup	graham wafer crumbs	150 mL
	FILLING	
1/2 cup	cream cheese, softened (4 oz/125 g)	125 mL
3 tbsp	granulated sugar	50 mL
1	egg	1
1/4 cup	sour cream	50 mL
2 tsp	grated tangerine rind	10 mL
1 tbsp	tangerine juice	15 mL
1-1/2 tsp	tangerine or orange liqueur (optional)	7 mL
	Tangerine segments	

● In bowl, combine butter with sugar; stir in crumbs. Firmly press 2 tsp (10 mL) crumb mixture into each of 24 paper-lined 1-3/4-inch (4.5 cm) tart tins. Bake in 325°F (160°C) oven for 5 to 10 minutes or until light golden.

● FILLING: Meanwhile, in bowl, beat cream cheese, sugar and egg until smooth. Blend in sour cream, tangerine rind and juice, and liqueur (if using).

● Spoon 1 tbsp (15 mL) filling over each base. Bake in 325°F (160°C) oven for about 20 minutes or until just firm to the touch. Let cool in pan on rack. Chill. *(Cheesecakes can be prepared to this point and refrigerated for up to 24 hours.)*

● Remove membranes from tangerine segments; garnish each cake with 2 segments. *(Garnished cheesecakes can be covered and refrigerated for up to 8 hours.)* Makes 2 dozen.

Lemon Mousse Cheesecake

This perfect little dessert serves four. Garnish with candied lemon slices and whipped cream.

❏ TIP: To candy lemon slices and rind, combine 1 cup (250 mL) granulated sugar with 1/4 cup (50 mL) water in saucepan; heat over medium-low heat until sugar is dissolved. Bring to boil; boil for 1 minute. Add lemon slices and rind; gently boil for 5 minutes or until fruit is translucent. Drain and let cool.

1/2 cup	graham wafer crumbs	125 mL
2 tbsp	butter, melted	25 mL
	FILLING	
1/2 lb	cream cheese, softened	250 g
1/2 cup	granulated sugar	125 mL
1 tsp	all-purpose flour	5 mL
1	egg	1
1 tbsp	grated lemon rind	15 mL
3 tbsp	lemon juice	50 mL
1/2 tsp	vanilla	2 mL
1/2 cup	sour cream	125 mL
	Candied lemon slices and rind	
	Whipped cream	

● Combine crumbs with butter; pat into bottom of 6-inch (750 mL) springform pan using back of spoon. Center pan on foil square; press to side of pan to keep out water when baking cheesecake.

● FILLING: In bowl, beat cream cheese with sugar for 2 to 3 minutes or until fluffy. Beat in flour and egg, scraping down side of bowl. Beat in lemon rind, lemon juice, vanilla and sour cream.

● Pour filling over crust; place pan in 8-inch (2 L) square baking dish. Pour in enough hot water to come 1 inch (2.5 cm) up sides of pan. Bake in 350°F (180°C) oven for 40 to 45 minutes or until set.

● Turn off oven; let cake cool in oven for 1 hour. Remove from oven; let cool to room temperature. Cover and refrigerate for at least 3 hours or up to 2 days.

● Gently run knife around edge of pan to loosen; remove cake from pan. Smooth sides with knife. Garnish with candied lemon slices and rind and whipped cream. Makes 4 servings.

CAKE BAKING TIPS

Following the Recipe

● Improvising is fun with most cooking, but not with cake baking. An extra pinch of this or that will disturb a carefully balanced cake recipe. Read through the recipe, assemble ingredients and follow directions carefully.

Measuring

● Measure ingredients carefully and accurately with standard measuring utensils. Use dry measures (the kind that come in a nest), measuring spoons (four in an imperial set, five in a metric set) and a liquid measure with a pouring spout and with the rim above the 1-cup (250 mL) mark.

Preparing Pans

● Prepare the pans before you start mixing. Always use the pan sizes called for. If the pan is too large, the cake will bake too quickly; if too small, the cake will not bake properly or may spill over in the oven. Use shiny metal pans, whenever possible.

● Unless otherwise specified, grease pans with shortening rather than butter or oil. Lining the bottoms with parchment or waxed paper makes removal of the cakes easy.

Using the Oven

● Preheat the oven before you start mixing. Check your oven's temperature occasionally with an oven thermometer to make sure it is accurate.

Flour Choices

● Cake-and-pastry flour produces fine-textured light cakes. If you wish to substitute all-purpose flour, use 1 cup (250 mL) less 2 tbsp (25 mL) of all-purpose for each cup of cake-and-pastry flour called for. All-purpose flour will give a slightly heavier texture.

● If the recipe calls for sifted flour, sift before measuring. Then spoon the flour lightly into a dry measure and level off the top with a knife. Don't tap or pack down.

Eggs

● Eggs separate more easily when cold, but should then be brought to room temperature before using. Our recipes were tested with large eggs.

● When beating egg whites, make sure the bowl and beaters have been carefully washed in warm soapy water, then rinsed and dried. Any trace of grease in the bowl or egg yolk in the whites will prevent the whites from forming stiff peaks. Use glass or metal bowls, not plastic.

Adding Ingredients

● Ingredients should be at room temperature.

● Add dry ingredients alternately with liquid ingredients, making three dry and two liquid additions, and blending lightly after each addition.

Baking

● Bake cakes in the middle of the oven. Arrange pans so that they are at least 1 inch (2.5 cm) from the edges of the oven and do not touch one another.

● Cakes are baked when the tops spring back when touched lightly with the fingers. A tester inserted into the center will come out clean, and usually the cake will have started to pull away from the edges of the pan.

Cooling

● Cool most cakes in the pan for about 5 minutes, then run a knife around the edge and turn out onto wire rack to let cool completely before filling or icing.

Black Currant Mousse Cake

Izabela Kalabis, chef for the Ontario winery, Inniskillin, created this gorgeous and refreshing dessert. It's equally good with raspberries.

❑ **TIP:** To make 1-1/2 cups (375 mL) black currant purée, purée 4 cups (1 L) black currants in food processor; press through sieve. Blend with 2 tbsp (25 mL) water and 2 tsp (10 mL) granulated sugar.

3	eggs	3
1/2 cup	granulated sugar	125 mL
2/3 cup	all-purpose flour	150 mL
	SYRUP	
1/4 cup	granulated sugar	50 mL
2 tbsp	water	25 mL
2 tbsp	cassis liqueur	25 mL
	MOUSSE	
4 tsp	unflavored gelatin	20 mL
1/3 cup	water	75 mL
1-1/4 cups	black currant purée	300 mL
1/2 cup	granulated sugar	125 mL
1 tbsp	cassis	15 mL
1 cup	whipping cream	250 mL
	GLAZE	
1/2 cup	water	125 mL
1 tsp	unflavored gelatin	5 mL
1/4 cup	granulated sugar	50 mL
1/4 cup	black currant purée	50 mL

● In bowl, beat eggs until foamy; gradually beat in sugar. Beat at high speed for 8 to 10 minutes or until pale yellow and batter falls in ribbons when beaters are lifted. Fold in flour in three additions.

● Pour batter into greased and floured 8-1/2-inch (2 L) springform pan; bake in 350°F (180°C) oven for 20 to 25 minutes or until cake pulls away from side of pan. Let cool on rack.

● SYRUP: In small saucepan, cook sugar and water over medium heat until sugar dissolves. Increase heat to high and boil for 1 minute. Remove from heat; stir in cassis. Set aside.

● MOUSSE: In small saucepan, combine gelatin and water; let stand for 5 minutes. Heat over low heat, stirring occasionally, until gelatin dissolves.

● In saucepan, bring black currant purée and sugar to boil over medium-high heat; remove from heat. Stir in gelatin mixture and cassis; transfer to bowl. Refrigerate, stirring occasionally, for 45 to 60 minutes or until chilled and starting to set. Whip cream; fold into black currant mixture.

● ASSEMBLY: Slice cake into 2 layers. Place bottom layer in clean springform pan; place waxed paper collar around cake inside pan, 1 inch (2.5 cm) higher than top of pan. Brush half of the syrup over cake; top with half of the mousse.

● Trim 1/4 inch (5 mm) from edge of second layer; place on top of mousse and brush with remaining syrup. Spread remaining mousse over top and sides of cake. Refrigerate.

● GLAZE: In small saucepan, combine half of the water with gelatin; let stand for 1 minute. Heat over low heat, stirring occasionally, until dissolved.

● In separate small saucepan, bring sugar and remaining water to boil over medium-high heat. Stir in black currant purée; boil, stirring, for 1 minute. Remove from heat; stir in gelatin. Refrigerate for 30 minutes or until cool but not set. Spoon evenly over mousse; refrigerate for at least 1 hour or until set. *(Cake can be made up to 1 day ahead.)* To serve, remove side of pan and collar.

VARIATION

RASPBERRY MOUSSE CAKE: Purée 3 cups (750 mL) raspberries and omit sugar when making the purée. Reduce sugar in mousse to 2 tbsp (25 mL). Use raspberry liqueur instead of cassis.

Photo, opposite page: slice of Chocolate Apricot Mousse Cake (p. 14)

13

Chocolate Apricot Mousse Cake

Use either amaretto or an orange liqueur in this grand-finale cake.

4	eggs, separated	4
1/2 cup	granulated sugar	125 mL
1 tsp	vanilla	5 mL
1 tsp	grated orange rind	5 mL
1/4 tsp	almond extract	1 mL
2/3 cup	all-purpose flour	150 mL
3 tbsp	unsweetened cocoa powder	50 mL

APRICOT SYRUP		
1/3 cup	apricot nectar	75 mL
1/4 cup	granulated sugar	50 mL
1/4 cup	amaretto	50 mL

APRICOT MOUSSE		
1-1/2 cups	dried apricots	375 mL
2	pkg unflavored gelatin	2
2 tbsp	amaretto	25 mL
1 tbsp	lemon juice	15 mL
3 cups	whipping cream	750 mL

CHOCOLATE GLAZE		
6 oz	semisweet chocolate, chopped	175 g
1/3 cup	whipping cream	75 mL
1 tbsp	amaretto	15 mL

● In large bowl, beat egg yolks with 1/4 cup (50 mL) of the sugar until very pale, 5 to 8 minutes. Beat in vanilla, orange rind and almond extract.

● In separate bowl, beat whites until soft peaks form; gradually beat in remaining sugar until stiff peaks form. Fold into yolk mixture. Sift flour and cocoa over top and gently fold in.

● Pour batter into greased 9-inch (2.5 L) springform pan. Bake in 350°F (180°C) oven for 30 to 35 minutes or until tester inserted into center comes out clean. Run knife around edge of cake. Let cake cool in pan on rack.

● APRICOT SYRUP: In saucepan, cook apricot nectar and sugar over medium-high heat until sugar dissolves, about 1 minute. Stir in amaretto. Set aside to let cool.

● APRICOT MOUSSE: In saucepan, cover apricots with 2-1/4 cups (550 mL) water; let soak for 1 hour. Bring to boil; reduce heat to medium-low and cook, covered, until tender, 30 to 40 minutes. In food processor or food mill, purée apricots and water to make about 2-1/2 cups (625 mL). Return to pan and keep warm.

● In small saucepan, sprinkle gelatin over 1/4 cup (50 mL) water; let stand for 1 minute to soften. Heat gently until gelatin dissolves; stir into apricot purée along with amaretto and lemon juice.

● Pour into large bowl set over larger bowl of ice water. Chill, stirring occasionally, until consistency of unbeaten egg whites, about 20 minutes. Whip cream; fold into cooled apricot mixture. Reserve 1/2 cup (125 mL) for garnish.

● ASSEMBLY: Remove side of springform pan and cut cake into 2 layers. Sprinkle cut side of layers with apricot syrup. Place one layer, syrup side up, in 10-inch (3 L) springform pan. Pour in half of the apricot mousse. Top with second layer of cake. Pour in enough of the remaining mousse to come almost to top of pan; smooth out surface. Refrigerate for about 2 hours or until firm.

● CHOCOLATE GLAZE: In saucepan over hot, not boiling, water, melt together chocolate, cream and amaretto, stirring until smooth. Let cool just until spreading consistency, about 15 minutes. Pour over top of cake, swirling gently with spatula. Chill for 30 minutes.

● Using pastry bag fitted with small star tip, pipe reserved mousse into tiny rosettes around edge of cake. Chill, covered, for up to 24 hours.

(left) Chocolate Chestnut Torte (p. 16);
Chocolate Apricot Mousse Cake

Chocolate Chestnut Torte

Indulge your passion for chocolate with this dark, rich, incredibly delicious cake. It's worth the effort — and the calories!

❑ **TIP:** Unsweetened chestnut purée or spread is sold in specialty food shops. You can buy candied violets in cake-decorating supply stores.

8 oz	semisweet chocolate, chopped	250 g
1/4 cup	butter	50 mL
1/2 cup	granulated sugar	125 mL
3	eggs, separated	3
1 cup	unsweetened chestnut purée or spread	250 mL
3 tbsp	orange liqueur	50 mL
1 tsp	vanilla	5 mL
1/3 cup	all-purpose flour	75 mL
	GLAZE	
6 oz	semisweet chocolate, chopped	175 g
1/3 cup	whipping cream	75 mL
2 tbsp	butter	25 mL
1 tbsp	orange liqueur	15 mL
	GARNISH	
6	candied violets Chocolate leaves (see p. 29)	6

● Grease 8-inch (2 L) springform pan; line with circle of parchment or waxed paper. Grease paper.

● In saucepan over hot, not boiling, water, melt chocolate, stirring until smooth. In large bowl, cream butter until light; beat in sugar. Beat in egg yolks, one at a time, beating well after each addition. Beat in chestnut purée, liqueur, vanilla and chocolate. Gently stir in flour.

● In separate bowl, beat egg whites until stiff peaks form; stir one-quarter into chocolate mixture. Gently fold in remaining egg whites.

● Pour batter into prepared pan; bake in 325°F (160°C) oven for 45 to 55 minutes or just until cake begins to come away from side of pan and springs back when touched lightly in center. Let cool in pan on rack. (If cake has puffed and fallen slightly, press down gently to level it.)

● Invert cake onto serving plate. Slide strips of waxed paper under cake to protect plate from glaze.

● GLAZE: In saucepan over hot, not boiling, water, melt chocolate, cream, butter and liqueur, stirring until smooth; let cool to room temperature. Spread over cake; let set for 30 minutes at room temperature. Remove paper strips.

● GARNISH: Arrange candied violets around edge of cake. Garnish with chocolate leaves.

GARNISHING WITH FLOWERS

A fragrant full-blown rose or a sprig of pretty pink geraniums can add a beautiful finishing touch to any special-occasion cake.

● *Make sure the flowers you pick are non-toxic. If in doubt, check with your local horticultural society. Any of the following are safe to use for garnishing desserts: Tulips, Impatiens, Nasturtium, Pansies, Day Lilies, Roses, Violas, Honeysuckle, Freesia, Gladiolus, Chrysanthemums, Borage Flowers, Cornflowers, Lavender, Baby's Breath, Violets, Marigolds, Sweet Peas, Carnations and Geraniums.*

● *Whenever possible, pick fresh unsprayed flowers from your own garden. Avoid using flowers from a florist's shop, since these have probably been sprayed with a pesticide.*

● *Pick flowers early in the day. Rinse blossoms and leaves in cold water, then dry and store in vase of water in refrigerator.*

● *Decorate cakes with individual blossoms, buds or petals. Or, arrange flowers in sprays (as with freesia, baby's breath or lavender).*

Four-Layer Chocolate Cake

Scrumptious on its own, this sour cream-and-chocolate iced cake is even more delicious served with Amaretto Cream Sauce (below) — as we did with the slice featured on our cover. It also makes a perfect birthday cake.

1 cup	butter, softened	250 mL
1-1/2 cups	granulated sugar	375 mL
2	eggs	2
1 tsp	vanilla	5 mL
2 cups	all-purpose flour	500 mL
1/2 cup	unsweetened cocoa powder	125 mL
1 tsp	baking powder	5 mL
1 tsp	baking soda	5 mL
1/4 tsp	salt	1 mL
1-1/2 cups	buttermilk	375 mL
	ICING	
1 lb	semisweet chocolate, coarsely chopped	500 g
2-1/3 cups	sour cream	575 mL
1/4 cup	granulated sugar	50 mL
1 tsp	vanilla	5 mL
	Toasted sliced almonds	
	White chocolate curls	

● In large bowl, cream butter; gradually beat in sugar until light and fluffy. Beat in eggs, one at a time; beat in vanilla. Sift together flour, cocoa, baking powder, baking soda and salt. With wooden spoon, stir into creamed mixture alternately with buttermilk, making 3 additions of dry and 2 of liquid.

● Spoon batter into two greased 8-inch (2 L) springform pans, smoothing tops. Bake in 350°F (180°C) oven for 30 to 35 minutes or until tester inserted into center comes out clean. Let cool on racks for 20 minutes. Remove from pans and let cool completely on racks.

● ICING: In top of double boiler or bowl set over hot, not boiling, water, melt chocolate; remove from heat. Whisk in sour cream, sugar and vanilla until smooth.

● Cut each cake horizontally into 2 layers. Place one layer, cut side up, on serving plate. Slide waxed paper strips under layer to protect plate from icing. Spread cut side with about 3/4 cup (175 mL) icing; cover with bottom half, cut side down, and spread top with 3/4 cup (175 mL) icing.

● Repeat with remaining layers, spreading remaining icing over side and top. Remove paper strips. Garnish border with almonds; garnish top with white chocolate curls. (For tips on making chocolate curls, see p. 27.)

Amaretto Cream Sauce

Change the flavor of this versatile sauce by substituting other liqueurs for the amaretto. For a non-alcoholic orange version, use orange juice concentrate.

3/4 cup	whipping cream	175 mL
1/4 cup	granulated sugar	50 mL
4 tsp	amaretto	20 mL
3/4 cup	plain yogurt	175 mL

● In bowl, whip cream with sugar and amaretto; gently fold in yogurt. *(Sauce can be covered and refrigerated for up to 1 day; whisk lightly before serving.)*
Makes 2-1/4 cups (550 mL).

CHOCOLATE

Types of Chocolate

There are five different kinds of chocolate for desserts and baking: **unsweetened, bittersweet, semisweet, sweet** *and* **white chocolate**. *Always use the chocolate called for in the recipe, and don't let the "bitter" in the bittersweet make you think it's the same as unsweetened chocolate — it's not.*

● *The two primary ingredients in chocolate are cocoa butter (a natural vegetable fat that gives chocolate its voluptuous smooth texture) and chocolate liquor (a thick brown paste that makes it taste like chocolate).*

● **Unsweetened chocolate** *is pure chocolate liquor;* **bittersweet, semisweet** *and* **sweet chocolate** *contain less chocolate liquor and an increasing amount of cocoa butter and sugar. Clearly, the more sugar, the less chocolate. Check labels when buying chocolate and don't be fooled into thinking that chocolate-flavored or artificial chocolate is chocolate.*

● *While* **white chocolate** *is treated like a chocolate, it contains no chocolate liquor. The resulting milder chocolate taste comes from its makeup of sugar, cocoa butter, vanilla*

and milk solids.

● *In recipes calling for* **milk chocolate**, *which is chocolate with milk protein*

added, use a good-quality chocolate bar.

Chocolate Chips

Available in a variety of flavors and sizes, chocolate chips should not be used interchangeably with baking chocolate. Since they do not reharden after heating, chocolate chips are a wonderful cookie, sauce and icing ingredient.

Unsweetened Cocoa Powder

Cocoa is refined pure chocolate liquor.

Storing Chocolate

Wrap chocolate well and store in a cool, dark place. Dark chocolate can be

stored for up to 1 year, while white and milk chocolates, because of their milk solids content, can be stored for up to 9 months.

Melting Chocolate

Chop chocolate and place in top of double boiler or in heatproof bowl set over hot, not boiling, water. When about half of the chocolate is melted, remove from heat and stir until smooth and melted. Or, melt chopped chocolate in microwaveable bowl at Medium (50%) for 45 to

60 seconds per 1 oz (30 g).

● *When melting chocolate, be wary of moisture, as even a single drop of condensation or a wet bowl can cause the chocolate to seize up. On the other hand, when combined with a sufficient amount of liquid (use 1/4 cup/50 mL for 6 oz/175 g of chocolate), it melts smoothly. If chocolate seizes, you can rescue it if you immediately add 1 tbsp (15 mL) vegetable oil per 6 oz (175 g) chocolate. Melt the mixture again and stir until smooth.*

Fast Chocolate Sauce

When you're caught short at dessert time, scoop some ice cream into bowls, add fruit and drizzle with this easy, glossy chocolate sauce.

● *In saucepan over low heat, melt together 1 cup (250 mL) semisweet chocolate chips, 1/4 cup (50 mL) corn syrup, 2 tbsp (25 mL) strong coffee and 1 tbsp (15 mL) butter. Or, microwave in 2-cup (500 mL) measure at Medium-High (70%) for 2 to 4 minutes or until smooth, stirring once.*

● *Sauce can be refrigerated for up to 1 week. Warm to pouring consistency. Makes about 1 cup (250 mL).*

No-Regrets Double Chocolate Cake

This fabulous chocolate-and-cream-filled dessert can be made up to 3 days ahead and stored in the refrigerator.

8 oz	bittersweet or semisweet chocolate	250 g
2 tbsp	water	25 mL
1/2 tsp	salt	2 mL
1/2 tsp	vanilla	2 mL
2 cups	all-purpose flour	500 mL
3/4 cup	cold butter, cut in 1-inch (2.5 cm) cubes	175 mL
	FILLING	
3 cups	whipping cream	750 mL
1-1/2 cups	sifted icing sugar	375 mL
3/4 cup	sifted unsweetened cocoa powder	175 mL
1/4 cup	coffee-flavored liqueur	50 mL
	GARNISH	
	Chocolate curls (see p. 27)	
	Icing sugar	

● In top of double boiler over hot, not boiling, water, melt chocolate; remove from heat. Add water, salt and vanilla; beat until smooth.

● In food processor, combine flour with butter; process with on/off motion until mixture resembles coarse crumbs. Add chocolate mixture; process until dough forms ball. (Alternatively, by hand, cut butter into flour. Make well in center and pour in chocolate mixture; stir just until soft dough forms.)

● Divide dough into three rounds; wrap and refrigerate until firm, about 20 minutes. Between two sheets of waxed paper, roll out each round to 1/8-inch (3 mm) thickness. Remove top sheet of waxed paper. With sharp knife, cut out 9-inch (23 cm) circle; remove excess dough. Carefully lift waxed paper and dough onto baking sheet. Bake in 350°F (180°C) oven for 15 to 20 minutes or until slightly firm to the touch. Transfer to rack; let cool completely. Turn over and remove paper.

● FILLING: In large bowl, beat together cream, sugar and cocoa; fold in liqueur.

● ASSEMBLY: Place one cake round on plate; slide waxed paper strips under round to protect from icing. Spread with one-quarter of the filling. Repeat with remaining rounds and filling; spread remaining filling over side of cake. Cover and refrigerate for at least 24 hours. *(Cake can be refrigerated for up to 3 days.)* Let stand at room temperature for 30 minutes before serving.

● Garnish with chocolate curls; dust with icing sugar.

Chocolate Banana Layer Cake

When it comes to sweet marriages, banana and chocolate are a match made in heaven! Take a classic moist banana cake and update it with two kinds of chocolate — dark chocolate both in and on the cake, plus a smooth white chocolate icing. For taste, this is simply the ultimate banana layer cake. For looks, this is spectacular and professional-looking — the crowning touch to any meal.

❏ **TIP: To protect the plate from icing, slip strips of waxed paper under the bottom cake layer and remove them before pouring the ganache (melted chocolate and cream glaze) over top.**

❏ **TIP: If ganache becomes too firm, gently rewarm over hot, not boiling, water until pourable.**

❏ **TIP: A palette knife is a broad-bladed knife that finishes icings smoothly.**

4	bananas, sliced	4
	Melted chocolate (about 1 oz/30 g)	

CAKE		
3/4 cup	butter, softened	175 mL
1 cup	granulated sugar	250 mL
3	eggs	3
1-1/2 tsp	vanilla	7 mL
1/2 cup	sour cream	125 mL
3 cups	sifted cake-and-pastry flour	750 mL
1-1/2 tsp	baking soda	7 mL
4 oz	semisweet chocolate, chopped	125 g
1-1/2 cups	mashed bananas	375 mL

WHITE CHOCOLATE ICING		
3 cups	whipping cream	750 mL
10 oz	white chocolate, chopped	300 g
1 tsp	vanilla	5 mL

DARK CHOCOLATE GANACHE		
1/2 cup	whipping cream	125 mL
4 oz	semisweet chocolate, chopped	125 g

● CAKE: In bowl, cream butter with sugar until fluffy. Beat in eggs, one at a time, then vanilla. Beat in sour cream. Combine flour, baking soda and chocolate; add in three additions to creamed mixture alternately with two additions of bananas, mixing just until flour is incorporated. Spoon into two greased 8-1/2-inch (2.25 L) springform pans, smoothing tops.

● Bake in 350°F (180°C) oven for 35 to 40 minutes or until tops spring back when touched. Let cool on rack for 20 minutes. Remove sides of pans; let cool completely.

● WHITE CHOCOLATE ICING: In saucepan, bring half of the cream to boil; pour over chocolate in bowl, whisking until melted. Add vanilla. Refrigerate until chilled, about 1 hour, whisking often.

● On medium speed, beat chocolate mixture just until ridges hold shape. Beat remaining cream just until soft peaks form; gently fold into chocolate mixture.

● With serrated knife, slice cakes in half horizontally. Place a top layer, cut side up, on plate; slide waxed paper strips under cake to protect plate. Spread top with 3/4 cup (175 mL) icing; cover with single layer of bananas, leaving 1/2-inch (1 cm) border. Cover with one bottom cake layer, cut side down; repeat with icing and bananas.

● Add remaining top layer, cut side up; repeat with the icing and bananas. Top with remaining cake layer, cut side down.

● Using palette knife, cover cake smoothly with remaining icing. Refrigerate until firm, 1-1/2 hours.

● DARK CHOCOLATE GANACHE: Meanwhile, bring cream to boil; pour over chocolate in small bowl, whisking until melted. Let cool for 20 minutes or until at room temperature and still pourable.

● Pour over center of cake, spreading to edge with clean palette knife if necessary, and letting some flow down sides. Refrigerate until firm, about 40 minutes, or up to 1 day.

● To serve, drizzle melted chocolate with fork over remaining bananas; let set. Arrange on cake. Slice with serrated knife.

Use serrated knife to cut cakes in half to make four layers.

Cover three layers with icing and bananas, then place remaining plain layer on top.

To ensure a smooth finish to the icing, wipe the palette knife often with a clean damp cloth.

Coffee Toffee Fudge Cake

This miniature cake is pure indulgence, and suits an intimate dinner for four.

❏ TIP: The recipe can be doubled to fit an 8-inch (2 L) springform pan. Bake this version for 10 minutes longer.

4 oz	semisweet chocolate, coarsely chopped	125 g
1/4 cup	butter, cut in pieces	50 mL
2 tbsp	coffee liqueur	25 mL
1-1/2 tsp	instant coffee granules	7 mL
1/4 cup	packed brown sugar	50 mL
2	eggs, separated	2
1/3 cup	all-purpose flour	75 mL
Pinch	each salt and cream of tartar	Pinch
2 tbsp	granulated sugar	25 mL
2	bars (each 39 g) milk chocolate-covered toffee, finely chopped	2

CHOCOLATE GLAZE		
2 tbsp	whipping cream	25 mL
1 tbsp	coffee liqueur	15 mL
1 tsp	instant coffee granules	5 mL
2 oz	semisweet chocolate, coarsely chopped	60 g

● In saucepan, heat semisweet chocolate, butter, liqueur and coffee granules over medium-low heat, stirring constantly, until smooth. Remove from heat; whisk in brown sugar until dissolved. Whisk in egg yolks, one at a time, whisking well after each addition. Whisk in flour in three additions; let cool for 5 minutes.

● In bowl and using electric mixer, beat together egg whites, salt and cream of tartar until soft peaks form; gradually beat in granulated sugar until stiff peaks form. Whisk one-third into chocolate batter; fold in remaining egg whites. Gently fold in half of the chopped chocolate bars.

● Pour into well-greased 5-inch (750 mL) round cake pan. Run knife through batter to remove air bubbles. Bake in 350°F (180°C) oven for 35 minutes or until top is firm to the touch and crust has formed. Let cool on rack for 10 minutes. Remove from pan and let cool completely.

● CHOCOLATE GLAZE: In small saucepan, bring cream, liqueur and coffee granules to boil over medium-high heat. Immediately stir in chocolate; remove from heat and whisk until smooth. Let cool to room temperature. Pour over cake, letting some drip down sides. Garnish with remaining chopped chocolate bar. Refrigerate for at least 1 hour or until glaze is set. *(Cake can be covered and refrigerated for up to 5 days or frozen for up to 1 week.)* Makes 4 servings.

LINING CAKE AND BAKING PANS

A smart baker always prepares the pan before preparing the recipe. There are three ways to ensure easy removal of cakes and loaves: greasing pans, flouring greased pans or lining prepared pans with paper.

Greasing
● *Grease pans well with shortening, including all corners. This is the most elementary method and works for most recipes.*

Flouring
● *Sprinkle about 1 tbsp (15 mL) all-purpose flour into greased pan and tilt the pan until well coated on bottom and sides. Tap any remaining flour back into flour storage container.*

Lining with Paper
● *When called for in the recipe, line the bottom of the prepared pan with parchment paper or greased waxed paper. Parchment paper costs more than waxed paper, but it can be wiped off and used over and over again.*

● *It's easy to run a knife around the sides of the pan, so lining the sides with paper is unnecessary unless it's called for in the recipe to keep the edges of a cake from drying out, protect the color of ingredients or provide a collar for the pan.*

Microwave Chocolate Cake

Topped with a rich but not-too-sweet chocolate icing, this delicious cake takes only 20 minutes to make. So, go ahead — serve it tonight!

❑ **TIP: For easy removal of the cake from the pan, line the bottom with waxed paper. If you secure the paper with a few dabs of shortening, it won't slip when you spread the thick batter.**

1/2 cup	butter, softened	125 mL
3/4 cup	packed brown sugar	175 mL
1	egg	1
1 cup	sour cream	250 mL
1 tsp	vanilla	5 mL
1-1/4 cups	all-purpose flour	300 mL
1/4 cup	unsweetened cocoa powder	50 mL
3/4 tsp	baking powder	4 mL
3/4 tsp	baking soda	4 mL
1/4 tsp	salt	1 mL

CHOCOLATE ICING

1 cup	semisweet chocolate chips	250 mL
1/4 cup	butter	50 mL
1/4 cup	sour cream	50 mL

SUGAR SYRUP

1/4 cup	granulated sugar	50 mL
1/4 cup	water	50 mL
2 tbsp	coffee or coffee liqueur	25 mL

GARNISH

White Chocolate Hearts (recipe follows)

● In bowl, cream together butter and sugar until fluffy; beat in egg, sour cream and vanilla. Sift together flour, cocoa, baking powder, baking soda and salt; stir into butter mixture.

● Spread in waxed paper-lined microwaveable 8-inch (2 L) square baking dish; microwave at Medium (50%) for 6 minutes, rotating once. Microwave at High for 2 to 3 minutes or until tester inserted into center comes out clean, rotating once. Let stand directly on counter for 10 minutes. Run knife around edges to loosen; turn out onto rack and let cool completely. Transfer to serving plate.

● CHOCOLATE ICING: Meanwhile, in 2-cup (500 mL) microwaveable measure, combine chocolate chips and butter; microwave at Medium (50%) for 1-1/2 to 2 minutes or until almost melted. Let stand, stirring often, until melted; blend in sour cream. Chill for 30 minutes or until spreading consistency.

● SUGAR SYRUP: Meanwhile, in separate 2-cup (500 mL) microwaveable measure, combine sugar and water; microwave at High for 1-1/2 to 2 minutes or until dissolved. Let cool; stir in coffee.

● GARNISH: Drizzle syrup over cake; spread icing over top and sides. Garnish with White Chocolate Hearts.

WHITE CHOCOLATE HEARTS
Pour 2 oz (60 g) melted white chocolate onto waxed paper; cover with another sheet of waxed paper. Lightly roll out to 1/8-inch (3 mm) thickness. Refrigerate on baking sheet until firm but not hard, about 3 minutes. Using heart-shaped cutter, cut out shapes.

Chocolate Cassata Cake

This sensational chilled cake is filled with a delicious mixture of ricotta cheese, brandied fruit, grated chocolate and nuts — then, it's slathered with chocolaty whipped cream. Definitely a holiday grand finale!

6	eggs	6
2 cups	granulated sugar	500 mL
2 cups	sifted cake-and-pastry flour	500 mL
2 tsp	baking powder	10 mL
1/2 tsp	salt	2 mL
1/2 cup	hot milk	125 mL
1 tsp	vanilla	5 mL
	RICOTTA FILLING	
1/2 cup	raisins	125 mL
1/4 cup	brandy or rum	50 mL
3 cups	ricotta cheese	750 mL
3/4 cup	icing sugar	175 mL
1/2 tsp	cinnamon	2 mL
2 oz	semisweet chocolate, grated	60 g
1/2 cup	chopped candied red cherries or candied ginger	125 mL
1/2 cup	slivered almonds, toasted	125 mL
1/2 cup	whipping cream, whipped	125 mL
	CHOCOLATE WHIPPED CREAM	
1-1/2 cups	whipping cream	375 mL
1/3 cup	unsweetened cocoa powder	75 mL
1/3 cup	granulated sugar	75 mL
	GARNISH	
1	good-quality milk chocolate bar (8 oz/250 g)	1

● In large bowl, beat eggs until pale and slightly thickened, about 2 minutes. Gradually beat in sugar; beat for 5 minutes longer or until batter falls in ribbons when beaters are lifted.

● Stir together flour, baking powder and salt; blend into egg mixture alternately with milk. Stir in vanilla.

● Pour batter into greased and floured 10-inch (4 L) tube pan. Bake in 350°F (180°C) oven for 50 to 60 minutes or until top springs back when lightly touched. Turn pan upside down and let cake hang until cool. Freeze in pan for 30 minutes. Remove from pan and slice into 4 layers.

● RICOTTA FILLING: In small bowl, soak raisins in brandy; set aside. In large bowl, beat ricotta until smooth; beat in sugar and cinnamon until well blended. Stir in chocolate, cherries, almonds, raisins and brandy. Fold in whipped cream.

● ASSEMBLY: Place one cake layer on plate; slide waxed paper strips under layer to protect plate. Top with one-third of the ricotta filling. Repeat with second and third layers. Top with remaining layer.

● CHOCOLATE WHIPPED CREAM: Meanwhile, in large bowl, combine whipping cream, cocoa and sugar. Refrigerate for 1 hour before whipping to stiff peaks. Frost cake immediately. Refrigerate cake for at least 6 hours or overnight.

● GARNISH: Warm chocolate in 200°F (100°C) oven for 2 to 3 minutes, or microwave at Medium (50%) for about 30 seconds, or until slightly softened but not melted. Using sharp vegetable peeler, peel off large curls from bottom of bar, rewarming chocolate if necessary. Garnish cake with curls. Serve chilled. Makes about 16 servings.

Fudgy Hanukkah Cake

This fabulous special-occasion cake is low in fat — but not in great taste! A sprinkling of edible gold glitter adds a festive touch.

❏ TIP: At Hanukkah, it's traditional to give children small gifts of money (called Hanukkah gelt), either real or chocolate. Tuck gold-wrapped chocolate coins into the batter to surprise your youngsters with a little treat.

1-1/2 cups	packed brown sugar	375 mL
1-1/4 cups	all-purpose flour	300 mL
1/2 cup	sifted unsweetened cocoa powder	125 mL
1-1/2 tsp	baking soda	7 mL
3/4 tsp	baking powder	4 mL
Pinch	each cinnamon and salt	Pinch
1	each egg and egg white	1
3/4 cup	buttermilk	175 mL
3/4 cup	strong coffee	175 mL
1/3 cup	vegetable oil	75 mL
	ICING	
1/4 cup	sifted unsweetened cocoa powder	50 mL
4 tsp	granulated sugar	20 mL
4 tsp	cornstarch	20 mL
1/2 cup	skim milk	125 mL
1/4 cup	corn syrup	50 mL
1 tsp	vanilla	5 mL
	Edible gold glitter (optional)	

● In bowl, combine brown sugar, flour, cocoa, baking soda, baking powder, cinnamon and salt. In separate bowl, beat together egg and egg white; beat in buttermilk, coffee and oil.

● Make a well in sugar mixture; pour coffee mixture into well and whisk just until blended. Pour into greased 8-inch (2 L) square cake pan. Tap pan gently on counter to eliminate air bubbles.

● Bake in 350°F (180°C) oven for 30 to 40 minutes or until tester inserted into center comes out clean and cake springs back when pressed. Let cool in pan on rack for 20 minutes. *(Cake can be frozen for up to 2 months.)*

● ICING: In small saucepan, combine cocoa, sugar and cornstarch. Whisk in milk until blended, then corn syrup and vanilla. Bring to boil over medium-high heat, whisking constantly; reduce heat to low and cook, whisking, for 1 to 2 minutes or until thickened and glossy. Let cool for 5 minutes. Spread evenly over cake. Sprinkle with glitter (if using). Makes 12 servings.

Chocolate Cake with Candied Orange and Ginger

Not many ingredients, not hard to make — and impossible to resist! Garnish this rich and moist chocolate cake with strips of orange rind.

6 oz	semisweet chocolate, coarsely chopped	175 g
3/4 cup	butter	175 mL
4	eggs, separated	4
3/4 cup	granulated sugar	175 mL
1 cup	ground toasted almonds	250 mL
1/4 cup	all-purpose flour	50 mL
3/4 cup	each candied orange peel and candied ginger, diced	175 mL
	GLAZE	
8 oz	semisweet chocolate, chopped	250 g
1/2 cup	whipping cream	125 mL
2 tbsp	orange liqueur	25 mL

● Grease 9-inch (2.5 L) springform pan; line with parchment or waxed paper.

● In top of double boiler over hot, not boiling, water, melt chocolate and butter; let cool to room temperature.

● In bowl, beat egg yolks with 1/2 cup (125 mL) of the sugar until light, about 5 minutes. Stir in chocolate mixture. Combine almonds and flour; stir into chocolate mixture along with candied peel and ginger.

● In bowl, beat egg whites until soft peaks form; gradually beat in remaining sugar until stiff peaks form. Stir one-quarter into chocolate mixture; gently fold in remaining egg white mixture.

● Spoon batter into prepared pan. Bake in 350°F (180°C) oven for 35 to 40 minutes or until edges are firm to touch. Let cool in pan on rack for 1 hour. Remove to serving plate.

● GLAZE: In double boiler over hot, not boiling, water, melt chocolate with cream and liqueur, whisking until smooth. Pour over cake, coating sides evenly.

MAKING CHOCOLATE CURLS

Chocolate curls are an impressive finishing touch for any dessert, including cakes. Here are several ways to make them.

With Blocks of Chocolate

● *Even with small blocks of chocolate, it is possible to make curls. The secret is warming the chocolate to the right temperature, and having enough chocolate. You will need about 5 oz (150 g) to cover the top of a 9-inch (23 cm) cake, cream pie or other dessert.*

● *Set chocolate, 1 oz (30 g) square at a time, on microwaveable plate;* microwave at High for 30 seconds. Or, handhold wrapped chocolate square for about 1 minute or until softened but not melted.

● *Hold the chocolate firmly and use firm, even pressure.* **For wide curls**, *slowly draw a vegetable peeler along the underside of square;* **for smaller curls**, *draw peeler along the narrow side.*

On Baking Sheets

● *Melt chocolate and spread evenly and thinly (less than 1/8 inch/3 mm) with palette knife over surface of clean baking* sheet. Refrigerate until set but not hard, about 5 minutes, letting warm again at room temperature if necessary.

● **For small curls**, *use a spoon held at 30° angle and scrape across chocolate toward you, forming curls.* **For large curls**, *scrape a knife or scraper across chocolate in opposite direction, forming curls of desired width.*

Grated Curls

● *These are the easiest to make, and are especially pretty on chilled desserts. You get the longest curls if* you use a large chunk of chocolate.

● *Either buy chunks in bulk and store for repeated use, or make your own block of chocolate by melting 12 oz (375 g) chopped chocolate over hot, not boiling, water and pouring into a small foil-lined loaf pan. Let harden thoroughly in refrigerator; peel off foil.*

● *Let block soften at room temperature for about 1 hour before grating. Use firm, even pressure and grate long side of chocolate block against coarse side of grater.*

Chocolate Wedding Cake

Make the happy day even more special by serving an elegant dark chocolate cake that will make chocolate lovers rejoice. Make one batch of the cake recipe for the top tier of the wedding cake and a double batch for the bottom one.

❏ **TIP: You can bake the cake up to 1 month ahead, then carefully wrap and freeze. Up to 2 days ahead, decorate thawed cake with icing and refrigerate until just before serving. Make sure that the refrigerator will be able to accommodate the assembled cake.**

❏ **TIP: To make decorating easier, place cake on a turntable.**

❏ **TIP: If you don't want to make chocolate roses and leaves, they can also be purchased at some cake-decorating supply stores. Or, garnish cake with fresh flowers (see p. 16).**

1 cup	butter, softened	250 mL
1-1/2 cups	granulated sugar	375 mL
2	eggs	2
1 tsp	vanilla	5 mL
2 cups	all-purpose flour	500 mL
1/2 cup	unsweetened cocoa powder	125 mL
1 tsp	each baking powder and baking soda	5 mL
1/2 tsp	salt	2 mL
1-1/2 cups	buttermilk	375 mL
6 cups	Chocolate Icing (recipe follows)	1.5 L
1-1/2 cups	finely chopped hazelnuts (optional)	375 mL

GARNISH

Chocolate Roses
(recipe follows)

Chocolate Leaves
(recipe follows)

● Top Cake Tier: Grease and flour 8-inch (2.5 L) round cake pan that is at least 3 inches (8 cm) deep. Line base with waxed paper and set aside.

● In large bowl, cream butter; gradually beat in sugar, beating until light. Beat in eggs, one at a time; beat in vanilla. Sift together flour, cocoa, baking powder, baking soda and salt; stir into butter mixture alternately with buttermilk, beginning and ending with flour mixture. Spoon into prepared pan.

● Bake in 350°F (180°C) oven for 70 to 80 minutes or until tester inserted into center comes out clean and top of cake springs back when lightly touched. Let cool for 5 minutes in pan on rack; loosen edges and invert cake onto rack. Peel off paper and let cool completely.

● Bottom Cake Tier: Grease and flour 12-inch (6 L) round cake pan that is at least 3 inches (8 cm) deep. Line base with waxed paper; set aside. Double all ingredients in cake recipe; prepare as directed, but bake for

85 to 95 minutes or until tester inserted into center comes out clean.

● Assembly: Place bottom tier on serving platter. Slide strips of waxed paper under cake to protect platter from icing. Place top tier on slightly smaller round of foil-lined cardboard. Spread icing over top and side of each tier, reserving enough for piping. Coat side of each tier with hazelnuts (if using).

● Insert plastic straw supports and stack tiers as directed in Carrot Wedding Cake (next page). Using pastry bag fitted with 1/4-inch (5 mm) star tip, pipe remaining icing around edges in shell pattern. Arrange chocolate roses and leaves over cake. Refrigerate for up to 2 days. Makes 50 to 60 servings.

CHOCOLATE ICING

3	pkg (350 g each) chocolate chips (6 cups/1.5 L)	3
3 cups	sour cream	750 mL
1/4 cup	hazelnut or coffee liqueur (optional)	50 mL

● In top of double boiler over hot, not boiling, water, melt chocolate chips. Stir in sour cream, and liqueur (if using); beat until smooth. Cover and refrigerate for about 15 minutes or until spreading consistency. Makes about 6 cups (1.5 L).

CHOCOLATE ROSES

4 oz	semisweet chocolate, chopped	125 g
3 tbsp	corn syrup	50 mL
1/8 tsp	water	0.5 mL

● In top of double boiler over hot, not boiling, water, melt chocolate; stir in corn syrup and water. Pour onto plastic wrap-lined baking sheet; cover with plastic wrap. Let stand for at least 6 hours or until no longer sticky. Remove plastic wrap and

place chocolate dough between sheets of waxed paper; roll out to 1/16-inch (1 mm) thickness. Using 1-1/2- or 2-inch (3.5 or 5 cm) round cutter, cut out circles for petals. Form trimmings into 1/2-inch (1 cm) balls; shape into cones for centers of roses.

● Using rolling pin, press outer edge of one half of each circle as thinly as possible. Wrap thick sides of several circles around cone, overlapping to form rose. Carefully curl back petals. Transfer to waxed paper-lined baking sheet; cover and refrigerate for up to 1 week.

CHOCOLATE LEAVES

Using pastry or paint brush, paint undersides of clean dry rose leaves with 4 oz (125 g) melted chocolate, taking care not to drip over edges or onto front of leaves. Place leaves, chocolate side up, on waxed paper-lined baking sheet and refrigerate until firm. Carefully peel rose leaves from chocolate.

Carrot Wedding Cake

A luscious cream cheese icing and a garnish of fresh flowers add the finishing touches to this elegant cake. Make one batch of the cake recipe for the top tier of the wedding cake and a double batch for the bottom one.

❑ **TIP:** To smooth icing, dip palette knife into hot water and wipe off. The heated knife sliding over the icing will melt it just enough to make surface smooth and shiny.

❑ **TIP:** To make cardboard round for top tier of cake, use cake pan as guide and cut out circle, trimming to make it slightly smaller than cake. Cover with foil, securing underside with tape.

❑ **TO SERVE CAKE:** Remove top tier with 2 metal spatulas and set aside. Cut circle on bottom tier about 2 inches (5 cm) from outside. Cut this border into small slices. Repeat once more. Cut center portion into wedges. Repeat with top tier, cutting only 1 circle.

4	eggs	4
1 cup	granulated sugar	250 mL
1 cup	packed brown sugar	250 mL
1 cup	vegetable oil	250 mL
2 cups	all-purpose flour	500 mL
2 tsp	baking powder	10 mL
1-1/2 tsp	cinnamon	7 mL
1 tsp	salt	5 mL
1/2 tsp	baking soda	2 mL
1/2 tsp	nutmeg	2 mL
3 cups	grated raw carrots	750 mL
1/2 cup	raisins	125 mL
1/2 cup	finely chopped pecans or walnuts (optional)	125 mL
6 cups	Cream Cheese Icing (recipe follows)	1.5 L

GARNISH

Fresh roses, fern leaves and baby's breath

● TOP CAKE TIER: Grease and flour 8-inch (2.5 L) round cake pan that is at least 3 inches (8 cm) deep. Line base with waxed paper and set aside.

● In large bowl, beat eggs well. Gradually beat in granulated and brown sugars, beating until light. Gradually beat in oil. Mix together flour, baking powder, cinnamon, salt, baking soda and nutmeg; stir into egg mixture. Stir in carrots, raisins, and pecans (if using). Spoon into prepared pan.

● Bake in 350°F (180°C) oven for 1-1/4 to 1-1/2 hours or until tester inserted into center comes out clean and cake springs back when lightly touched. Let cool for 5 minutes in pan on rack; loosen edges and invert cake onto rack. Peel off paper and let cool completely.

● BOTTOM CAKE TIER: Grease and flour 12-inch (6 L) round cake pan that is at least 3 inches (8 cm) deep. Line base with waxed paper; set aside. Double all ingredients in cake recipe; prepare as directed, but bake for 1-1/2 to 1-3/4 hours or until tester inserted into center comes out clean.

● ASSEMBLY: Place bottom tier on serving platter. Slide strips of waxed paper under cake to protect platter from icing. Place top tier on slightly smaller round of foil-lined cardboard. Spread icing over top and side of each tier, reserving enough for piping.

● Invert same small cake pan over center of bottom tier and lightly trace outline. Cut 6 plastic straws exact height of bottom tier. Evenly space 5 straws 1 inch (2.5 cm) inside marked circle; insert remaining straw in center. Using 2 spatulas, center top tier on bottom. Remove waxed paper strips. Using pastry bag fitted with 1/4-inch (5 mm) star tip, pipe remaining icing around edges in shell pattern. Refrigerate for up to 2 days.

● GARNISH: Just before serving, garnish cake with flowers and leaves. Makes 50 to 60 servings.

CREAM CHEESE ICING

2 lb	cream cheese, softened	1 kg
1 cup	butter, softened	250 mL
1 tbsp	vanilla	15 mL
12 cups	(approx) sifted icing sugar	3 L

● In bowl, cream together cream cheese, butter and vanilla. Gradually beat in enough of the icing sugar to give smooth spreadable consistency. Makes about 6 cups (1.5 L).

Strawberry Buttercream Cake

Celebrate summer and berry season with this beautiful strawberry-layered cake. Ice it the day it's served and use a serrated knife for cutting.

❏ **TIP:** Serve your favorite fruit and wine punch with this strawberry cake.
To dress up the punch bowl, make an ice ring instead of simply adding ice cubes. Fill ring mould one-third full with cooled boiled water. Float strawberry slices and mint leaves on top; freeze. Add cooled boiled water to cover strawberry slices; freeze. Repeat layering of strawberry slices, then fill with cooled boiled water and freeze.

6	eggs	6
1 cup	granulated sugar	250 mL
1 tsp	vanilla	5 mL
1 cup	all-purpose flour	250 mL
1/2 tsp	baking powder	2 mL
Pinch	salt	Pinch
1/3 cup	butter, melted	75 mL

BUTTERCREAM ICING		
4 cups	strawberries	1 L
2	egg whites	2
1-1/2 cups	granulated sugar	375 mL
1/3 cup	water	75 mL
1/4 tsp	cream of tartar	1 mL
1 lb	unsalted butter	500 g
1 tsp	vanilla	5 mL

● Grease and flour two 9-inch (1.5 L) round cake pans. Line bottoms with waxed paper.

● In large deep bowl, beat eggs at high speed until foamy. Gradually beat in sugar, then beat at high speed for 8 to 10 minutes or until pale and batter falls in ribbons when beaters are lifted. Beat in vanilla.

● Sift together flour, baking powder and salt; sift one-third over egg mixture and fold in. Repeat twice. Fold in melted butter. Pour into prepared pans and spread. Bake in 325°F (160°C) oven for 25 to 30 minutes or until tops spring back when lightly touched. Let cool in pans on racks for 5 minutes. Turn out onto racks; remove paper and let cool completely.

● BUTTERCREAM ICING: Set aside 3 berries for garnish. In food processor or blender, purée 2 cups (500 mL) of the berries. Pass through sieve; set aside. Halve remaining berries; set aside.

● In large bowl and using electric mixer, beat together egg whites, sugar, water and cream of tartar for 1 minute. Place bowl over hot, not boiling, water; beat for 7 minutes or until very thick and fluffy. Remove from heat; beat for 4 minutes or until cooled to room temperature.

● In separate bowl, beat butter until softened; gradually beat into egg white mixture until thickened and spreadable. Blend in vanilla. Gradually beat in strawberry purée.

● ASSEMBLY: Set aside 1 cup (250 mL) icing for piping. Place one layer of cake, top side down, on serving platter. Slide strips of waxed paper under cake to protect platter. Spread about 1 cup (250 mL) icing over top. Arrange halved berries on top. Spread about 1 cup (250 mL) icing over berries.

● Place second cake layer on top. Spread remaining icing over top and side of cake. Using pastry bag fitted with 1/4-inch (5 mm) open star tip, pipe reserved icing into 12 rosettes around top edge of cake. Garnish with reserved whole berries. Remove paper strips. *(Cake can be refrigerated for up to 8 hours; let stand at room temperature for 30 minutes before serving.)*

Classic Angel Food Cake

Served with fresh fruit or Warm Orange Sauce (next page), this light-as-a-feather cake makes a dessert special enough for any occasion.

1 cup	sifted cake-and-pastry flour	250 mL
1-1/2 cups	granulated sugar	375 mL
1-1/2 cups	egg whites, at room temperature (about 11 eggs)	375 mL
1 tbsp	lemon juice	15 mL
1 tsp	cream of tartar	5 mL
1/2 tsp	salt	2 mL
1 tsp	vanilla	5 mL
1/2 tsp	almond extract	2 mL

● Into bowl, sift together flour and 3/4 cup (175 mL) of the sugar; sift again. Set aside.

● In large mixing bowl (not plastic), beat egg whites until foamy. Add lemon juice, cream of tartar and salt; beat until soft peaks form.

● Gradually add remaining sugar, 2 tbsp (25 mL) at a time, beating until stiff glossy peaks form.

● A quarter at a time, sift flour mixture over egg whites, gently folding in each addition until well blended. Gently fold in vanilla and almond extract. Pour into ungreased 10-inch (4 L) tube pan.

● Run spatula through batter to eliminate any large air pockets. Smooth top with spatula. Bake in 350°F (180°C) oven for 40 to 45 minutes or until cake springs back when lightly touched.

● Turn pan upside down and let hang on legs attached to pan, or on inverted funnel or bottle, until completely cool. Remove from pan. *(Cake can be stored in airtight container for up to 2 days or frozen for up to 1 month.)*

VARIATIONS

CITRUS ANGEL FOOD CAKE: Fold in 1 tbsp (15 mL) each grated lemon and lime rind with vanilla. Omit almond extract.

CHOCOLATE-FLECKED ANGEL FOOD CAKE: Omit almond extract; fold in 1 oz (30 g) finely grated semisweet chocolate along with vanilla.

Warm Orange Sauce

Spoon this tangy dessert sauce over slices of angel food or pound cake.

2	seedless oranges	2
1/2 cup	orange juice	125 mL
1/4 cup	granulated sugar	50 mL
2 tsp	cornstarch	10 mL
1	cinnamon stick	1

● Using vegetable peeler, peel off thin outer rind of half of one orange. Cut into matchstick-size strips to make about 1/4 cup (50 mL). Cover strips with boiling water. Let stand until cool.

● Peel oranges, cutting away outside membrane. Slice thinly.

● In saucepan, combine orange juice, sugar, cornstarch, cinnamon stick and drained rind. Bring to boil, stirring; cook for 1 minute. Add orange slices and heat just to warm through. Discard cinnamon. Makes about 1 cup (250 mL).

Banana Spice Cake

We've lightened this quick and easy cake by using yogurt instead of sour cream to lower the fat.

❏ TIP: Ripe yellow bananas, freckled and fragrant, make all the difference in this cake. Plan ahead to let bananas ripen a few days at room temperature.
For faster ripening, place bananas in bag.

1/3 cup	butter, softened	75 mL
1 cup	granulated sugar	250 mL
1	each egg and egg white	1
1/3 cup	yogurt	75 mL
1 tsp	vanilla	5 mL
2 cups	sifted cake-and-pastry flour	500 mL
2 tsp	baking powder	10 mL
3/4 tsp	cinnamon	4 mL
1/2 tsp	baking soda	2 mL
Pinch	each nutmeg, allspice and salt	Pinch
1 cup	mashed bananas	250 mL
1 tbsp	icing sugar	15 mL

● In bowl, cream together butter and sugar. Beat in egg and egg white, one at a time, beating well after each addition. Add yogurt and vanilla.

● Stir together flour, baking powder, cinnamon, baking soda, nutmeg, allspice and salt; fold into egg mixture alternately with bananas.

● Spoon into greased 6-cup (1.5 L) bundt pan or 8-inch (2 L) springform pan, spreading higher at edges.

● Bake in 350°F (180°C) oven for 35 to 40 minutes or until cake springs back when touched. Remove to rack and let cool. Dust with icing sugar.

Windblown Cake

This pretty apricot-flavored cake is as light and airy as the name suggests.

❏ TIP: Foam cakes, baked in ungreased tube pans, should be inverted immediately after removal from the oven. They should be cooled completely this way before removing them from the pan.

3	eggs, separated	3
3/4 cup	cold water	175 mL
1 cup	granulated sugar	250 mL
1-2/3 cups	sifted cake-and-pastry flour	400 mL
1 tsp	baking powder	5 mL
1/2 tsp	vanilla	2 mL
1/4 tsp	almond extract	1 mL
1/4 tsp	cream of tartar	1 mL
	Apricot Purée (recipe follows)	

BUTTERCREAM		
1/4 cup	butter	50 mL
1 cup	sifted icing sugar	250 mL
1 tbsp	(approx) apricot liqueur, orange juice or milk	15 mL
1/2 tsp	vanilla	2 mL

● In large bowl, beat egg yolks with cold water for 5 minutes or until thickened and pale. Gradually add sugar, 2 tbsp (25 mL) at a time, beating well after each addition. Combine flour and baking powder; blend into egg mixture at low speed. Add vanilla and almond extract.

SIFTING

When a recipe calls for sifting ingredients, use a sifter especially designed for baking or sift through a fine mesh sieve. We prefer to sift cocoa and icing sugar to eliminate lumps. When using cake-and-pastry flour, our recipes are based on sifting the flour before measuring. All-purpose flour does not require sifting.

● In separate bowl, beat egg whites with cream of tartar until stiff peaks form; fold into batter. Pour into ungreased 9-inch (3 L) tube pan. Bake in 350°F (180°C) oven for 40 to 45 minutes or until top springs back when lightly touched. Turn pan upside down on rack; let cake hang until cool.

● Remove cake from pan. With serrated knife, carefully slice cake horizontally into three layers; slide waxed paper strips under cake to protect plate. Spread two cake layers with one-third each of the apricot purée. Top with remaining cake layer.

● BUTTERCREAM: In bowl, beat together butter and icing sugar until light and fluffy; beat in liqueur and vanilla. Spread on side of cake. Pipe or spoon more buttercream around top of edge to form rim. Cover top with remaining apricot purée.

APRICOT PURÉE		
1-1/2 cups	dried apricots	375 mL
1-1/2 cups	water	375 mL
1 tsp	grated orange rind	5 mL
1/2 cup	granulated sugar	125 mL
1 tbsp	apricot liqueur or orange juice	15 mL

● In saucepan over low heat, simmer apricots, water and orange rind for about 20 minutes or until apricots are tender. Add sugar; cook for 10 minutes or until thickened. Purée in blender or food processor. Add liqueur; let cool until spreadable. Makes 2 cups (500 mL).

(In center) Windblown Cake

Summer Fruit Flan

Arrange your favorite fresh fruit over a pastry cream or lemon cream filling in a delicate sponge cake flan. Brushed lightly with a glaze, this lovely dessert makes a perfect sweet ending to a summer meal.

❏ TIP: You can also bake the cake in an 8-inch (1.2 L) round layer cake pan. Split the cake in half and fill with pastry cream and fresh fruit. Dust with icing sugar and serve in wedges.

2	eggs (at room temperature)	2
2/3 cup	granulated sugar	150 mL
1/3 cup	warm water	75 mL
1 tsp	vanilla	5 mL
1 cup	all-purpose flour	250 mL
2 tsp	baking powder	10 mL
Pinch	salt	Pinch

PASTRY CREAM FILLING

3	egg yolks	3
1/4 cup	granulated sugar	50 mL
2 tbsp	all-purpose flour	25 mL
1 cup	milk	250 mL
1 tsp	vanilla	5 mL
1/2 cup	whipping cream	125 mL

TOPPING

3 cups	mixed fresh fruit (strawberries, blueberries, raspberries or sliced peaches, kiwifruit or bananas)	750 mL
2 tbsp	apple or red currant jelly	25 mL

● Grease 11-inch (1.2 L) flan pan with raised center. Dust with flour; place round of parchment or waxed paper in raised center.

● In bowl and using electric mixer, beat eggs, sugar and water for 10 minutes or until batter leaves ribbon trail when beaters are lifted. Blend in vanilla. Stir together flour, baking powder and salt; sift half over egg mixture and fold in until blended. Repeat with remaining flour mixture.

● Pour batter into prepared pan and spread evenly to edge. Bake in 350°F (180°C) oven for 20 to 30 minutes or until top springs back when lightly touched. Let cool in pan for 5 minutes. Loosen edges and invert onto rack. Peel away paper and let cool completely.

● PASTRY CREAM FILLING: In bowl, whisk together egg yolks, sugar, flour and 1/4 cup (50 mL) of the milk. In heavy saucepan, heat remaining milk just until bubbles appear around edge; gradually whisk into egg mixture. Return to saucepan; cook over medium heat, whisking constantly, for 3 minutes or until thickened and bubbly. Transfer to bowl; stir in vanilla. Place waxed paper directly on surface; let cool completely.

● Whip cream; whisk one-quarter into cooled pastry cream until smooth. Fold in remaining whipped cream. Spread evenly over indented part of cake.

● TOPPING: Arrange fruit over pastry cream. In small saucepan, melt apple jelly over low heat. Using pastry brush, brush jelly glaze over fruit. Serve immediately or refrigerate for up to 2 hours.

VARIATION

LEMON CREAM FILLING: In heavy saucepan, whisk together 1 egg, 1 egg yolk and 1/4 cup (50 mL) granulated sugar until foamy. Stir in 2 tsp (10 mL) grated lemon rind and 1/3 cup (75 mL) lemon juice. Cook over medium heat, stirring constantly, for 6 to 8 minutes or until thickened and bubbly. Remove from heat and stir in 2 tbsp (25 mL) softened butter; let cool completely. Whip 1/2 cup (125 mL) whipping cream; whisk one-quarter into lemon mixture until smooth, then fold in remaining whipped cream.

Beat eggs, sugar and water until batter leaves ribbon trail when beaters are lifted.

With rubber spatula, spread pastry cream evenly over indented portion of cake.

Arrange fruit as desired over pastry cream. Using pastry brush, brush fruit with jelly glaze.

Classic Strawberry Shortcake

Fill this old-fashioned biscuit shortcake with strawberries or with lightly sweetened blueberries, raspberries or peaches.

	Strawberries	
	Whipped Cream	
	SHORTCAKE	
2 cups	all-purpose flour	500 mL
2 tbsp	granulated sugar	25 mL
1 tbsp	baking powder	15 mL
1/2 tsp	baking soda	2 mL
1/4 tsp	salt	1 mL
1/2 cup	butter	125 mL
1/2 cup	sour cream	125 mL
1/4 cup	milk	50 mL
	GLAZE	
	Milk	
	Granulated sugar	

● In bowl, combine flour, sugar, baking powder, baking soda and salt. Using pastry blender or two knives, cut in butter finely.

● Combine sour cream and milk; add all at once to dry mixture, stirring with fork to make soft, slightly sticky dough. Gather into ball.

● On lightly floured surface, knead dough gently about 8 times or until smooth. Roll out or pat into 8-inch (20 cm) circle. (Alternatively, with 3-inch/8 cm round cookie cutter, cut out 6 rounds.) Place on baking sheet.

● GLAZE: Lightly brush dough with milk; sprinkle with sugar. Bake in 425°F (220°C) oven for 20 to 25 minutes for large shortcake (15 to 20 minutes for small) or until top is golden brown. While still warm, slice in half horizontally.

● To serve, spoon strawberries over bottom half; add dollop of whipped cream. Top with upper half; add more strawberries and whipped cream. Makes about 6 servings.

Italian Fruited Rice Cake

This rice pudding-like cake can be made ahead and reheated briefly just before serving.

1/2 cup	chopped candied orange peel	125 mL
1/2 cup	raisins	125 mL
1/4 cup	brandy	50 mL
3 cups	milk	750 mL
3/4 cup	short-grain rice	175 mL
2/3 cup	granulated sugar	150 mL
1/4 cup	butter	50 mL
4	eggs, separated	4
1/2 cup	amaretti or gingersnap cookie crumbs	125 mL
1 tbsp	icing sugar	15 mL
1 cup	whipping cream	250 mL

● In bowl, soak peel and raisins in brandy; set aside.

● Meanwhile, in saucepan, bring milk and rice to boil; cover, reduce heat to low and cook for 20 minutes, stirring, or until creamy and tender. Stir in sugar and butter; cook, stirring, for 15 to 20 minutes or until almost all liquid is absorbed. Stir in raisin mixture.

● Transfer to large bowl; let cool to room temperature. Beat in egg yolks. In bowl, beat egg whites until soft peaks form; fold into rice mixture.

● Dust greased 10-inch (3 L) springform pan with amaretti crumbs; pour in batter. Bake in 350°F (180°C) oven for 1-1/4 hours or until top springs back when lightly touched. Let cool in pan on rack for 10 minutes. Turn out onto serving plate; let cool for 15 minutes. Sift icing sugar over top. Whip cream; serve on the side. *(Cake can be refrigerated for up to 1 day.)*

White Chocolate Petits Fours

For a pretty sweet tray, decorate petits fours with borage flowers or candied violets — as we did in the photo on p. 153.

❏ **TIP: Borage flowers are just one of many fresh flowers that can be used safely — and to great effect — to garnish cakes and other desserts (see GARNISHING WITH FLOWERS, p. 16).**

5	eggs	5
1 cup	butter, softened	250 mL
1-1/2 cups	granulated sugar	375 mL
1 tsp	vanilla	5 mL
2 cups	sifted cake-and-pastry flour	500 mL
WHITE CHOCOLATE GLAZE		
8 oz	white chocolate, chopped	250 g
1 cup	whipping cream (at room temperature)	250 mL
Borage flowers		

● Cover eggs with warm water; let stand for 5 minutes. Drain.

● In bowl, cream butter with sugar until fluffy; beat in eggs, one at a time, beating well after each addition. Stir in vanilla. Stir in flour just until blended.

● Spoon into greased and floured 9- x 5-inch (2 L) loaf pan; bake in 350°F (180°C) oven for 1 to 1-1/4 hours or until tester inserted into center comes out clean.

Let cool in pan for 10 minutes. Turn out onto rack; let cool completely.

● WHITE CHOCOLATE GLAZE: In top of double boiler over hot, not boiling, water, melt chocolate. Whisk in cream all at once until smooth. Refrigerate for about 20 minutes or until slightly thickened, whisking occasionally.

● Meanwhile, cut cake into 3/4-inch (2 cm) thick slices. Using 1-3/8-inch (3.5 cm) cookie cutter, cut out three or four rounds from each slice (freeze leftover cake to use in a trifle).

● Place cake rounds 1 inch (2.5 cm) apart on rack set over jelly roll pan. Spoon heaping tablespoonful (20 mL) glaze over each round, covering completely. Pour glaze drippings from jelly roll pan through fine sieve to remove any crumbs; reuse to complete glazing. Refrigerate for at least 2 hours or until chilled. *(Petits fours can be refrigerated for up to 3 days or frozen for up to 2 weeks.)* Garnish with borage flowers. Makes about 40.

Chocolate Cupcake Cones

Kids will love these fun chocolate cake-filled cones. And you'll love our one-bowl, quick and easy cake batter. For crisp cones, bake the day of the party.

13	ice cream cones (with flat bottoms)	13
1-1/2 cups	all-purpose flour	375 mL
1 cup	granulated sugar	250 mL
1/2 cup	unsweetened cocoa powder	125 mL
1-1/2 tsp	baking soda	7 mL
3/4 cup	water	175 mL
1/3 cup	vegetable oil	75 mL
1 tbsp	vinegar	15 mL
2 tsp	vanilla	10 mL
	ICING	
1/4 cup	butter, softened	50 mL
2 oz	semisweet chocolate, melted	60 g
3/4 cup	icing sugar	175 mL
1/2 tsp	vanilla	2 mL
	Colored candy sprinkles	

● Stand ice cream cones in muffin cups; set aside.

● In bowl, whisk together flour, sugar, cocoa and baking soda. Combine water, oil, vinegar and vanilla; whisk into dry ingredients just until smooth.

● Spoon into ice cream cones to within 1/2 inch (1 cm) of tops; bake in 325°F (160°C) oven for 30 to 35 minutes or until tops spring back when lightly touched. Let cool on rack.

● ICING: In bowl, whisk butter into chocolate; whisk in sugar and vanilla until smooth. Spread over tops of cupcakes; dip tops into sprinkles to coat lightly. Makes 13.

In photo, above: Chocolate Cupcake Cones (left); make-your-own banana splits

---

MAKE IT A COOL KIDS' PARTY!

Make your child's next get-together or birthday party a sure-fire hit with make-your-own banana splits.

● On washable or covered table, set out banana-split boats, serving spoons and all the fixings for the best banana splits in town! — bananas, peeled and sliced lengthwise (brush lightly with lemon juice to prevent discoloration); bowls of candy-coated chocolate, chocolate and butterscotch chips, nuts, colored sprinkles and raisins; and lots of fruit on a plate (pineapple tidbits, fresh strawberries, raspberries, blueberries, grapes).

● And for the crowning touch — chocolate and butterscotch sauces (recipes, p. 112), plus freshly whipped cream.

Dress-Up Cupcakes

It's hard to beat cupcakes that are as much fun to decorate as they are to eat!

❏ JUST FOR KIDS! Make a cupcake Easter Bunny using candy-coated chocolate pieces for eyes and nose, and candy strips for whiskers. To make ears, cut pink marshmallows into four quarters with scissors.

● For flowerpot cupcakes, sprinkle tops with 1 cup (250 mL) flaked coconut that you've shaken with 4 drops of green food coloring in a large jar. Arrange cut-up gumdrops to form petals.

1-1/2 cups	sifted cake-and-pastry flour	375 mL
1 cup	granulated sugar	250 mL
2 tsp	baking powder	10 mL
1/2 tsp	salt	2 mL
1/2 cup	butter, softened	125 mL
1/2 cup	milk	125 mL
2	eggs	2
1 tsp	vanilla	5 mL
	EASY FLUFFY ICING	
1/2 cup	corn syrup	125 mL
1	egg white	1
1 tsp	lemon juice	5 mL

In photo above (clockwise from right): Easter Bunny Cupcakes; Flowerpot Cupcakes; Tangerine Sponge Pudding (p. 130)

● In bowl, combine flour, sugar, baking powder and salt. Using electric mixer at low speed, blend in butter, milk, eggs and vanilla; beat for 2 minutes at medium speed.

● Spoon batter into 16 large greased or paper-lined muffin cups. Bake in 375°F (190°C) oven for 12 to 16 minutes or until tester inserted into centers comes out clean. Transfer to rack and let cool.

● EASY FLUFFY ICING: In saucepan over high heat, heat corn syrup (or microwave at High for 1-1/2 to 2 minutes) until boiling. In bowl, beat egg white with lemon juice until frothy; gradually blend in boiling corn syrup and beat until stiff peaks form, about 4 minutes.

● Dip tops of cooled cupcakes into icing. Decorate as desired. Makes 16 cupcakes.

Easy Orange Dacquoise

Smothered luxuriously with orange-flavored whipped cream, this meringue cake, or dacquoise, with its nutty meringue layers, makes a show-stopping finale for any celebration. Best of all, it's make-ahead — and easy enough for a beginner baker!

❏ **TIP: For the most even baking of meringues, place oven racks as close to the center of oven as possible.**

PECAN MERINGUE

2-1/4 cups	toasted pecans or walnuts (see p. 51)	550 mL
1-1/2 cups	granulated sugar	375 mL
2 tbsp	cornstarch	25 mL
9	egg whites	9
1 tsp	vanilla	5 mL

ORANGE CREAM

2 cups	whipping cream	500 mL
3/4 cup	sifted icing sugar	175 mL
2 tbsp	orange liqueur or orange juice	25 mL
1 tbsp	grated orange rind	15 mL

GARNISH

Orange or kumquat slices
Mint or orange leaves

● PECAN MERINGUE: Line 2 baking sheets with parchment paper or greased and floured foil. Using 8-inch (20 cm) cake pan as guide, draw 2 circles on each paper; set aside.

● In food processor, process 1-1/2 cups (375 mL) of the pecans, 1/2 cup (125 mL) of the sugar and cornstarch until finely ground.

● In bowl and using electric mixer, beat egg whites until soft peaks form. Gradually beat in remaining sugar until stiff glossy peaks form. Add vanilla. Sprinkle with half of the nut mixture; using rubber spatula, fold into egg whites. Repeat with remaining nut mixture.

● Divide meringue mixture among circles on baking sheets; spread evenly to fill circles. Bake in 275°F (140°C) oven for 60 to 75 minutes or until tops are firm to the touch, switching baking sheets between top and bottom racks midway through baking.

● Using sharp knife and same cake pan as guide, trim meringues into even circles while still hot. Slide long metal spatula under meringues to loosen; carefully transfer to rack and let cool completely. *(Meringues can be stored in airtight container for up to 1 week.)*

● ORANGE CREAM: In bowl and using electric mixer, beat together cream, sugar and orange liqueur; stir in orange rind. Center 1 meringue layer on serving plate. Place strips of waxed paper underneath meringue to protect plate from splatters.

● Sandwich meringues with two-thirds of the orange cream. Spread remaining cream over top and side. Chop remaining pecans and press into side of cake. Refrigerate for at least 1 hour or up to 8 hours. Remove waxed paper. Garnish with orange and mint. To serve, slice with serrated knife. Makes 10 servings.

VARIATIONS

MOCHA CREAM MERINGUE CAKE: Prepare meringues as directed. Dissolve 2 tbsp (25 mL) instant coffee granules in 1 tbsp (15 mL) hot water; let cool. Beat together 2 cups (500 mL) whipping cream, 1 cup (250 mL) sifted icing sugar and coffee mixture. Assemble cake and garnish with candied coffee beans.

CHOCOLATE CREAM MERINGUE CAKE: Prepare meringues as directed. Beat together 2 cups (500 mL) whipping cream, 1 cup (250 mL) sifted icing sugar, 1/2 cup (125 mL) sifted unsweetened cocoa powder and 1 tsp (5 mL) vanilla. Assemble cake and garnish with chocolate curls. (For tips on making chocolate curls, see p. 27.)

Using palette knife, spread meringue mixture evenly among circles drawn on paper-lined baking sheet.

Using sharp knife and cake pan as guide, trim baked meringues into even circles while still hot.

Ice cake with orange cream. With hand, press chopped pecans into side of cake.

45

Christmas Pavlova

Pavlova is a soft baked meringue that's topped with whipped cream and fruit. Red and green fruit give this easy-to-make dessert Christmas glamor (see photo, p. 125). You can also use blueberries, pitted cherries, sliced peaches or well-drained pineapple or mandarin orange sections.

6	egg whites	6
1/4 tsp	salt	1 mL
1/4 tsp	cream of tartar	1 mL
1-1/2 cups	granulated sugar	375 mL
2 tbsp	cornstarch	25 mL
1 tbsp	vinegar	15 mL
1-1/2 tsp	vanilla	7 mL
1-1/2 cups	whipping cream	375 mL
1 cup	raspberries or strawberries	250 mL
2	kiwifruit, sliced	2

● Line baking sheet with parchment paper. Place bottomless 8-inch (2 L) or 9-inch (2.5 L) springform pan on top; set aside.

● In bowl, beat egg whites, salt and cream of tartar until soft peaks form. Gradually beat in sugar in thin steady stream until stiff glossy peaks form. Fold in cornstarch, vinegar and vanilla.

● Spoon batter into prepared pan; smooth top. Bake in 275°F (140°C) oven for 2 to 2-1/2 hours or until crisp and lightly browned on outside but still soft in middle. Let cool completely (meringue may deflate). Run knife around meringue; remove pan. Carefully remove paper. *(Meringue can be loosely covered and stored for up to 3 days.)*

● Remove loose bits from meringue. Whip cream; spread over top of meringue, swirling into peaks. Garnish with raspberries and kiwifruit. Makes 6 to 8 servings.

SUBSTITUTIONS

When you don't have all the necessary ingredients for a recipe, consider using the following substitutions. Remember to measure accurately — and allow for a slight variation in taste or appearance.

1 cup (250 mL) cake-and-pastry flour = 1 cup (250 mL) all-purpose flour less 2 tbsp (25 mL)

1 cup (250 mL) buttermilk = 1 cup (250 mL) milk mixed with 1 tbsp (15 mL) vinegar or lemon juice (let stand for 10 minutes)

1 cup (250 mL) self-rising flour (flour that already contains baking powder) = 1 cup (250 mL) all-purpose flour plus 1 tsp (5 mL) baking powder and 1/4 tsp (1 mL) salt

1 oz (30 g) unsweetened chocolate = 3 tbsp (45 mL) unsweetened cocoa powder plus 2-1/2 tsp (12 mL) butter

1 tsp (5 mL) lemon juice = 1/2 tsp (2 mL) vinegar

1 cup (250 mL) milk = 1 cup (250 mL) fruit juice, in baking

1 cup (250 mL) milk = 1/2 cup (125 mL) evaporated milk plus 1/2 cup (125 mL) water

1 tsp (5 mL) baking powder = 1/4 tsp (1 mL) baking soda plus 1/2 tsp (2 mL) cream of tartar

1 cup (250 mL) buttermilk = 1 cup (250 mL) plain yogurt

1 cup (250 mL) sour cream = 3 tbsp (45 mL) butter plus 7/8 cup (220 mL) buttermilk

1 cup (250 mL) cream cheese = 1 cup (250 mL) cottage cheese plus 1/4 cup (50 mL) butter or margarine

4 cups (1 L) homogenized milk = 4 cups (1 L) skim milk plus 3 tbsp (45 mL) cream

1 lb (500 g) apples = 1 lb (500 g) any hard fruit such as pears

1 cup (250 mL) granulated sugar = 1 cup (250 mL) packed brown sugar

Meringues on Apricot Coulis

A delicate web of chocolate adds the finishing touch to this attractive, yet surprisingly light, dessert. A coulis is a puréed fruit sauce that is served under, not over, the dessert it's saucing.

❏ TIP: Use ice-cream scoop to shape meringue into balls.

❏ TIP: The baking time given here will produce meringues with slightly chewy centers; for crisp dry centers, bake the meringues for two hours.

4	egg whites	4
1/4 tsp	cream of tartar (or 1 tsp/5 mL white vinegar)	1 mL
Pinch	salt	Pinch
1 cup	granulated sugar	250 mL
	APRICOT COULIS	
3/4 cup	whipping cream	175 mL
1	can (14 oz/398 mL) apricots, drained	1
2 tbsp	apricot brandy	25 mL
6 oz	semisweet chocolate, melted	175 g

● In bowl, beat egg whites, cream of tartar and salt until soft peaks form. Gradually beat in sugar, 2 tbsp (25 mL) at a time, beating until stiff glossy peaks form.

● Using ice-cream scoop or spoon, scoop meringue onto parchment paper- or foil-lined baking sheet. Bake in 250°F (120°C) oven for 1-1/2 hours or until pale golden. Turn off oven; let meringues stand in oven for 1 hour.

● APRICOT COULIS: Whip cream; set aside. In food processor, purée apricots. With machine running, gradually pour in whipped cream and apricot brandy; process just until mixed. Spoon onto dessert plates; drizzle or pipe some of the chocolate decoratively over top. Place meringues on top; drizzle with remaining chocolate. Makes 6 servings.

Frozen Lemon Meringue Torte

Garnish this luscious make-ahead dessert with candied violets or mint leaves. (For other fresh flower suggestions, see sidebar, p. 16.)

1-1/4 cups	granulated sugar	300 mL
1/3 cup	butter	75 mL
1 tbsp	grated lemon rind	15 mL
1 cup	lemon juice	250 mL
6	eggs	6
1-1/2 cups	whipping cream	375 mL

MERINGUES

1-1/2 cups	granulated sugar	375 mL
2 tbsp	cornstarch	25 mL
2 tsp	grated lemon rind	10 mL
6	egg whites	6
1 tsp	vanilla	5 mL

● Trace four 8-inch (20 cm) circles on parchment paper; place on baking sheets.
● MERINGUES: Combine 3/4 cup (175 mL) of the sugar, cornstarch and rind; set aside.
● In bowl, beat egg whites until soft peaks form; gradually beat in remaining sugar until stiff peaks form. Add vanilla; fold in reserved sugar mixture. Spoon meringue onto circles, smoothing tops. Bake in 300°F (150°C) oven for 1 hour or until dry and lightly golden. Let cool. *(Meringues can be stored in cool, dry place for up to 3 days.)*
● In saucepan over medium-high heat, heat sugar, butter, lemon rind and juice, stirring, until sugar dissolves.
● In bowl, beat eggs; whisk in lemon mixture. Return to saucepan and cook, stirring, just until boiling; simmer for 1 minute. Pour into bowl. Place plastic wrap directly on surface; chill in refrigerator to room temperature. *(Mixture can be refrigerated for up to 1 day.)* Whip cream; fold into lemon mixture.
● ASSEMBLY: Crumble least-attractive meringue for garnish; set aside. Fit one meringue into 9-inch (2.5 L) springform pan. Pour one-third of the lemon mixture over top. Repeat layers twice. Sprinkle crumbled meringue over top. Freeze for at least 8 hours. *(Torte can be removed from pan, wrapped well and frozen for up to 1 week.)* Let soften in refrigerator for 45 minutes before serving. Makes 12 servings.

MAKING PERFECT MERINGUES

Warming Eggs
● *Remove eggs from refrigerator and let stand at room temperature for about 30 minutes, or in warm water for 5 minutes, before beating the whites; they will reach a higher volume than cold egg whites.*

Preparation
● *Before beating egg whites, prepare baking pans, preheat oven and chop all ingredients such as nuts or cherries. Make sure mixing bowl and beaters are clean and dry.*

Lining Pans
● *Use brown paper, parchment paper or lightly greased foil to line baking pans for large meringues or cake layers. This makes removal of cooled meringues easy.*

Sugar
● *To avoid a grainy texture, use instant dissolving (fruit/berry) sugar or fine granulated sugar to sweeten.*

Bowls
● *Use a small, round deep bowl made of glass or stainless steel; plastic bowls can absorb grease which hinders the foaming action of egg whites.*

Baking
● *To maintain a high volume, bake meringues as soon as possible after egg whites are beaten.*
● *Maintain a low oven temperature so meringues bake until crisp and dry without browning. Reduce temperature if meringues start to brown.*
● *Keep oven door closed if possible until meringues are completely baked.*

(Top) Raspberry Truffle Trifle (p. 126); Frozen Lemon Meringue Torte

Frozen Hazelnut Cream Torte

This elegant dessert can be made up to 3 days ahead, wrapped in foil and kept frozen until shortly before serving. Prepare the chocolate sauce just before serving and drizzle over dessert or pass separately.

3	egg whites (at room temperature)	3
Pinch	each cream of tartar and salt	Pinch
3/4 cup	granulated sugar	175 mL
	FILLING	
4	egg yolks	4
3/4 cup	granulated sugar	175 mL
1/4 cup	cold water	50 mL
1 cup	whipping cream	250 mL
1/4 cup	Frangelico (hazelnut liqueur)	50 mL
1 tsp	vanilla	5 mL
1/2 cup	ground or sliced hazelnuts, toasted	125 mL
	CHOCOLATE SAUCE	
6 oz	semisweet chocolate, coarsely chopped	175 g
1/2 cup	light cream	125 mL
1/4 cup	light corn syrup	50 mL
1 tsp	vanilla	5 mL

● Line two baking sheets with parchment paper. Using 8-inch (1.2 L) round cake pan as guide, draw 3 circles on paper.

● In bowl, beat egg whites, cream of tartar and salt until soft peaks form. Gradually beat in sugar, 2 tbsp (25 mL) at a time, until stiff peaks form.

● With spatula or pastry bag, spread or pipe meringue evenly over circles on baking sheets. Bake in 250°F (120°C) oven for 1 hour. Turn off heat; leave in oven for at least 3 hours or overnight. Carefully remove parchment from meringues; place on racks.

● FILLING: In bowl, beat egg yolks; set aside. In small heavy saucepan, bring sugar and cold water to boil; boil, stirring and brushing down any crystals clinging to side of pan with brush dipped in cold water, until soft ball stage and candy thermometer registers 238°F (114°C). Add hot syrup to yolks in thin steady stream, beating constantly until completely cool. Transfer to large bowl.

● Whip cream; stir in liqueur and vanilla. Stir one-quarter into yolk mixture; fold in remaining whipped cream. Fold in nuts.

● ASSEMBLY: Place 1 meringue in 9- or 10-inch (2.5 or 3 L) springform pan. Spread with one-third of the filling. Repeat with remaining meringues and filling. Cover with foil; freeze until firm, about 8 hours. Transfer to serving plate; place in refrigerator for 30 minutes before serving to soften slightly.

● CHOCOLATE SAUCE: In top of double boiler over hot, not boiling, water, combine chocolate, cream and corn syrup; heat until melted and smooth. Stir in vanilla. Drizzle over dessert or pass separately. Makes 6 to 8 servings.

Chocolate Icebox Cake

If soft ladyfingers are not available, use small thin gingersnaps or chocolate wafer cookies.

2 cups	whipping cream	500 mL
1 cup	sifted icing sugar	250 mL
1/2 cup	sifted unsweetened cocoa powder	125 mL
1	pkg (3 oz/85 g) soft ladyfingers	1
1 tsp	vanilla	5 mL
2 cups	fresh strawberries or raspberries (or 1/2 cup/125 mL toasted sliced almonds)	500 mL

● In bowl, combine whipping cream, icing sugar and cocoa; refrigerate for 1 hour.

● Cut ladyfingers in half crosswise; line bottom and side of greased 8-inch (2 L) springform pan with some of the ladyfingers, flat sides facing in.

● Whip cream mixture; blend in vanilla. Spread half in prepared pan; cover with remaining ladyfingers. Top with remaining cream. Refrigerate until firm, about 4 hours.

● Top with fresh berries or toasted almonds. Remove side of pan; serve in wedges.

Celebration Ice Cream Cake

Three shades of ice cream dress up this easy-to-make dessert that's sure to please kids of all ages. We used chocolate, strawberry and vanilla, but why not choose your own favorite flavors? Add a variety of crispy, caramel, chocolate and peanut butter candy bars.

8 oz	semisweet chocolate, coarsely chopped	250 g
3/4 cup	whipping cream	175 mL
2 tbsp	corn syrup	25 mL
3	containers ice cream (each 1 L)	3
9	candy bars (each about 50 g)	9
16	chocolate sandwich cookies	16
1/4 cup	slivered almonds, toasted	50 mL

● In top of double boiler over hot, not boiling, water, melt together chocolate, cream and corn syrup, whisking until smooth; let cool.

● Let ice cream soften at room temperature for 30 minutes.

● Meanwhile, cover 10-inch (25 cm) cardboard circle with waxed paper; place in 11-inch (3.5 L) springform pan. Chop candy bars and cookies.

● Spread one container of ice cream in pan; sprinkle with half of the candy bars and cookies. Drizzle with 1/2 cup (125 mL) of the sauce. Repeat layers.

● Spread third container of ice cream on top; drizzle with remaining sauce. Sprinkle with almonds. Freeze for at least 3 hours. *(Cake can be removed from pan, wrapped well and frozen for up to 1 month.)* Let soften in refrigerator for 30 minutes before serving. Makes 16 to 20 servings.

TOASTING NUTS

Toasting nuts before using them in a recipe intensifies their flavor and enhances the overall taste of the finished dessert.

In Oven
● *Spread shelled pecans, walnuts, almonds, hazelnuts, peanuts, pistachios, cashews or Brazil nuts on baking sheet or in cake pan and toast in 350°F (180°C) oven for 10 minutes or until fragrant.*

In Microwave
● *Spread shelled nuts on plate; microwave, uncovered, at High for 8 to 10 minutes (5 to 7 minutes for cashews or Brazil nuts) or until lightly browned and fragrant, stirring every 2 minutes.*

Hazelnut Mocha Torte

This creamy multilayered cake has its origins in the famous coffee houses and bake shops of Austria. Serve it as an elegant ending to any special occasion.

1-1/2 cups	hazelnuts	375 mL
6	eggs	6
1 cup	granulated sugar	250 mL
1/3 cup	all-purpose flour	75 mL
1 tbsp	baking powder	15 mL
	FILLING	
1/4 cup	butter, softened	50 mL
2 cups	sifted icing sugar	500 mL
1/4 cup	strong coffee	50 mL
2 tbsp	unsweetened cocoa powder	25 mL
1 tsp	vanilla	5 mL
	TOPPING	
1 cup	whipping cream	250 mL
2 tbsp	coffee liqueur	25 mL
1 tsp	granulated sugar	5 mL
1/4 cup	hazelnuts, chopped	50 mL
	Chocolate curls (see p. 27)	

● Grease two 9-inch (1.5 L) round cake pans; line bottoms with parchment or waxed paper. Set aside.

● Spread hazelnuts on baking sheet; bake in 350°F (180°C) oven for 8 minutes. Transfer to terry cloth towel and rub off skins. In food processor or blender, finely chop hazelnuts.

● In large bowl and using electric mixer, beat eggs with sugar for about 10 minutes or until thickened, pale and batter falls in ribbons when beaters are lifted. Add flour, baking powder and hazelnuts; mix well.

● Pour batter into prepared pans. Bake in 350°F (180°C) oven for 20 to 25 minutes or until tester inserted into centers comes out clean. Let cool on racks for 5 minutes. Carefully run knife around edge of cakes; turn out onto racks and remove paper. Let cool completely. Cut each cake in half to make four layers.

● FILLING: In bowl, cream butter with icing sugar; beat in coffee, cocoa and vanilla. Place one cake layer on serving plate; slide waxed paper strips under cake to protect plate. Spread with one-third of the filling. Repeat with second and third layers. Top with fourth layer.

● TOPPING: In bowl, whip cream with liqueur and sugar. Spread over top and side of cake. Sprinkle top with hazelnuts. Arrange chocolate curls on top of cake. *(Cake can be covered and refrigerated for up to 1 day.)*

(Top) Hazelnut Mocha Torte;
Lemon Raisin Bundt Cake (next page)

Lemon Raisin Bundt Cake

Studded with raisins and scented with lemon rind, this buttery cake keeps well for several days. (See previous page for photo.)

3/4 cup	unsalted butter, softened	175 mL
1-1/4 cups	(approx) icing sugar	300 mL
2 tsp	lemon rind	10 mL
2 tbsp	lemon juice	25 mL
2 tbsp	rum	25 mL
4	eggs, separated	4
1/2 cup	raisins	125 mL
1/2 cup	finely chopped blanched almonds	125 mL
2-1/2 cups	sifted cake-and-pastry flour	625 mL
2 tsp	baking powder	10 mL
1/2 cup	milk	125 mL
	Icing sugar	

● In large bowl and using electric mixer, cream butter. Sift 1-1/4 cups (300 mL) icing sugar over butter; beat until smooth. Add lemon rind and juice, rum and egg yolks; beat until pale in color. Stir in raisins and almonds.

● Stir together flour and baking powder; alternately fold into batter with milk. In mixing bowl, beat egg whites until soft peaks form; fold into batter.

● Spoon into greased and floured 8-inch (2 L) bundt pan. Bake in 375°F (190°C) oven for 45 to 50 minutes or until tester inserted into center comes out clean. Let cool in pan for 5 minutes; invert cake onto rack and let cool completely. Dust with icing sugar.

Lightened Lemon-Yogurt Coffee Cake

We've cut back on the butter — but not the great taste! — of this light and delicious cake.

2/3 cup	granulated sugar	150 mL
3 tbsp	butter	50 mL
2	egg whites	2
1	egg	1
3/4 cup	plain yogurt	175 mL
2 tsp	grated lemon rind	10 mL
2 tsp	lemon juice	10 mL
3/4 tsp	vanilla	4 mL
1-1/2 cups	all-purpose flour	375 mL
3/4 tsp	baking powder	4 mL
3/4 tsp	baking soda	4 mL
1/4 tsp	salt	1 mL
3 tbsp	packed brown sugar	50 mL
1/2 tsp	cinnamon	2 mL
1/2 tsp	nutmeg	2 mL
1/4 cup	chopped dates	50 mL

● In large bowl, beat granulated sugar and butter until combined. Beat in egg whites and egg, one at a time, beating well after each addition. Beat in yogurt, lemon rind, lemon juice and vanilla.

● Stir together flour, baking powder, baking soda and salt; set aside.

● In bowl, blend together brown sugar, cinnamon and nutmeg; mix in dates.

● Stir flour mixture into yogurt mixture just until combined. Pour into lightly greased 8-inch (2 L) square cake pan. Sprinkle with brown sugar mixture; swirl slightly with spatula.

● Bake in 350°F (180°C) oven for 35 minutes or until tester inserted into center comes out clean. Let cool in pan on rack for 10 minutes.

Cranberry Coffee Cake

Feathery light, with the sweet crunch of caramel and pecans and the tang of cranberries, this coffee cake is an easy-to-make brunch or breakfast treat. It's great with a mug of tea in the afternoon, too!

❑ TIP: Wrap foil around bottom of pan before baking cake to prevent any batter or topping from leaking into oven.

1/2 cup	butter, softened	125 mL
3/4 cup	granulated sugar	175 mL
2	eggs	2
1 tsp	vanilla	5 mL
1-1/2 cups	all-purpose flour	375 mL
1-1/2 tsp	baking powder	7 mL
1 tsp	baking soda	5 mL
1/2 tsp	cinnamon	2 mL
1/4 tsp	salt	1 mL
1 cup	sour cream	250 mL
	TOPPING	
2/3 cup	packed brown sugar	150 mL
1/3 cup	butter	75 mL
1/4 tsp	cinnamon	1 mL
1-1/4 cups	cranberries	300 mL
1/2 cup	chopped pecans	125 mL

● TOPPING: In saucepan, bring sugar, butter and cinnamon to boil over medium heat, stirring. Pour into greased 9-inch (2.5 L) springform pan. Sprinkle with cranberries and pecans. Wrap foil around bottom of pan; set aside.

● In large bowl, cream butter with sugar until fluffy. Beat in eggs, one at a time; beat in vanilla.

● Stir together flour, baking powder, baking soda, cinnamon and salt. Using wooden spoon, stir half of the flour mixture into creamed mixture; stir in sour cream. Stir in remaining flour mixture.

● Spread batter over cranberry layer, pushing batter higher around edge. Bake on baking sheet in 350°F (180°C) oven for about 1 hour or until tester inserted into center comes out clean and cake springs back when lightly touched. Let cool in pan for 10 minutes. Invert onto serving platter and serve warm.

GETTING A RISE IN YOUR BAKING

● *Baking powder is a popular leavener. It is a combination of an alkali, usually baking soda plus an acid such as cream of tartar, and a moisture absorber such as cornstarch. When combined with liquid, it produces carbon dioxide gas bubbles that make cakes, quick breads and cookies rise.*

● *The most common baking powder in Canada is a **continuous action** kind, formulated so that the acids in it react continuously when moistened and during heating time. Another kind of baking powder is called* **double action**, *which releases bubbles in two stages, first when moistened, then when heated. Continuous and double action baking powders are interchangeable.*

● *Stored in a cool dry place with the lid tightly closed, baking powder remains potent for two years. However, heat and moisture can diminish its strength. To test, dissolve 1 tsp (5 mL) in 1/3 cup (75 mL) hot tap water. If it bubbles with vim and vigor, it's fine. If not, throw it out before it ruins expensive ingredients, such as for a cake.*

● *Recipes with an acid ingredient, such as buttermilk, sour milk, vinegar, molasses or lemon juice, often call for baking soda to produce leavening. Other acidic ingredients, such as honey and chocolate, often don't produce enough leavening with baking soda alone, so a little cream of tartar or baking powder is also called for.*

● *In a pinch, you can substitute 1/2 tsp (2 mL) each baking soda and cream of tartar for 1 tsp (5 mL) baking powder.*

Blueberry Cinnamon Coffee Cake

Serve this small fruity cake for a special breakfast, or make individual bundt cakes and tuck into lunch boxes for a sweet treat. The cake can be wrapped and refrigerated for up to one week.

1 cup	fresh or frozen unsweetened blueberries	250 mL
1 tsp	cinnamon	5 mL
1/2 cup	butter, softened	125 mL
1 cup	granulated sugar	250 mL
2	eggs	2
1-1/2 tsp	vanilla	7 mL
1-1/2 cups	all-purpose flour	375 mL
2 tsp	baking powder	10 mL
1/4 tsp	salt	1 mL
2/3 cup	milk	150 mL
	Icing sugar	

● Toss blueberries with cinnamon; set aside.

● In bowl, beat butter with sugar for 1 minute. Beat in eggs, one at a time, beating well after each addition. Stir in vanilla.

● Stir together flour, baking powder and salt; fold into butter mixture alternately with milk, making three additions of each. Fold in blueberry mixture, leaving some streaks.

● Spoon into greased 6-cup (1.5 L) bundt pan or six 1-cup (250 mL) bundt pans, spreading batter higher at edges. Bake in 350°F (180°C) oven for 40 to 45 minutes (25 to 35 minutes for individual cakes) or until tester inserted into center comes out clean. Let cool in pan on rack for 15 minutes; invert onto serving plate. Sprinkle with icing sugar and serve warm. Makes 6 servings.

Snacking Honey Spice Cake

This easy cake is generously spread with a delicious cream cheese icing.

❑ **TIP: To help honey slide out of measuring cups easily, rinse the cup with hot water first or use it to measure oil or shortening first.**

1	egg	1
1 cup	sour cream	250 mL
1 cup	liquid honey	250 mL
1/4 cup	melted butter or vegetable oil	50 mL
2-1/2 cups	all-purpose flour	625 mL
2 tsp	ginger	10 mL
1 tsp	baking powder	5 mL
1 tsp	baking soda	5 mL
1 tsp	cinnamon	5 mL
1/2 tsp	salt	2 mL
1/4 tsp	cloves	1 mL
1/4 tsp	nutmeg	1 mL

CREAM CHEESE ICING		
8 oz	cream cheese, softened	250 g
1/3 cup	liquid honey	75 mL
1 tsp	grated orange rind	5 mL
1/3 cup	chopped walnuts, toasted (see p. 51)	75 mL

● In large bowl, beat egg; blend in sour cream, honey and butter. Combine flour, ginger, baking powder, baking soda, cinnamon, salt, cloves and nutmeg; stir into honey mixture.

● Pour into greased 9-inch (2.5 L) square cake pan; bake in 350°F (180°C) oven for 30 to 40 minutes or until tester inserted into center comes out clean. Let cool in pan on rack.

● CREAM CHEESE ICING: In bowl, blend together cream cheese, honey and orange rind. Spread over cake. Sprinkle with walnuts. Cut into squares to serve.

Orange Pecan Cake

This moist cake is a must-add to any household's file of delicious foolproof desserts. It's a prizewinning creation of Joanne Anderson of Richmond Hill, Ontario, and it's great for brunch, snacks or entertaining.

2 cups	all-purpose flour	500 mL
1-3/4 cups	packed brown sugar	425 mL
2 tbsp	coarsely grated orange rind	25 mL
1/2 tsp	allspice	2 mL
1/2 tsp	salt	2 mL
1/2 cup	butter	125 mL
1	egg	1
1 cup	sour cream	250 mL
1 tsp	baking soda	5 mL
1 cup	pecan halves	250 mL
	GLAZE	
1 tbsp	liquid honey	15 mL
1/2 tsp	orange juice concentrate	2 mL
	ORANGE SAUCE	
1/2 cup	whipping cream	125 mL
1/2 cup	sour cream	125 mL
2 tbsp	icing sugar	25 mL
2 tbsp	orange liqueur or orange juice concentrate	25 mL
1 tsp	grated orange rind	5 mL

● In large bowl, sift together flour and sugar; stir in orange rind, allspice and salt. With pastry blender or two knives, cut in butter until crumbly. Press 2-1/2 cups (625 mL) of the mixture onto bottom of 8-inch (2 L) springform pan.

● Whisk together egg, sour cream and baking soda; stir into remaining mixture in bowl. Spoon over crust in pan. Arrange pecans over top.

● Bake in 350°F (180°C) oven for about 1 hour and 15 minutes or until tester inserted into center comes out clean. Let cool slightly on rack.

● GLAZE: Stir together honey and orange juice concentrate. Lightly brush over cake.

● ORANGE SAUCE: Whip cream; stir in sour cream, icing sugar, liqueur and orange rind. *(Sauce can be refrigerated for up to 1 hour.)* Serve cake warm with sauce.

Orange Gateau Breton

This French classic is simple to make and wonderfully crumbly. Almost like shortbread, it's best served plain, along with fruit and a dessert wine. The flavor and texture mellow if cake stands, covered, overnight. If desired, omit the glazed oranges and dust the cake with icing sugar instead.

1 cup	butter	250 mL
3/4 cup	granulated sugar	175 mL
2	eggs	2
2	egg yolks	2
2 tsp	orange liqueur	10 mL
1 tsp	vanilla	5 mL
1/3 cup	ground almonds	75 mL
1-1/2 cups	all-purpose flour, sifted	375 mL

GLAZED ORANGE SLICES

1 cup	granulated sugar	250 mL
1/4 cup	water	50 mL
1	orange (unpeeled), thinly sliced	1

● In large bowl, cream butter with sugar until light and fluffy. Beat in 1 of the eggs and 2 yolks, one at a time, beating well after each addition. Add liqueur and vanilla. Mix in almonds, blending well. Fold in flour.

● Spoon batter into greased 9-inch (23 cm) fluted flan pan with removable bottom, spreading evenly. Lightly beat remaining egg; brush generously over batter. Bake in 350°F (180°C) oven for 30 minutes or until top is golden. Let cool in pan on rack.

● GLAZED ORANGE SAUCE: In saucepan, stir sugar with water over high heat until boiling and sugar dissolves. Reduce heat to low. Simmer a few orange slices at a time for 1 to 2 minutes or until softened and translucent. Remove to waxed paper and let cool; reserve syrup. Remove seeds. Arrange slices on top of cooled cake; brush with some of the reserved syrup.

Lemon Almond Pound Cake

Bakers, both new and experienced, will want to add this moist lemon cake to their repertoire — and to their freezer, when baking ahead for company or special occasions.

1 cup	butter, softened	250 mL
1 cup	granulated sugar	250 mL
4	eggs	4
2-1/4 cups	sifted cake-and-pastry flour	550 mL
1 tsp	baking powder	5 mL
1/2 tsp	salt	2 mL
1-1/4 cups	sliced almonds	300 mL
1 tbsp	coarsely grated lemon rind	15 mL
3 tbsp	lemon juice	50 mL

GLAZE

1/2 cup	icing sugar	125 mL
2 tbsp	lemon juice	25 mL

● In bowl, cream butter with sugar until fluffy; beat in eggs, one at a time.

● In separate bowl, stir together flour, baking powder and salt. Mix in 1 cup (250 mL) of the almonds. Stir half of the flour mixture, lemon rind and juice into butter mixture; stir in remaining flour mixture.

● Spoon into parchment- or waxed paper-lined 9- x 5-inch (2 L) loaf pan, smoothing top. Sprinkle with remaining almonds.

● Bake in 350°F (180°C) oven for 40 to 45 minutes or until tester inserted into center comes out clean.

● GLAZE: Pierce cake all over with tester. Combine icing sugar with lemon juice; spoon evenly over top of hot cake. Let cool on rack before removing from pan. Wrap and store at room temperature for 1 day before slicing.

Golden Fruit Pound Cakes

These moist and fruity miniature pound cakes need no aging and are a perfect size for holiday bazaars and gift-giving. They also freeze well.

❏ **TIP:** To make one large cake, use 9- x 5-inch (2 L) loaf pan. Bake in 300°F (150°C) oven for 1-1/2 to 2 hours or until firm and tester inserted into center comes out clean.

3/4 cup	butter, softened	175 mL
3/4 cup	granulated sugar	175 mL
1/4 cup	ground almonds	50 mL
4	eggs	4
1 cup	currants	250 mL
1 cup	chopped seeded raisins (Lexia)	250 mL
1/2 cup	slivered dried apricots	125 mL
1/4 cup	lemon juice	50 mL
2 tbsp	finely chopped crystallized ginger	25 mL
2 tbsp	grated orange rind	25 mL
2 cups	sifted cake-and-pastry flour	500 mL
1 tsp	baking powder	5 mL
1/2 tsp	nutmeg or mace	2 mL
1/4 tsp	salt	1 mL
	TOPPING	
1 cup	(approx) blanched almonds	250 mL
1 tbsp	milk	15 mL
1 tbsp	granulated sugar	15 mL

● Grease three 5-3/4- x 3-1/4-inch (625 mL) mini loaf pans; line bottoms with waxed paper.

● In large bowl, beat butter until creamy; gradually beat in sugar for about 5 minutes or until fluffy. Beat in almonds alternately with eggs, beating well after each addition.

● Combine currants, raisins, apricots, lemon juice, ginger and orange rind; stir into batter.

● Combine flour, baking powder, nutmeg and salt; stir into batter. Spoon into prepared pans, smoothing tops.

● TOPPING: Arrange almonds over loaves. Bake in 300°F (150°C) oven for about 50 minutes or until tops are firm and light golden. Blend milk with sugar; brush over tops. Bake for 20 to 25 minutes longer or until tester inserted into centers comes out clean. Let cool in pans on rack for 30 minutes. Turn out and let cool completely on rack. Makes 3 little loaves.

Chocolate Date and Nut Loaf

A slice of this rich chocolate-laced pound cake is an excellent pick-me-up with tea, coffee or a glass of icy cold milk.

3/4 cup	butter	175 mL
1 cup	granulated sugar	250 mL
2	eggs	2
2 tsp	vanilla	10 mL
2 cups	all-purpose flour	500 mL
1/4 cup	unsweetened cocoa powder	50 mL
1 tsp	baking soda	5 mL
1/2 tsp	salt	2 mL
2/3 cup	buttermilk	150 mL
1 cup	chopped toasted pecans (see p. 51)	250 mL
1 cup	chocolate chips	250 mL
1 cup	chopped dates	250 mL
	Icing sugar	

● In large bowl, cream together butter and sugar; beat in eggs, one at a time. Beat in vanilla.

● Stir together flour, cocoa, baking soda and salt; add to creamed mixture alternately with buttermilk, making three additions of flour mixture and two of buttermilk. Stir in pecans, chocolate chips and dates.

● Spoon into waxed paper-lined 9- x 5-inch (2 L) loaf pan; smooth top and tap pan gently on counter. Bake in 350°F (180°C) oven for 1 hour and 10 minutes or until tester inserted into center comes out clean. Let cool in pan for 10 minutes; turn out onto rack and let cool completely. Wrap and store for 1 day in airtight container before serving. Dust with icing sugar.

Peach Cream Roll

The cake can be made the day before and wrapped, towel and all, in foil or plastic wrap. After filling, be sure to refrigerate dessert because of the whipped cream.

❏ **TIP: When fresh peaches are not available, use drained canned peaches and omit the icing sugar in the filling.**

3	eggs	3
1 cup	packed brown sugar	250 mL
1/3 cup	water	75 mL
1 tsp	vanilla	5 mL
1 cup	sifted cake-and-pastry flour	250 mL
1 tsp	baking powder	5 mL
1 tsp	cinnamon	5 mL
1/2 tsp	nutmeg	2 mL
1/4 tsp	ground cloves	1 mL
1/4 tsp	salt	1 mL
	TOPPING	
1/4 cup	icing sugar	50 mL
1/2 tsp	cinnamon	2 mL
	FILLING	
3	peaches	3
1/2 cup	whipping cream	125 mL
1 tbsp	icing sugar	15 mL
	GARNISH	
	Whipped cream	
	Sliced peaches	

● Line 15- x 10-inch (40 x 25 cm) jelly roll pan with parchment or waxed paper; grease paper.

● In bowl, beat eggs until thickened and pale, about 5 minutes. Gradually beat in sugar. On low speed, blend in water and vanilla. Gradually beat in flour, baking powder, cinnamon, nutmeg, cloves and salt, beating just until smooth. Pour into pan, spreading into corners.

● Bake in 375°F (190°C) oven for 12 to 15 minutes or until tester inserted into center comes out clean.

● TOPPING: Mix icing sugar with cinnamon; sprinkle over cake. Loosen edges of cake and invert onto clean tea towel; peel off paper. Trim any crusty edges. Starting at narrow side, immediately roll up cake in towel. Let cool on rack.

● FILLING: Peel and chop peaches. Whip cream; fold in peaches and icing sugar. Unroll cake and spread with peach mixture; roll up. Transfer to serving plate, seam side down. Arrange peaches decoratively on top of cake; spoon or pipe whipped cream on top.

THE SCOOP ON SUGAR

● **Granulated sugar** *is the sugar of everyday use in Canada, and is the type most often called for in recipes.*

● *More finely granulated sugar, often called for in meringues and whipped cream, goes under a variety of names depending on the region of Canada —* **berry, fruit, superfine and instant dissolving** *being the most common. Equal quantities of* any of these can be used in place of granulated sugar. In a pinch, make your own finer granulated sugar by processing regular granulated sugar in food processor until desired fineness.

● **Icing sugar** *is powdered sugar blended with enough cornstarch to keep it from clumping together. A reliable sweetener for whipped* cream, it's the essential ingredient for icings.

● **Brown sugar**, *both the gentler flavored light and the stronger flavored dark, is a blend of granulated sugar and molasses. Store in airtight container to keep it soft. A packed measure of brown sugar equals the same amount of granulated sugar.*

Honey Hazelnut Roulade

Transform a basic sponge cake into a delicious roll with a creamy hazelnut filling. Since this cake can be frozen, it's perfect for last-minute entertaining.

4	eggs, separated	4
1/4 cup	warm water	50 mL
3/4 cup	granulated sugar	175 mL
1 tsp	vanilla	5 mL
1/4 tsp	cream of tartar	1 mL
1/2 cup	all-purpose flour	125 mL
1/4 cup	cornstarch	50 mL
1/4 tsp	baking powder	1 mL

HONEY HAZELNUT FILLING

2 cups	hazelnuts	500 mL
1/3 cup	creamed honey	75 mL
1-1/2 cups	whipping cream	375 mL
1/4 cup	dark rum or Frangelico (hazelnut liqueur)	50 mL
	Icing sugar	

● Grease 17-1/2 x 11-1/2-inch (45 x 29 cm) jelly roll pan and line with parchment paper. Grease paper and lightly dust with flour.

● In mixing bowl, beat egg yolks with water until pale; beat in 1/2 cup (125 mL) of the sugar until thickened. Blend in vanilla.

● In separate bowl, beat egg whites with cream of tartar until foamy. Beat in remaining sugar until stiff peaks form; fold into egg yolk mixture. Sift together flour, cornstarch and baking powder; fold into egg mixture.

● Spread batter evenly in prepared pan; bake in 400°F (200°C) oven for 15 minutes or until puffed, browned and firm to the touch. Let cool in pan for 10 minutes. Loosen edges of cake and invert onto second piece of parchment paper. Let cool completely.

● HONEY HAZELNUT FILLING: Meanwhile, spread nuts on baking sheet; bake in 350°F (180°C) oven for 10 minutes. While still warm, place in terry cloth towel and rub off skins. Chop nuts finely.

● In bowl, combine hazelnuts, honey, 1/2 cup (125 mL) of the cream and 2 tbsp (25 mL) of the rum to make thick, somewhat sticky mixture. Whip remaining cream with remaining rum.

● Spread hazelnut mixture over cooled cake; spread whipped cream over top. Gently roll up cake, starting from long side; transfer to serving plate, seam side down. Sift with icing sugar. To serve, cut into diagonal slices.

HIGH-ALTITUDE BAKING

High altitude affects cake baking in several ways:

● *The leavening agent (yeast, baking powder, baking soda) releases more and larger gas bubbles that expand quickly and collapse easily, causing cakes to fall.*

● *Moisture vaporizes at a lower temperature, causing a drier texture.*

● *The internal temperature of the cake being baked at a high altitude is much lower, so the cake will take longer than the time specified in a regular recipe.*

Adapt your regular recipes by following these simple guidelines:

Reduce Leavening Agent

● *For cake batters, reduce the baking powder or baking soda by 1/8 tsp (0.5 mL) for each teaspoon (5 mL) called for in the recipe.*

Line Pans

● *Line bottoms of baking pans with waxed paper or grease well and dust with flour. Because moisture vaporizes more quickly, baked goods tend to stick more easily.*

Cut Back on Sugar

● *Reduce the amount of sugar in butter cakes if the quantity given is much more than half the quantity of flour given. Reduce sugar by about 1 tbsp (15 mL) for each cup (250 mL) called for. Excess sugar weakens the structure.*

Increase Baking Time

● *Increase the baking time by a few minutes for most baked goods. Do not adjust the temperature.*

Banana Split Roll

All the flavors of a banana split — banana, strawberry, chocolate and whipped cream — are in this '90s update of an old-fashioned soda fountain favorite.

❑ **TIP:** For a quick and easy chocolate sauce, see CHOCOLATE sidebar, p. 18. For the strawberry sauce, use our recipe for Strawberry Purée (p. 107).

1/3 cup	butter, softened	75 mL
3/4 cup	granulated sugar	175 mL
3	egg yolks	3
2/3 cup	mashed bananas (about 2)	150 mL
1/2 cup	buttermilk	125 mL
1 cup	all-purpose flour	250 mL
3/4 tsp	each baking powder and baking soda	4 mL
1/2 tsp	salt	2 mL
6	egg whites	6
	FILLING	
1 cup	whipping cream	250 mL
2 tbsp	icing sugar	25 mL
1 tsp	vanilla	5 mL
	GARNISH	
	Strawberry sauce	
	Banana slices	
	Pineapple slices	
	Chocolate sauce	

● Grease 17-1/2- x 11-1/2-inch (45 x 29 cm) jelly roll pan and line with waxed paper. Grease and lightly dust with flour. Set aside.

● In large bowl, beat butter until creamy; gradually beat in sugar until light and fluffy. Beat in egg yolks, one at a time, beating well after each addition. Mix in bananas and buttermilk. Stir together flour, baking powder, baking soda and salt; add to batter all at once, stirring just until combined.

● In separate bowl and using clean beaters, beat egg whites until soft peaks form. Stir about one-quarter into banana mixture; fold in remaining egg whites. Spoon into prepared pan, smoothing top.

● Bake in 350°F (180°C) oven for about 20 minutes or until golden. Loosen edges with knife; let cool in pan on rack for 5 minutes. Invert onto clean tea towel; peel off paper. Starting at long side, roll up cake in towel. Let cool completely on rack.

● FILLING: Whip cream; beat in sugar and vanilla. Unroll cake and spread with cream mixture; roll up gently. *(Roll can be covered and refrigerated for up to 8 hours.)*

● To serve, pool strawberry sauce on each plate. Top with 3 thin slices or 1 thick slice banana roll; garnish with banana and pineapple slices. Drizzle with chocolate sauce.

Glazed Nutty Fruitcake

Glazed fruit and nuts top a fruitcake that's sure to become a Christmas favorite year after year.

❏ TIP: Wrap cake well and store in a cool, dry place for up to one month. Remove paper and reglaze with more melted honey, if desired.

❏ TIP: It's easier to cut fruit cake when it's cold.

4 cups	quartered pitted dates (1 lb/500 g)	1 L
2 cups	candied pineapple chunks (1 lb/500 g)	500 mL
2 cups	halved candied cherries (1 lb/500 g)	500 mL
2 cups	slivered dried apricots (1/2 lb/250 g)	500 mL
2 cups	sliced dried figs (1/2 lb/250 g)	500 mL
1/3 cup	rum	75 mL
3-1/2 cups	whole Brazil nuts (1 lb/500 g)	875 mL
1 cup	butter, softened	250 mL
1-1/4 cups	packed brown sugar	300 mL
4	eggs	4
2 tsp	vanilla	10 mL
1-1/2 cups	all-purpose flour	375 mL
1-1/2 tsp	baking powder	7 mL
1/4 tsp	salt	1 mL
3 tbsp	liquid honey	50 mL

● In large bowl, toss together dates, pineapple, cherries, apricots, figs and rum. Cover and let stand overnight. Mix in nuts.

● Line bottom and side of deep 8-inch (3 L) round fruitcake pan with heavy brown paper or two layers of parchment or waxed paper, leaving 1-inch (2.5 cm) collar above pan. Grease paper.

● In large bowl, cream butter with sugar until fluffy; beat in eggs, one at a time. Beat in half of the vanilla. Stir together flour, baking powder and salt; stir into batter. Mix in about two-thirds of the fruit mixture.

● Pack into prepared pan; tap pan gently on counter. Bake in 300°F (150°C) oven for about 2 hours or until tester inserted into center comes out clean.

● In small saucepan, heat honey; mix with remaining fruit and vanilla. Spread over cake. Bake for 30 minutes longer or until topping firms. Let cool in pan on rack. Remove from pan.

Brandied Mincemeat Ring

When there's little time left before Christmas to ripen a fruitcake, try this quick and easy fruity cake instead.

3/4 cup	butter, softened	175 mL
3/4 cup	packed brown sugar	175 mL
4	eggs	4
1-1/2 cups	mincemeat	375 mL
1 tbsp	coarsely grated lemon rind	15 mL
2 cups	diced mixed candied fruit	500 mL
1 cup	coarsely chopped walnuts, toasted (see p. 51)	250 mL
2 cups	whole wheat flour	500 mL
2 tsp	baking powder	10 mL
1/2 tsp	salt	2 mL
1/3 cup	brandy or apple juice	75 mL

● In large bowl, cream butter with sugar until fluffy. Beat in eggs, one at a time, mincemeat and lemon rind, beating well.

● In bowl, toss together candied fruit, walnuts and 1/2 cup (125 mL) of the flour; set aside.

● Stir together remaining flour, baking powder and salt; add alternately with brandy to creamed mixture, stirring just until combined. Fold in fruit mixture.

● Turn into greased 10-inch (3 L) bundt pan or 9-inch (3 L) tube pan; bake in 325°F (160°C) oven for 1 to 1-1/4 hours or until tester inserted into center comes out clean. Let cool completely on rack. *(Cake can be wrapped well and refrigerated for up to 2 weeks or frozen for up to 2 months. Remove from refrigerator and slice 1 hour before serving.)*

ALWAYS REMEMBER TO MEASURE ACCURATELY!

If you've ever had a recipe fail, improper measuring techniques may have been the problem. Baked goods are especially sensitive to changes in fat, liquid and dry ingredient proportions. For best results, follow these standard techniques.

Liquid and dry measures

● *Whether metric or imperial, there are two types of measures. Dry ingredient measures come in sets of graduated sizes. Liquid measuring cups leave a space between the cup mark and the rim to prevent spills; the different levels are marked on the outside.*

● *Use standard measuring spoons for both dry and liquid ingredients.*

● *Be sure to stick to one measurement system, whether metric or imperial, throughout the recipe.*

Measuring dry ingredients

● *Lightly spoon dry ingredients, such as flour, into dry measure without packing or tapping — a packed cup of flour may contain 1/4 cup (50 mL) more flour than a lightly filled one. Fill measure until heaping; level off with straight edge of knife.*

● *Brown sugar is the exception — pack brown sugar so that it keeps cup shape when turned out.*

Measuring fats

● *For firm fats, such as butter, it's easiest to slice off the amount required*

using the package markings as a guide.

● *You can also measure hard fats using the displacement method: For example, if you want 1/2 cup (125 mL) butter, fill measuring cup with 1/2 cup (125 mL) cold water; add enough butter, submerging it in water, until water reaches the 1-cup (250 mL) mark. Drain off water.*

● *For softened fats, pack into dry measure, pressing firmly with the back of a spoon to eliminate any gaps; level off.*

Measuring liquids

● *Place liquid measure on counter and pour in liquid to desired level; bend down to check measurement at eye level.*

Creamy Maple Pecan Yule Log

Bring this centerpiece Christmas cake to the table before coffee and liqueurs are poured so that your guests have time to enjoy your artistry before the first slice is cut and served. We guarantee that it tastes even better than it looks!

❏ TIP: If you're making the log ahead of time, assemble and ice it, then either refrigerate or freeze it. Prepare the Pecan Meringue Mushrooms and store them in airtight containers.

1/2 cup	pecans	125 mL
1/4 cup	sifted cake-and-pastry flour	50 mL
1 tsp	baking powder	5 mL
5	eggs, separated	5
3/4 cup	granulated sugar	175 mL
1 tsp	vanilla	5 mL
	Icing sugar	
	BUTTERCREAM	
1-3/4 cups	cold butter	425 mL
1-1/2 cups	pure maple syrup	375 mL
6	egg yolks	6
	GARNISH	
1/4 cup	finely chopped pecans	50 mL
	Pecan Meringue Mushrooms (recipe follows)	

● Grease 15- x 10-inch (40 x 25 cm) jelly roll pan; line bottom with parchment or waxed paper. Turn paper over to grease both sides; lightly dust with flour, shaking out excess.

● In food processor or blender, combine pecans, flour and baking powder; process until nuts are finely ground. Set aside.

● In large bowl, beat egg yolks with 1/2 cup (125 mL) of the granulated sugar for about 5 minutes or until pale and batter falls in ribbons when beaters are lifted. Blend in vanilla.

● In separate bowl, beat egg whites until soft peaks form. Gradually beat in remaining granulated sugar until stiff glossy peaks form; fold into egg yolk mixture along with pecan mixture. Spread batter evenly in prepared pan.

● Bake in 350°F (180°C) oven for about 20 minutes or until top springs back when lightly touched. Let cool in pan for 10 minutes. Dust with icing sugar.

● Loosen edges of cake with knife and turn out onto clean tea towel; carefully remove paper. Using serrated knife, trim edges of cake. Starting at long side, immediately roll up in tea towel; let cool on rack.

● BUTTERCREAM: In bowl, beat butter until softened; set aside. In deep heavy saucepan, boil maple syrup over medium-high heat, without stirring, for 5 to 10 minutes or until soft ball stage and candy thermometer registers 234°F (112°C). Remove from heat and let bubbles subside.

● Place yolks in large bowl; gradually pour in hot syrup, beating constantly at medium speed. Increase speed to high and continue beating for 5 to 10 minutes or until thickened and cool. Beat in reserved butter. Set 1 cup (250 mL) buttercream aside.

● ASSEMBLY: Unroll cake and spread with one-third of the buttercream. Roll up again and place, seam side down, on serving platter. Spread remaining buttercream evenly over cake. Pipe or spoon two mounds of some of the reserved buttercream decoratively on cake to form "knots." Run fork lengthwise along log to simulate bark. Refrigerate for 30 to 60 minutes or until buttercream is firm.

● Using serrated knife, cut off end of log at an angle. Place cut end alongside log to form branch, securing with some of the reserved buttercream. (Use remaining buttercream to secure meringue mushrooms to log.) Trim off other end of log to balance appearance. *(Recipe can be prepared to this point, covered and refrigerated for up to 3 days or frozen for up to 1 month. Let stand at room temperature for 30 minutes or thaw in refrigerator for 2 hours before serving.)*

● GARNISH: Sprinkle chopped pecans over log; surround with meringue mushrooms. Makes 8 servings.

PECAN MERINGUE MUSHROOMS

1/2 cup	pecans	125 mL
1/4 cup	granulated sugar	50 mL
2	egg whites	2
1/2 tsp	cream of tartar	2 mL
1/4 cup	packed brown sugar	50 mL
1/2 tsp	vanilla	2 mL
	Unsweetened cocoa powder	
	Buttercream	

● In food processor or blender, combine pecans and granulated sugar; process until nuts are finely ground.

● In bowl, beat egg whites with cream of tartar until soft peaks form. Gradually beat in brown sugar until stiff glossy peaks form. Fold in vanilla and pecan mixture.

● Using piping bag fitted with 1/2-inch (1 cm) plain tip, pipe half of the mixture in small rounds for mushroom caps onto foil-lined or greased and floured baking sheet. Dust with cocoa.

● Using remaining meringue mixture, form upright stems, about 1 inch (2.5 cm) tall, by drawing piping bag upward while squeezing gently. Bake in 250°F (120°C) oven for about 45 minutes or until crisp. Let cool on rack. Just before serving, stick stems onto caps with reserved buttercream. Makes about 20 mushrooms.

Pies, Tarts and Pastries

Pies are a Canadian dessert tradition. Today's double-crusted pies may be cut into smaller wedges but their flaky pastry and luscious filling are just as appealing now as they were a hundred years ago. So is the satisfying art of pie-making — from rolling out a light and perfect pastry to fluting the edges and adding a topping and a rich golden glaze. You'll find all of these time-honored techniques clearly explained in this chapter. Use them for our delicious fruit and cream tarts, too. Or try elegant but surprisingly easy choux pastry éclairs, profiteroles and light-as-air cream puffs.

Crunchy Pecan Pie

Quite simply, this is the best! The pastry is light and flaky, and the filling is deliciously crunchy and just sweet enough to satisfy. No lover of pecan pies could ask for more!

3-1/3 cups	sifted cake-and-pastry flour	825 mL
1/2 tsp	salt	2 mL
1/2 cup	cold butter, cubed	125 mL
1/2 cup	cold lard or shortening, cubed	125 mL
1	egg	1
3 tbsp	(approx) ice water	50 mL
2 tsp	white vinegar	10 mL
	FILLING	
3	eggs	3
3/4 cup	packed brown sugar	175 mL
3/4 cup	corn syrup	175 mL
2 tbsp	butter, melted	25 mL
1 tsp	vanilla	5 mL
1-1/2 cups	pecan halves	375 mL
	GLAZE	
2 tbsp	corn syrup, warmed	25 mL

● In large bowl, combine flour and salt. Using pastry blender or two knives, cut in butter and lard until mixture resembles coarse crumbs with a few larger pieces. Beat together egg, water and vinegar.

● Add egg mixture, 1 tbsp (15 mL) at a time, to flour mixture, stirring briskly with fork until dough holds together when pressed. Add more water, a few drops at a time, if necessary. Press into ball; divide in half and flatten into discs. Wrap and refrigerate 1 disc for at least 30 minutes or up to 3 days. Freeze remaining disc for up to 3 months for another use.

● For dough refrigerated for more than 8 hours, let stand at room temperature for about 15 minutes or until pliable before rolling out. On lightly floured heavy pastry cloth or work surface and using stockinette-covered rolling pin, roll out dough from center toward edge to 1/8-inch (3 mm) thickness, lifting rolling pin at edge of dough to maintain even thickness. Dust work surface and dough with flour as you work.

● Loosely roll pastry around rolling pin; unroll into 9-inch (23 cm) pie plate. Trim edge evenly, leaving 1-inch (2.5 cm) overhang. Tuck pastry overhang under to make double layer around rim; flute crust. Refrigerate while making filling.

● FILLING: Blend eggs, sugar, corn syrup, butter and vanilla; stir in pecans. Pour into pie shell. Bake in bottom third of 375°F (190°C) oven for 40 to 45 minutes or until pastry is golden and filling is just firm to the touch, shielding edge with foil if necessary.

● GLAZE: Brush filling with corn syrup; let cool. Cut with serrated knife.

PASTRY MAKING IS EASY AS PIE

1 **Cutting in fat.** Using pastry blender or two knives, cut fat into flour until mixture resembles coarse crumbs with a few larger pieces.

5 **Trimming edge of pastry.** Using sharp knife, trim edge evenly, leaving 1-inch overhang.

2 **Adding liquid.** Sprinkle on 1 tbsp (15 mL) at a time, tossing with a fork where liquid hits flour mixture, until dough holds together when pressed.

6 **Tucking in edge of pastry.** Tuck pastry overhang under to make a raised double layer around rim.

3 **Rolling out pastry.** On lightly floured pastry cloth, roll out dough from center to edge, lifting rolling pin at edge to maintain even thickness.

7 **Fluting.** Place index finger and thumb 3/4 inch (2 cm) apart on edge of pastry. With other index finger, push pastry toward outside to form scalloped edge.

4 **Fitting pastry into plate.** Loosely roll pastry around rolling pin; unroll into pie plate.

8 **Filling shell with weights.** Prick unbaked pie shell with fork; line with large piece of foil and fill evenly with pie weights or dried beans (see sidebar, p. 92).

Perfect Pastry Every Time

Even experienced pie makers — like prizewinners in the annual Apple Pie Contest at Black Creek Pioneer Village and the Perfect Pie Contest in Warkworth, Ontario — use this never-fail recipe.

6 cups	cake-and-pastry flour (or 5-1/4 cups/1.3 L all-purpose flour)	1.5 L
1-1/2 tsp	salt	7 mL
2-1/3 cups	lard or shortening (1 lb/454 g)	575 mL
1	egg	1
1 tbsp	white vinegar	15 mL
	Ice water	

● In large bowl, combine flour with salt. Using pastry blender or two knives, cut in lard until mixture resembles fine crumbs with a few larger pieces.

● In measuring cup and using fork, beat together egg and vinegar until blended. Add enough ice water to make 1 cup (250 mL).

● Stirring briskly with fork, gradually add just enough egg mixture, 1 tbsp (15 mL) at a time, to flour mixture to make dough hold together. Divide into 6 portions and press each into disc. Wrap and refrigerate for at least 30 minutes. *(Dough can be refrigerated for up to 3 days or frozen for up to 3 months. Let cold pastry stand for 15 minutes at room temperature before rolling out.)* Makes enough for six single-crust or three double-crust 9-inch (23 cm) pies.

Perfect Processor Pastry

A Canadian Living test kitchen favorite, this recipe makes enough for one double-crust or two single-crust 9- or 10-inch (23 or 25 cm) pies.

3 cups	all-purpose flour	750 mL
1 tsp	salt	5 mL
1/2 cup	cold butter, cubed	125 mL
1/2 cup	cold lard or shortening, cubed	125 mL
1	egg	1
2 tsp	white vinegar	10 mL
	Ice water	

● In food processor fitted with metal blade, combine flour and salt; process to mix.

● Using on/off motion, cut in butter and lard until mixture resembles fine crumbs with a few larger pieces.

● In measuring cup, beat egg until foamy; add vinegar and enough ice water to make 2/3 cup (150 mL). With motor running, add egg mixture all at once; process just until dough starts to clump together. Do not let it form a ball.

● Remove; press together into 2 discs. Wrap and chill for at least 30 minutes or for up to 3 days, or freeze for up to 3 months.

● Let cold pastry stand for 15 minutes at room temperature before rolling out.

PASTRY PRINCIPLES

In pastry making, the purpose of cutting fat into flour is to produce both tenderness and flakiness. The fat can be lard, shortening, butter, margarine or a combination of these.

● ***Shortening and lard*** *are easiest to work with and produce a good "short" (tender) texture. They can be interchanged in most recipes. Lard is animal fat and adds an old-fashioned flavor; shortening is usually made from vegetable oils (hardened by hydrogenation) and adds little flavor.*

● ***Butter*** *is used when a buttery flavor is desired; it has a higher moisture content than shortening and lard, must be kept cold and handled quickly (using a little shortening along with butter makes the pastry easier to work with).*

● ***Regular margarine*** *(not soft) can be substituted for butter in most recipes, but the pastry will not be as "short" nor have the same flavor. Butter is animal fat (made from cream); margarine is made from vegetable oils. Recipes using salted butter or margarine will, of course, call for less salt than those using shortening or lard.*

THAT PERFECT PIE

The Right Touch

Speed and lightness count when it comes to making pastry. The tricky point is adding the liquid. Sprinkle it on 1 tbsp (15 mL) at a time, tossing with a fork where the liquid hits the flour mixture, until all flour has been incorporated and dough forms moist clumps. Avoid worrying the dough by overstirring. At once, use your fingertips to gather the dough into a ball, pressing gently, and wrap it well.

The Big Chill

Ever wonder why a pastry recipe tells you to chill the dough before rolling it out? That rest in the cool of the refrigerator sets the fat and relaxes the gluten content of the flour, making for easier rolling and a tender pie crust that's less likely to shrink. If the dough's too hard when it comes straight out of the refrigerator, let it rest for a few minutes at room temperature.

Rolling Stock

A good tip for beginner pie makers is to roll out the dough on a sturdy well-floured pastry cloth. A stockinette covering on the rolling pin helps keep sticking to a minimum. You can also roll out the dough on a lightly floured kitchen counter, the cool of a laminate surface being better than wood, but better yet would be marble. Or for very delicate dough, roll between two large sheets of waxed paper or plastic wrap. Avoid short, light rolling pins in favor of sturdy longer ones (at least 12 inches/30 cm) that will give years of service.

Roll Around The Clock

Keep a light touch with the rolling pin. Avoid pressing down — this is not ironing! Flatten and shape the portion of dough into a disc. Start rolling from the middle to the edge, as though pastry were a clock and you roll to 12, then to 3, 6, 9 and 12 again. Continue rolling until pastry is a little less than 1/4-inch (5 mm) thick, lifting the rolling pin as it nears the edges for even thickness.

Pizzazz For Your Pies

1. Edging in

A pie is just a pie until the baker puts on the finishing touches. These can be as simple as a pretty crimped edge, of which the easiest is to press the edge with a fork. You can also flute the edge with your fingers (see page 70), or trim the pastry at the edge of the pie plate and brush with water, then cover the edge with small cutout hearts, leaves, stars, half-moons or a pastry braid.

2. Slashing with style

Make the upper crust picture-perfect with some stylish slashing, as we did with the Prizewinning Sour Cherry Pie on the cover (recipe, p. 73).

3. Instead of lattices

Weaving a lattice is nice, but an attractive topping can be made just as easily with pastry scraps and a favorite cookie cutter (as we did with the blueberry pie on this page). Cut out a dozen hearts and place them over the pie, letting edges overlap slightly. You can do the same thing with maple leaves, Christmas trees, stars or shamrocks.

Make-Ahead Pastry

All well-wrapped unbaked pastry keeps perfectly for up to 3 days in the refrigerator or for up to 3 months in the freezer. Thaw the pastry in the refrigerator and let it soften at room temperature before rolling.

Prize-Winning Sour Cherry Pie

Each November, Warkworth, Ontario hosts the Perfect Pie Contest, and pie makers brush off their rolling pins. This cherry pie, made with frozen unsweetened cherries, is adapted from prizewinner Velma Massey's masterpiece and is featured on our cover.

❏ **TIP: You need to thaw 8 cups (2 L) frozen cherries for this pie. Thawing the cherries and thickening the juice before baking the pie ensures just the right thickness to hold the cherries nicely between the flaky bottom and top crusts.**

	Pastry for 9-inch (23 cm) double-crust pie	
1	egg, beaten	1
	Granulated sugar	
	FILLING	
1-1/2 cups	sour cherry juice (from thawed cherries)	375 mL
1 cup	granulated sugar	250 mL
1/3 cup	cornstarch	75 mL
Pinch	salt	Pinch
4 cups	drained thawed pitted sour cherries (see Tip)	1 L
2 tbsp	butter	25 mL
2 tbsp	lemon juice	25 mL
1/4 tsp	almond extract	1 mL

● FILLING: In saucepan, heat 3/4 cup (175 mL) of the cherry juice over medium heat until steaming. Meanwhile, combine sugar, cornstarch and salt; stir in remaining cherry juice until smooth. Whisk into saucepan; cook, whisking, for 6 to 8 minutes or until boiling and thickened.

● Add cherries and remove from heat; stir in butter, lemon juice and almond extract. Let cool, stirring occasionally.

● On lightly floured surface, roll out half of the pastry and fit into 9-inch (23 cm) pie plate; pour in cherry filling. Roll out remaining pastry. Moisten rim of pastry shell with water; cover with top pastry and trim to leave 1/2-inch (1 cm) border. Tuck border under and flute edge.

● With paring knife, cut four leaf shapes out of top pastry; arrange each leaf beside cutouts. With back of knife, press leaf design onto each leaf. From pastry scraps, form a few pea-size balls and arrange in middle of top.

● Brush pastry with egg; sprinkle lightly with granulated sugar. Bake in 425°F (220°C) oven for 15 minutes; reduce heat to 350°F (180°C) and bake for 40 to 50 minutes longer or until crust is golden brown and filling bubbly. Let cool on rack.

Peach Pie with Peach Coulis

The inspiration for this bountiful pie comes from Langdon Hall in the rolling hills of Waterloo County, Ontario. You'll need about 14 peaches (3-1/2 lb/1.75 kg).

❑ **TIP: Let pie cool for four to five hours so juices thicken before serving.**

	Pastry for deep 9-inch (23 cm) double-crust pie	
1 tsp	light cream	5 mL
1 tsp	granulated sugar	5 mL
2	peaches, peeled	2
	FILLING	
8 cups	thickly sliced peeled peaches	2 L
1 tbsp	lemon juice	15 mL
2/3 cup	granulated sugar	150 mL
1/3 cup	all-purpose flour	75 mL
1/4 tsp	nutmeg (optional)	1 mL
1 tbsp	butter	15 mL

● On lightly floured surface, roll out half of the pastry; fit into deep 9-inch (23 cm) pie plate.

● FILLING: In large bowl, toss sliced peaches with lemon juice. Stir together sugar, flour, and nutmeg (if using); combine with peaches and spoon into pie shell. Dot with butter.

● Roll out remaining pastry. Moisten rim of shell with water and cover with top pastry. Trim pastry about 1/2 inch (1 cm) beyond rim; tuck under rim of bottom pastry and flute edge.

● Brush pastry with cream; sprinkle with sugar. Cut vents in top for steam to escape. Bake in 425°F (220°C) oven for 15 minutes; reduce heat to 375°F (190°C) and bake for 50 minutes longer or until crust is golden brown and filling bubbly. Let cool on rack.

● To serve, purée peaches; spoon around each serving.

Strawberry Rhubarb Pie

For extra-juicy fruit like this, quick-cooking tapioca makes the ideal thickener.

❑ **TIP: Wine and cheese get better with age but not pies or tarts. Except for pies that need to chill to set or are meant to mellow, the best pie is a fresh pie, preferably one that has just cooled down from baking.**

	Pastry for 9-inch (23 cm) double-crust pie	
3/4 cup	granulated sugar	175 mL
3 tbsp	quick-cooking tapioca	50 mL
3 cups	strawberries, hulled and halved	750 mL
3 cups	sliced rhubarb	750 mL
1 tsp	lemon juice	5 mL
1 tbsp	butter	15 mL
1	egg, beaten	1

● On lightly floured surface, roll out half of the pastry; fit into 9-inch (23 cm) pie plate.

● In bowl, stir sugar with tapioca; add strawberries, rhubarb and lemon juice, tossing to coat. Spoon into pie crust; dot with butter.

● Roll out remaining pastry and fit over top of pie; trim and flute edge. Brush egg over pastry; cut vents in top for steam to escape. Bake on baking sheet in 425°F (220°C) oven for 15 minutes. Reduce heat to 375°F (190°C); bake for 35 to 45 minutes longer or until golden and filling is bubbly.

Peach Pie with Peach Coulis

Down-Home Seeded Raisin Pie

The secret of a perfect raisin pie is all in the raisins — only seeded raisins deliver the reputation-making, rich wine-like flavor that's at the heart of of this old-time Canadian favorite. Use muscat or Lexia raisins for tastiest results.

	Pastry for 9-inch (23 cm) double-crust pie	
	FILLING	
2 cups	seeded raisins	500 mL
2 cups	boiling water	500 mL
2 tsp	coarsely grated orange rind	10 mL
Pinch	salt	Pinch
1 cup	packed brown sugar	250 mL
3 tbsp	cornstarch	50 mL
1/3 cup	orange juice	75 mL
1 tbsp	lemon juice	15 mL
1 tbsp	butter	15 mL

● FILLING: In saucepan, combine raisins, water, orange rind and salt; cover and bring to boil. Reduce heat and simmer for 10 minutes.

● Combine sugar with cornstarch; gradually stir into raisin mixture until smooth. Cook over medium heat until thickened, clear and no taste of cornstarch remains; remove from heat. Stir in orange juice, lemon juice and butter. Let cool.

● On lightly floured surface, roll out half of the pastry; fit into 9-inch (23 cm) pie plate. Add raisin filling. Roll out remaining pastry and fit over top; trim and flute edge. Cut vents in top for steam to escape.

● Bake in 425°F (220°C) oven for 15 minutes. Reduce heat to 375°F (190°C) and bake for 20 to 25 minutes longer or until pastry is golden.

Warm Rhubarb Cheesecake Pie

This delicious springtime dessert originated in a Stratford, Ontario restaurant, The Old Prune. Quark is a creamy low-fat cheese (see Tip, p. 107).

1-1/2 cups	all-purpose flour	375 mL
1/2 cup	granulated sugar	125 mL
Pinch	salt	Pinch
1/2 cup	cold butter, diced	125 mL
2	egg yolks	2
1 tbsp	milk	15 mL
	FILLING	
5 cups	chopped rhubarb	1.25 L
1/2 cup	granulated sugar	125 mL
2	eggs	2
1/3 cup	granulated sugar	75 mL
1/3 cup	quark or light cream cheese	75 mL
1/3 cup	sour cream	75 mL
1 tbsp	cornstarch	15 mL
1 tsp	vanilla	5 mL
2 tbsp	stale cake crumbs or crushed ladyfingers	25 mL

● In large bowl, combine flour, sugar and salt; cut in butter until mixture resembles coarse crumbs. Beat egg yolks with milk; add all at once to flour mixture, mixing with fork and then fingertips until dough can be pressed together. Press into bottom and 1 inch (2.5 cm) up sides of 10-inch (3 L) springform pan. Chill.

● FILLING: Meanwhile, in stainless steel saucepan, cook rhubarb and 1/2 cup (125 mL) sugar over medium heat, stirring, until boiling. Reduce heat and simmer, stirring occasionally, for about 3 minutes or until rhubarb is tender but still holds its shape. Drain; reserve liquid for another use.

● In food processor or in large bowl using electric mixer, blend eggs, 1/3 cup (75 mL) sugar, quark, sour cream, cornstarch and vanilla.

● Sprinkle cake crumbs over crust. Arrange rhubarb in crust; pour cheese mixture over top. Bake in 375°F (190°C) oven for 40 to 45 minutes or until set. Let cool on rack.

Perfect Double-Crust Fruit Pies

With this handy chart and our simple step-by-step instructions, it really is as easy as pie to make a perfect summer fruit pie — with the berries and fruit just the right juiciness, the bottom crust flaky and the top crust a crisp golden brown.

Type of Pie	Prepared Fruit	Granulated Sugar	All-purpose Flour	Flavorings
Blueberry	5 cups (1.25 L)	3/4 cup (175 mL)	1/4 cup (50 mL)	1/2 tsp (2 mL) each grated lemon rind and cinnamon
Peach	5 cups (1.25 L), peeled and sliced	3/4 cup (175 mL)	1/4 cup (50 mL)	2 tbsp (25 mL) chopped candied ginger
Plum	5 cups (1.25 L), quartered if large, halved if small	1 cup (250 mL)	1/4 cup (50 mL)	1/2 tsp (2 mL) cinnamon
Raspberry	4 cups (1 L)	1 cup (250 mL)	3 tbsp (45 mL)	none needed
Apple	6 cups (1.5 L), peeled and sliced	3/4 cup (175 mL)	1 tbsp (15 mL)	1/4 tsp (1 mL) nutmeg and 1/2 tsp (2 mL) cinnamon

● Line 9-inch (23 cm) pie plate with pastry.

● In large bowl, combine prepared fruit, sugar, flour, 1 tbsp (15 mL) lemon juice and flavoring (see chart above for amounts.)

● Fill pastry shell with fruit mixture; dot filling with 1 tbsp (15 mL) butter.

● Moisten edges of bottom crust. Cover with top crust. Trim and flute edge. Cut steam vents. Brush top with milk or cream; sprinkle lightly with granulated sugar.

● Bake in 425°F (220°C) oven for 15 minutes; reduce heat to 350°F (180°C) and bake for 35 to 45 minutes longer or until fruit is tender, filling thickened and crust golden.

FREEZING PIES

● You can freeze well-wrapped unbaked fruit pies for up to 4 months, with the following changes: increase the amount of flour in each pie by 1 tbsp (15 mL) and don't cut steam vents until just before baking. Bake still-frozen pies in 450°F (230°C) oven for 15 minutes; reduce heat to 375°F (190°C) and bake for up to 60 minutes longer or until filling is thickened and crust golden brown.

EASY GLAZING

● A pie with a beautiful gloss and golden color is especially appealing. There are several ways to get a professional-looking glaze.

● Whisk together an egg yolk with 1-1/2 tsp (7 mL) cream for a deep gold color. Milk or water can replace the cream, but the glaze will be less golden. Or, use a whole beaten egg (the white adds particular gloss), cream or milk. Just before baking, brush the top pastry with choice of glaze.

● For fruit pies, especially cherry and apple, and winter-time pies such as raisin, sprinkle granulated sugar over the glaze to make the pie glitter (as we did with the Prize-winning Sour Cherry Pie on the cover).

Country-Style Apple Pie

With country-style pies, the pastry is left untrimmed and is, instead, folded back over the filling (see photo, next page) to form an attractive ragged edge. For a change of taste, substitute raspberries for the cranberries.

❏ TIP: For baking, select apples that keep their shape. Northern Spy, Ida Red, Golden Delicious, Rome Beauty and Newtown are good choices for pies, strudels, baked apples and crisps.

1/2 cup	granulated sugar	125 mL
1/3 cup	ground almonds	75 mL
2 tbsp	all-purpose flour	25 mL
6	apples	6
1-1/2 cups	cranberries	375 mL
4 tsp	butter	20 mL
1 tbsp	light cream	15 mL
	Icing sugar	
	PASTRY	
2-1/4 cups	sifted cake-and-pastry flour	550 mL
1 tbsp	granulated sugar	15 mL
1/2 tsp	salt	2 mL
1/3 cup	cold butter, cubed	75 mL
1/3 cup	cold shortening, cubed	75 mL
1	egg yolk	1
1 tsp	lemon juice	5 mL
	Ice water	

● PASTRY: In large bowl, stir together flour, sugar and salt. Using pastry blender or two knives, cut in butter and shortening until mixture resembles fine crumbs with a few larger pieces. In measure, combine egg yolk, lemon juice and enough water to make 1/4 cup (50 mL). With fork, stir liquid briskly into flour mixture, 1 tbsp (15 mL) at a time, until dough holds together.

● On floured pastry cloth, roll out pastry into 14-inch (35 cm) circle, leaving edges rough. Transfer to 12-inch (30 cm) pizza pan, letting pastry hang over edge.

● Reserve 2 tbsp (25 mL) of the sugar; combine remaining sugar with almonds and flour. Sprinkle about half over pastry. Peel, core and cut apples into eighths; arrange in single layer over almond mixture. Sprinkle with cranberries and remaining almond mixture and sugar; dot with butter.

● Fold pastry overhang over filling to form attractive ragged edge; brush top of pastry with cream. Bake in 425°F (220°C) oven for 15 minutes. Reduce heat to 375°F (190°C); bake for 35 minutes longer or until apples are tender and pastry golden. Let cool on rack; dust with icing sugar. Makes 12 servings.

Almond and Red Currant Pie

With its tart taste, appealing color and almond crunchiness, this delicious pie is sure to become a summer favorite. Replace half the currants with raspberries, if desired.

	Pastry for 10-inch (25 cm) double-crust pie	
3/4 cup	toasted blanched slivered almonds	175 mL
4 cups	stemmed red currants	1 L
1-3/4 cups	granulated sugar	425 mL
1/4 cup	all-purpose flour	50 mL
1/2 tsp	almond extract	2 mL
2 tbsp	butter	25 mL
	GLAZE	
1	egg white (or 1 tbsp/15 mL light cream)	1
1 tbsp	granulated sugar	15 mL

● On lightly floured surface, roll out pastry and fit into 10-inch (25 cm) pie plate. Scatter almonds over pie shell.

● In bowl, mix red currants, sugar, flour and almond extract; spread over almonds. Dot with butter.

● Roll out remaining pastry and fit over top; trim and flute edge.

● GLAZE: Mix egg white with sugar; brush over pastry. Cut four steam vents in top. Bake in 425°F (220°C) oven for 15 minutes. Reduce heat to 350°F (180°C) and bake for 30 to 40 minutes longer or until pastry is golden and filling bubbly.

Caramel-Topped Pear Pie

Firm, just-ripe pears are perfect for this delicious pie. So is a scoop of vanilla ice cream!

❑ TIP: A 9- or 10-inch (23 or 25 cm) pie serves 6 to 8.

1	unbaked 10-inch (25 cm) pie shell	1
1 cup	packed brown sugar	250 mL
3/4 cup	all-purpose flour	175 mL
1 tsp	cinnamon	5 mL
1/3 cup	butter	75 mL
6	pears	6
2 tbsp	lemon juice	25 mL
1/4 cup	whipping cream	50 mL

● In bowl, stir together sugar, 1/2 cup (125 mL) of the flour and cinnamon. Using pastry blender, cut in butter until crumbly. Set aside.

● Peel, core and slice pears; toss with lemon juice and remaining flour. Arrange pears in pie shell. Spoon sugar mixture evenly over top; drizzle with cream.

● Bake on lowest rack in 425°F (220°C) oven for 20 to 25 minutes or until pastry is golden. Reduce temperature to 350°F (180°C); bake for 25 to 30 minutes longer or until topping is golden brown and filling bubbly.

Berry Crisp Pie

With frozen berries, it's easy to enjoy the taste of this summer pie all year long. The recipe originated with Vancouver caterer Susan Mendelson.

1	unbaked 10-inch (25 cm) pie shell	1
	CRISP TOPPING	
2/3 cup	packed brown sugar	150 mL
1/2 cup	all-purpose flour	125 mL
1/3 cup	rolled oats	75 mL
1/3 cup	butter	75 mL
	FILLING	
3 cups	frozen blueberries	750 mL
2 cups	frozen raspberries	500 mL
1 cup	frozen strawberries, quartered	250 mL
3/4 cup	granulated sugar	175 mL
3 tbsp	quick-cooking tapioca	50 mL
1/4 tsp	nutmeg	1 mL

● CRISP TOPPING: In bowl, stir together sugar, flour and rolled oats. Using pastry blender or two knives, cut in butter until crumbly.

● FILLING: In large bowl, combine blueberries, raspberries and strawberries. Stir together sugar, tapioca and nutmeg; sprinkle over berries, tossing to coat evenly. Spoon into pie shell.

● Sprinkle topping over fruit. Bake 425°F (220°C) oven for 15 minutes. Reduce heat to 350°F (180°C); bake for about 1 hour or until pastry is golden, topping crisp and brown, and filling bubbly. Let cool on rack.

Lemon Meringue Pie

This old-fashioned lemon meringue pie is a classic, with a very full-flavored and lemony filling.

❏ **FOR A PERFECT LEMON FILLING EVERY TIME:** Sometimes a lemon pie filling will thin out because it's been cooked for too long in the saucepan or at too high a temperature. Cornstarch reaches maximum thickness at boiling point. After that, you should boil gently only long enough to thicken the mixture and dispel the starchy taste. Vigorous or prolonged cooking will cause the starch granules to shrink; vigorous stirring will also cause the mixture to thin out by breaking down the swollen granules.

1	9-inch (23 cm) baked pie shell (see Pre-Baking Pie Shells, p. 92)	1
	FILLING	
1-1/4 cups	granulated sugar	300 mL
6 tbsp	cornstarch	100 mL
1/2 tsp	salt	2 mL
2 cups	water	500 mL
3	egg yolks, lightly beaten	3
3 tbsp	butter	50 mL
1 tbsp	grated lemon rind	15 mL
1/2 cup	lemon juice	125 mL
	MERINGUE	
3	egg whites	3
1/4 tsp	cream of tartar	1 mL
6 tbsp	granulated sugar	100 mL

● FILLING: In heavy-bottomed saucepan, combine sugar, cornstarch and salt; gradually stir in water. Bring to boil over medium-high heat, stirring constantly. Reduce heat to medium-low; boil gently for 3 minutes, stirring almost constantly.

● Remove from heat. Whisk a little hot mixture into egg yolks; whisk back into saucepan. Cook over medium heat, stirring constantly, for 2 minutes. (There should be no raw taste of starch or yolk.) Remove from heat; stir in butter, lemon rind and juice. Let cool slightly, about 3 minutes. Pour into baked pie shell. Let cool slightly while making meringue.

● MERINGUE: In bowl, beat egg whites with cream of tartar until soft peaks form. Gradually beat in sugar, about 1 tbsp (15 mL) at a time, until stiff peaks form. Spread over hot filling, sealing to crust to prevent shrinking. With spatula, knife or back of spoon, swirl meringue into attractive peaks.

● Bake in 350°F (180°C) oven for 12 to 15 minutes or until lightly browned. Let cool thoroughly (at least 2 hours); do not refrigerate.

Harvest Pumpkin Pie

Update a classic pumpkin pie with a pretty decorative flourish. Our smooth and creamy dark pumpkin pie is easy to make — or, try the honey variation. Both pies will taste as luscious as they look!

❏ TIP: A fabulous pumpkin pie combines a crisp flaky crust with a smooth creamy custard. For guaranteed success, quick-chill and prebake the crust at a high temperature before adding the pumpkin custard and baking the pie at a lower temperature.

	Pastry for 9-inch (23 cm) single-crust pie	
	FILLING	
2	eggs	2
1-1/2 cups	cooked pumpkin purée	375 mL
1 cup	packed dark brown sugar	250 mL
3/4 cup	light cream	175 mL
1 tsp	cinnamon	5 mL
1/2 tsp	cloves	2 mL
1/2 tsp	ginger	2 mL
1/2 tsp	nutmeg	2 mL
1/2 tsp	salt	2 mL
2 tbsp	sour cream	25 mL
1-1/2 tsp	milk	7 mL

● On pastry cloth and using stockinette-covered rolling pin, roll out pastry and fit into 9-inch (23 cm) pie plate. Trim pastry, leaving 1-inch (2.5 cm) overhang; fold under and flute edge. With fork, prick shell all over. Place in freezer for 30 minutes.

● Line pastry shell with foil; fill evenly with pie weights or dried beans. Bake on lowest rack in 400°F (200°C) oven for 10 minutes; lift out foil with weights and bake for about 10 minutes longer or until pastry is set.

● FILLING: Meanwhile, in large bowl, beat eggs lightly. Blend in pumpkin, sugar, light cream, cinnamon, cloves, ginger, nutmeg and salt; pour into pastry shell.

● Combine sour cream with milk; pour into funnel with narrow tube, blocking opening with finger. Remove finger and quickly drizzle mixture in spiral pattern over filling.

● Beginning at center, pull tip of knife shallowly through filling and sour cream mixture at 8 evenly spaced intervals.

Beginning at outside, pull knife through middle of intervals toward center to create web pattern.

● Bake on lowest rack in 350°F (180°C) oven for about 1 hour or until filling is set and point of knife inserted into center comes out clean. Let cool on rack.

VARIATION

HONEY PUMPKIN PIE: Substitute 3/4 cup (175 mL) honey for all the brown sugar. Reduce light cream to 1/2 cup (125 mL).

No-Bake Pumpkin Cream Pie

This luscious Thanksgiving pie is so creamy and delicious, no one will guess how easy it was to make!

1-1/2 cups	ginger cookie crumbs	375 mL
1/4 cup	butter, melted	50 mL
	FILLING	
3/4 cup	packed brown sugar	175 mL
1	pkg unflavored gelatin	1
1 tsp	cinnamon	5 mL
1/4 tsp	each salt, ginger and nutmeg	1 mL
Pinch	cloves	Pinch
1	can (14 oz/398 mL) pumpkin	1
3/4 cup	milk	175 mL
3	egg yolks, lightly beaten	3
1/2 cup	whipping cream	125 mL

● Mix together ginger cookie crumbs and melted butter; press onto bottom and side of 9-inch (1.5 L) deep pie plate. Refrigerate.

● FILLING: Meanwhile, in heavy saucepan, stir together brown sugar, gelatin, cinnamon, salt, ginger, nutmeg and cloves; blend in pumpkin, milk and egg yolks. Bring just to boil over medium heat, stirring constantly, about 5 minutes. Set pan in ice water or refrigerate until cooled enough to just start mounding when stirred.

● In bowl, beat cream; whisk one-quarter into pumpkin mixture. Fold in remaining whipped cream; pour into pie crust. Refrigerate for at least 4 hours or until set, or overnight. Pipe whipped cream around pie, if desired.

Coconut Cream Pie

This slice-of-heaven cream pie is made even better with toasted coconut and white chocolate curls on the whipped cream topping. For a change of taste, try the Banana Cream variation.

❏ **TIP: Toasting coconut gives it a gorgeous golden color and extra flavor. Spread the coconut on baking sheet and bake in 350˚F (180˚C) oven for 5 minutes or until golden, tossing once or twice. Or, spread on microwaveable plate and microwave at High for 5 to 7 minutes or until golden, stirring once or twice.**

1	baked 9-inch (23 cm) single-crust pie shell	1
3/4 cup	whipping cream	175 mL
1/3 cup	flaked coconut, toasted	75 mL
1 oz	white chocolate (optional)	30 g
	FILLING	
3 cups	milk	750 mL
1 cup	flaked coconut	250 mL
3/4 cup	granulated sugar	175 mL
1/3 cup	cornstarch	75 mL
1/2 tsp	salt	2 mL
3	egg yolks	3
2 tbsp	butter	25 mL
1 tsp	vanilla	5 mL

● FILLING: In saucepan, heat milk with coconut until bubbles appear around edge; remove from heat.

● In bowl, combine sugar, cornstarch and salt; whisk in milk mixture. Return to saucepan; cook over medium heat, whisking constantly, for 4 to 7 minutes or until boiling and thickened. Remove from heat.

● Whisk a quarter of the hot mixture into egg yolks; whisk back into saucepan. Reduce heat and simmer for about 1 minute or until no raw taste of starch remains. Remove from heat; stir in butter and vanilla. Pour into bowl and cover surface with waxed paper; refrigerate until cold and set.

● Spoon filling into baked pie shell, spreading evenly. Whip cream. Spread or pipe over filling. *(Pie can be prepared to this point, covered and refrigerated for up to 1 day.)* Sprinkle with coconut.

● Shave white chocolate (if using) to form curls. Sprinkle over pie. (For tips on making chocolate curls, see sidebar, p. 27.)

VARIATION

BANANA CREAM FILLING: Prepare Coconut Cream Filling, but omit coconut and increase vanilla to 2 tsp (10 mL). No more than 4 hours before serving, toss 2 cups (500 mL) thinly sliced bananas with about 2 tbsp (25 mL) orange juice; fold into cream filling. Garnish whipped cream topping with grated nutmeg and sliced bananas just before serving.

Raspberry Mousse Pie

*Garnish this luscious
dessert with raspberries
and chocolate leaves.
(To make chocolate leaves,
see p. 29.)*

1-1/2 cups	graham wafer crumbs (about 25 wafers)	375 mL
1/3 cup	butter, melted	75 mL
2 tbsp	granulated sugar	25 mL
2 tbsp	unsweetened cocoa powder	25 mL
	MOUSSE	
2	pkg (300 g each) frozen unsweetened raspberries, thawed	2
1/2 cup	granulated sugar	125 mL
1	pkg unflavored gelatin	1
1 cup	plain yogurt	250 mL
1/2 cup	whipping cream	125 mL

● Combine crumbs, butter, sugar and cocoa; press into lightly greased 9-inch (23 cm) pie plate. Bake in 350°F (180°C) oven for about 10 minutes or until set. Let cool on rack.

● MOUSSE: In food processor or blender, purée raspberries and juices; strain through sieve into saucepan. Stir in sugar. Sprinkle with gelatin; let stand for 1 minute. Warm over medium heat, whisking occasionally, for about 3 minutes or until dissolved. Chill for about 45 minutes or until slightly thickened, whisking often. Stir in yogurt.

● Whip cream and whisk one-third into purée; fold in remaining whipped cream. Spoon into crust; chill until set, about 6 hours.

Strawberry Meringue Custard Pie

Fresh and light, this pretty pie has a taste of summer in every slice.

❏ TIP: Pies with custard filling like this one are best eaten as soon as they are cool from baking. Be sure to refrigerate any leftovers.

1	baked 9-inch (23 cm) single-crust pie shell (see Pre-Baking Pie Shells, p. 92)	1

FILLING		
2 cups	milk	500 mL
1/2 cup	granulated sugar	125 mL
1/4 cup	cornstarch	50 mL
2	egg yolks, lightly beaten	2
1 tbsp	butter	15 mL
1 tsp	vanilla (or 1 tbsp/15 mL orange liqueur)	5 mL
2 cups	sliced strawberries	500 mL
2 tsp	granulated sugar	10 mL
1 tsp	grated orange rind	5 mL

MERINGUE		
2	egg whites	2
Pinch	cream of tartar	Pinch
1/4 cup	instant dissolving (fruit/berry) sugar	50 mL

GARNISH		
1/2 cup	sliced strawberries	125 mL
1 tbsp	strawberry or red currant jelly, melted	15 mL
	Mint sprigs	
	Strawberries	

● FILLING: In heavy saucepan, combine milk, 1/2 cup (125 mL) sugar and cornstarch; cook over medium heat, stirring constantly, for 5 to 10 minutes or until boiling and thickened. Whisk about one-third of the hot mixture into egg yolks; return to saucepan. Cook over low heat for 2 minutes. Remove from heat; stir in butter and vanilla until butter has melted.

● Spread sliced berries in baked pie shell; sprinkle with sugar and orange rind. Pour hot filling over top; set aside to let cool slightly.

● MERINGUE: In bowl, beat egg whites with cream of tartar until soft peaks form. Gradually beat in sugar until stiff shiny peaks form. Drop spoonfuls of meringue around edge of filling to form ring, sealing edge of meringue to pie crust. Bake in 400°F (200°C) oven for 10 to 12 minutes or until meringue is golden. Let cool completely, 1 to 2 hours.

● GARNISH: Arrange sliced strawberries over filling in center of pie. Spoon melted jelly over berries. Garnish with mint and a few whole berries.

Double Whammy Chocolate Cream Pie

A flaky chocolate crust covered with creamy chocolate filling, whipped cream and an elegant finish of chocolate curls — this rich and satisfying chocolate pie is a chocoholic's dream come true!

❑ **TIP: Always use a good pie plate. Glass, enamel or pottery pie plates work well and are widely available. Avoid foil plates — the shiny surface reflects heat, preventing the pastry from setting and browning, and their flimsy structure allows the pie filling to seep under the bottom crust, making your pie soggy.**

3/4 cup	whipping cream	175 mL
1 oz	semisweet chocolate	30 g
	FILLING	
3 cups	milk	750 mL
1/2 cup	granulated sugar	125 mL
1/3 cup	cornstarch	75 mL
1/2 tsp	salt	2 mL
4 oz	bittersweet chocolate, chopped	125 g
3	egg yolks	3
2 tbsp	butter	25 mL
2 tsp	vanilla	10 mL
	CHOCOLATE CRUST	
1 cup	all-purpose flour	250 mL
1/4 cup	unsweetened cocoa powder	50 mL
1/4 cup	granulated sugar	50 mL
1/4 tsp	salt	1 mL
1/4 cup	cold butter, cubed	50 mL
1/4 cup	cold shortening, cubed	50 mL
3 tbsp	cold water	45 mL

● CHOCOLATE CRUST: In bowl, combine flour, cocoa, sugar and salt. Using pastry blender or two knives, cut in butter and shortening until mixture resembles fine crumbs with a few larger pieces.

● Sprinkle with water, stirring quickly with fork just until mixture is moistened and clumps together when pressed. Knead lightly 5 or 6 times to form ball; flatten into disc. Wrap and refrigerate for 30 minutes.

● On lightly floured surface, roll out dough to 1/4-inch (5 mm) thickness. Fit into 9-inch (23 cm) pie plate; trim and flute edge. Chill until firm.

● Using fork, prick pastry all over. Line with foil; fill with pie weights or dried beans. Bake in 400°F (200°C) oven for 20 minutes. Lift out foil with weights. Bake for about 10 minutes longer or until browned and no longer doughy in center. Let cool on rack.

● FILLING: Meanwhile, in saucepan, heat milk until bubbles form around edge. In bowl, combine sugar, cornstarch and salt; gradually add milk, whisking to remove any lumps. Return to saucepan. Add chocolate; cook over medium heat, whisking constantly, for 4 to 7 minutes or until boiling and thickened. Remove from heat.

● Whisk a quarter of the hot mixture into egg yolks; whisk back into saucepan. Reduce heat and simmer for about 1 minute or until no raw taste of starch remains. Remove from heat; stir in butter and vanilla. Pour into bowl and cover surface with waxed paper; refrigerate until cold and set.

● Spoon filling into baked pie shell, spreading evenly. Whip cream; spread or pipe over filling. Shave semisweet chocolate to form curls: sprinkle over cream. (For tips on making chocolate curls, see p. 27.) Cover loosely and refrigerate until filling is set, about 2 hours, or for up to 1 day.

Ice Cream Sundae Pie

This is a deliciously decadent variation of an all-time favorite dessert. Serve it after a meal, as an afternoon treat or at your child's next birthday party. One pie goes a long way, although you can count on most people wanting seconds. Be sure to use good-quality ice cream. Substitute vanilla ice cream for the coffee, if desired.

1-1/4 cups	fine chocolate wafer crumbs	300 mL
1/4 cup	finely ground toasted almonds	50 mL
3 tbsp	granulated sugar	50 mL
1/3 cup	butter, melted	75 mL
	FILLING	
4 cups	strawberry ice cream, softened	1 L
1/2 cup	mashed strawberries	125 mL
2 tsp	granulated sugar	10 mL
4 cups	coffee or chocolate ice cream, softened	1 L
	SAUCE	
1 cup	granulated sugar	250 mL
3/4 cup	unsweetened cocoa powder	175 mL
1 tsp	instant coffee granules	5 mL
1 cup	whipping cream	250 mL
1/4 cup	butter	50 mL

● In small bowl, combine crumbs, almonds and sugar; toss lightly with butter until blended. Press evenly onto bottom and side of deep 9- or 10-inch (23 or 25 cm) pie plate. Chill for 30 minutes.

● FILLING: Spread half of the strawberry ice cream evenly over crust; freeze until firm. Mix strawberries with sugar; spread over ice cream. Spread remaining strawberry ice cream over top. Freeze until firm.

● With ice cream scoop, arrange scoops of coffee ice cream over frozen strawberry ice cream. Freeze for 4 hours or until firm, or overnight.

● SAUCE: Meanwhile, in saucepan, combine sugar, cocoa and instant coffee; whisk in half of the cream to smooth paste. Blend in remaining cream. Cook over medium heat, stirring constantly, until sugar dissolves completely. Add butter and cook, stirring, until smooth and thickened, 5 to 8 minutes; let cool. *(Sauce can be refrigerated for up to 2 days. Rewarm to pouring consistency.)*

● TO SERVE: Let pie soften slightly in refrigerator for 30 minutes. Drizzle with sauce; garnish servings with dollop of whipped cream and strawberry, if desired.

Summer Berry Tart

This summer-fresh tart is sublime with Canada's favorite berry, the strawberry. It's equally delicious with blueberries or raspberries. And the easy press-in pastry is a no-fuss plus. This recipe makes one large tart or 4 smaller ones.

PRESS-IN PASTRY

1 cup	all-purpose flour	250 mL
3 tbsp	granulated sugar	50 mL
1/2 cup	cold butter, cubed	125 mL
1/2 tsp	white vinegar	2 mL

CREAM FILLING

3	egg yolks	3
1/2 cup	granulated sugar	125 mL
1/4 cup	all-purpose flour	50 mL
1-1/2 cups	hot milk	375 mL
1 tbsp	butter	15 mL
1 tsp	vanilla	5 mL

TOPPING

4 cups	strawberries (or 1-1/2 cups/375 mL blueberries or raspberries)	1 L
3 tbsp	red currant jelly	50 mL
1-1/2 tsp	water	7 mL

● CREAM FILLING: In heavy saucepan, whisk egg yolks; gradually whisk in sugar, then flour. Gradually whisk in milk and bring to boil, whisking constantly. Reduce heat to low and cook, stirring constantly, for 2 minutes. Stir in butter and vanilla. Pour into bowl and cover surface with waxed paper: refrigerate until cool or for up to 2 days.

● PRESS-IN PASTRY: In food processor, mix together flour and sugar. Using on/off motion, cut in butter until mixture resembles fine meal. Pour in vinegar; process on/off twice, being careful dough does not come together. Transfer to bowl and refrigerate for 20 minutes.

● With floured hands, squeeze handfuls of dough until it comes together into ball. Press evenly onto bottom and side of 9-inch (23 cm) tart pan with removable bottom, or four 4-1/2-inch (11 cm) ones. Refrigerate for 30 minutes or until firm.

● Prick bottom of shell with fork; bake in 400°F (200°C) oven for 25 to 30 minutes, or 15 to 20 minutes for 4-1/2-inch (11 cm) pans, or until golden. Let cool completely.

● Spoon cream filling into baked crust, spreading evenly. Hull berries and arrange over top. Melt together jelly and water; brush over berries. Refrigerate for up to 1 hour before serving.

STRAWBERRY FIELDS

An outing to a strawberry patch is a perfect way to celebrate the arrival of summer.

● *Contact your provincial department of agriculture for information about pick-your-own farms near you.*

● *Schedule your visit during the week to avoid crowds.*

● *Call ahead on the day you want to go to ensure picking is available.*

● *Pick berries in the morning or evening when the berries are firmer and the weather is cooler.*

● *Choose containers carefully if you bring your own. Avoid plastic bags or too large a container. Most farms will weigh your container before you start picking, and sell berries by weight, not measure.*

● *Pick only red berries; strawberries don't ripen after picking.*

Handle With Care

● *Don't leave berries in the sun or a hot car.*

● *Refrigerate in a shallow uncovered container.*

● *To clean berries, spray or rinse with cool water before hulling. Do not soak berries.*

● *Hull berries just before serving. The caps help preserve flavor, texture and nutritional value.*

Freezing Tips

● ***With sugar:*** *Hull berries. Mix 4 cups (1 L) sliced berries with 3/4 cup (175 mL) granulated sugar; or 4 cups (1 L) whole berries with 1/2 cup (125 mL) sugar. Let stand for a few minutes before sealing and freezing.*

● ***Without sugar:*** *Hull berries. Place whole dry berries in container and freeze.*

Maple Walnut Tart

This impressive tart was created by Toronto's Bistro 990 for Feast of Fields — a spectacular annual autumn progressive picnic that celebrates the local agriculture of southern Ontario. Instead of the chocolate garnish, you can pipe whipped cream around the border.

❏ **TIP: For fresh walnuts that are not rancid, avoid bagged ones in favor of vacuum-sealed walnuts in cans. In the fall and early winter, crack your own.**

2-1/4 cups	sifted cake-and-pastry flour	550 mL
1 tbsp	granulated sugar	15 mL
1/4 tsp	salt	1 mL
3/4 cup	cold butter	175 mL
1	egg	1
1 tbsp	ice water	15 mL
	MAPLE WALNUT FILLING	
2 cups	walnut pieces	500 mL
1/3 cup	whipping cream	75 mL
1/2 cup	maple syrup	125 mL
1/3 cup	granulated sugar	75 mL
1/4 cup	water	50 mL
2 oz	semisweet chocolate	60 g

● In bowl, combine flour, sugar and salt. Using pastry blender or two knives, cut in butter until mixture resembles coarse meal. Stir egg with ice water; stir into flour mixture until dough holds together. Knead lightly into ball; wrap and refrigerate for at least 30 minutes. *(Dough can be refrigerated for up to 3 days or frozen for up to 3 months; let stand at room temperature for 15 minutes before rolling out.)*

● On lightly floured surface, roll out pastry to 1/8-inch (3 mm) thickness; fit into 10-inch (25 cm) flan pan with removable bottom. Refrigerate for 30 minutes. Line pastry with foil; add pie weights or dried beans. Bake in 375°F (190°C) oven for 25 minutes. Lift out foil with weights. Prick pastry; bake for 10 to 15 minutes longer or until golden brown. Let cool.

● MAPLE WALNUT FILLING: Meanwhile, in food processor, chop half of the walnuts, 2 tbsp (25 mL) of the cream and half of the maple syrup until nuts are fine; set aside.

● In small saucepan, cook sugar and water over medium heat, stirring, until sugar dissolves. Boil over high heat, without stirring, for 5 to 7 minutes or until light caramel color. Whisk in remaining cream and maple syrup; cook, whisking, for 2 to 4 minutes or until slightly thickened.

● Whisk in nut mixture; cook, whisking, for 1 minute. Remove from heat; stir in remaining nuts. Pour into pie shell; refrigerate for 2 hours.

● In saucepan over hot, not boiling, water, melt chocolate; drizzle over tart.

PRE-BAKING PIE SHELLS

● *To bake single-crust pie shell unfilled (blind), first prick it all over with fork. This helps prevent pastry from shrinking or puffing up during baking.*

● *Line with piece of foil large enough to lift out easily. Fill evenly with pie weights, or with dried beans or rice (these can be used again).*

● *Bake pastry shell in 400°F (200°C) oven for 20 minutes. Remove from oven and carefully lift out foil with weights. Prick*

shell again if puffed, then return to oven for 10 minutes longer or until golden brown. Let cool before filling.

Plum Tart

Ground walnuts, flour and sugar sprinkled on the crust help absorb juices and prevent the crust from becoming soggy.

❏ TIP: Pick fresh-looking, plump, full-colored plums. They shouldn't be shrivelled or punctured but should be soft enough at the tip to yield to gentle pressure from your thumb. Plums don't change color or become any sweeter after being picked; they only become softer. If you get firm plums, leave them at room temperature to soften, then store in the refrigerator and use them as soon as possible. Wash plums just before using.

2 cups	all-purpose flour	500 mL
1/2 tsp	salt	2 mL
1/2 cup	butter, cubed	125 mL
2 tbsp	shortening, cubed	25 mL
1/2 cup	(approx) ice water	125 mL
	FILLING	
1/4 cup	ground walnuts	50 mL
1/4 cup	granulated sugar	50 mL
2 tbsp	all-purpose flour	25 mL
1 lb	red or purple plums, quartered	500 g
	CUSTARD	
1	egg	1
1/4 cup	granulated sugar	50 mL
1/3 cup	hot light cream	75 mL
1/4 tsp	vanilla	1 mL

● In large bowl, combine flour and salt. Using pastry blender or two knives, cut in butter and shortening until mixture resembles fine crumbs with a few larger pieces. With fork, stir in enough ice water to make dough hold together. Press into ball and flatten into disc; wrap and refrigerate for 30 minutes.

● On lightly floured surface, roll out dough to 1/4-inch (5 mm) thickness. Fit into 9-inch (23 cm) flan pan with removable bottom, building up sides about 1/4 inch (5 mm) above rim of pan. Cover and freeze for 30 minutes.

● FILLING: Stir together walnuts, 2 tbsp (25 mL) of the sugar and flour; sprinkle over tart shell. Arrange plums on top; sprinkle with remaining sugar. Bake in 400°F (200°C) oven for 20 to 30 minutes or until pastry is lightly browned.

● CUSTARD: In bowl, beat together egg and sugar. Stir in hot cream and vanilla; pour over plums. If necessary, shield edge of pastry with foil to prevent browning. Return to oven and bake for 20 to 25 minutes or until custard is set. Let cool on rack for 5 minutes. Remove side of pan and let cool slightly. Serve warm or chilled.

Bite-Size Lemon Tarts

These tiny tarts are a lemon-lover's delight. The recipe originated with writer Helen Gougeon.

2 tbsp	butter, softened	25 mL
3/4 cup	granulated sugar	175 mL
2 tsp	grated lemon rind	10 mL
1/4 cup	lemon juice	50 mL
2	eggs, well beaten	2
1 tsp	dried mint, crumbled	5 mL
18	unbaked mini (2-inch/5 cm) tart shells	18

● In bowl and using wooden spoon, cream butter with sugar until combined. Stir in lemon rind and juice; whisk in eggs and mint to make filling that will appear curdled.

● Spoon into tart shells, filling three-quarters full. Bake in 400°F (200°C) oven for 12 to 15 minutes or until filling is set and pastry golden. Makes 18 tarts.

Fresh Blueberry Tart

A buttery pat-in shortbread crust holds a double shot of blueberries — one cooked right in the crust, and a second scattered over the baked tart for a burst of fresh berry deliciousness.

1-1/2 cups	all-purpose flour	375 mL
2 tbsp	granulated sugar	25 mL
1/2 tsp	salt	2 mL
3/4 cup	butter	175 mL
	FILLING	
5 cups	blueberries	1.25 L
1 cup	granulated sugar	250 mL
1 tbsp	all-purpose flour	15 mL
2 tsp	cinnamon	10 mL
2 tbsp	icing sugar	25 mL

● In large bowl, combine flour, sugar and salt. Using pastry blender or two knives, cut in butter until crumbly. Pat firmly and evenly on bottom and side of 10-inch (25 cm) flan or quiche pan with removable base, or 1/2 inch (1 cm) up side of same-size pie plate. Bake in 350°F (180°C) oven for 20 to 25 minutes or until light golden.

● FILLING: Reserve 2 cups (500 mL) of the blueberries. In large bowl, lightly toss remaining berries with sugar, flour and cinnamon. Spoon into crust; cover edge with foil.

● Bake in 400°F (200°C) oven for 30 to 35 minutes or until bubbly and crust is golden brown. Let cool on rack.

● Remove side of pan and transfer to serving plate. Spoon reserved berries evenly over pie. Using sieve, dust with icing sugar. Garnish with mint sprig, if desired.

Berry Cream Chocolate Tarts

For a last-minute dessert, simply fill the tart shells with a dollop of whipped cream and top with a fresh summer berry.

❏ TIP: The chocolate pastry tart shells can be made up to 1 day ahead and stored in airtight container at room temperature.

4 cups	strawberries, raspberries or blackberries	1 L
	CHOCOLATE PASTRY	
8 oz	semisweet chocolate	250 g
2 tbsp	water	25 mL
1/2 tsp	vanilla	2 mL
2 cups	all-purpose flour	500 mL
1/2 tsp	salt	2 mL
3/4 cup	cold butter	175 mL
	CREAMY CHEESE FILLING	
3/4 cup	cream cheese, softened	175 mL
4 tsp	icing sugar	20 mL
1/3 cup	whipping cream	75 mL
1/2 tsp	vanilla	2 mL

● CHOCOLATE PASTRY: In double boiler over hot, not boiling, water, melt chocolate; remove from heat. Stir in water and vanilla until smooth.

● In food processor or in bowl using pastry blender, combine flour and salt; cut in butter until crumbly. Add chocolate and process or stir until soft dough forms. Divide into 4 balls; flatten, wrap and chill until firm, at least 30 minutes. *(Dough can be refrigerated for up to 3 days or frozen for up to 3 months.)*

● Remove dough from refrigerator 15 minutes before rolling out. Between sheets of waxed paper, roll out each portion to 1/8-inch (3 mm) thickness; remove top sheet of paper. Using floured 2-1/2-inch (6 cm) cutter, cut out rounds. Fit into 2-1/4-inch (5.5 cm) miniature tart shells. Prick bottoms and sides with fork.

● Bake in 350°F (180°C) oven for 10 minutes. Prick again on bottom if puffed. Bake for about 5 minutes longer or until slightly firm. Let cool in pans for 2 minutes; transfer to racks and let cool completely.

● CREAMY CHEESE FILLING: In bowl, blend together cream cheese and sugar; gradually beat in cream until smooth. Stir in vanilla. Chill for 30 minutes. Spoon rounded teaspoonful (5 mL) into each pastry shell. Top each with berry. Makes about 48.

Old-Time Butter Tarts

These classic butter tarts are a cinch to make — so why not bake more than one batch. We guarantee they'll disappear quickly!

18	unbaked 2-1/4-inch (5.5 cm) tart shells	18
	FILLING	
3/4 cup	packed brown sugar	175 mL
1/4 cup	corn syrup	50 mL
1	egg	1
2 tbsp	butter, softened	25 mL
1 tsp	vanilla	5 mL
1 tsp	vinegar	5 mL
Pinch	salt	Pinch
1/4 cup	currants, raisins or chopped nuts	50 mL

● FILLING: In bowl, whisk together brown sugar, corn syrup, egg, butter, vanilla, vinegar and salt; whisk vigorously. Stir in currants. Spoon into pastry-lined tart shells, filling three-quarters full.

● Bake in 450°F (220°C) oven for 10 to 12 minutes or until filling is puffed and bubbly and pastry is lightly golden. Let cool on racks. Makes 18 tarts.

Strawberry Cream Layers

Gossamer-light phyllo layered with lemony whipped cream and fresh berries floats on a pool of sabayon — what a tantalizing dessert to behold!

❏ **TIP:** Just before dinner, flavor and whip the cream and measure out the sabayon ingredients. Assemble the dessert at serving time, then whisk up the fast sabayon and serve immediately.

2 cups	strawberries	500 mL
1 tbsp	icing sugar	15 mL
8	mint sprigs	8
	PHYLLO ROUNDS	
3	sheets phyllo pastry	3
2 tbsp	butter, melted	25 mL
2 tbsp	granulated sugar	25 mL
	LEMON CREAM	
1-1/2 cups	whipping cream	375 mL
2 tbsp	granulated sugar	25 mL
1 tsp	finely chopped fresh mint	5 mL
1/4 tsp	finely grated lemon rind	1 mL
	SABAYON	
6	egg yolks	6
2 tbsp	lemon juice	25 mL
2 tbsp	white wine	25 mL
1 tbsp	Drambuie or brandy	15 mL
4 tsp	granulated sugar	20 mL

● PHYLLO ROUNDS: Place 1 phyllo sheet on damp tea towel, keeping remaining sheets covered with damp tea towel to prevent drying out. Brush sheet lightly with butter; sprinkle with sugar.

● Lay second sheet over first; repeat butter and sugar steps. Top with third sheet; repeat butter and sugar. Using 3-inch (8 cm) round cookie cutter, carefully cut out 16 rounds.

● Bake on parchment paper-lined or greased baking sheets in 375°F (190°C) oven for about 5 minutes or until golden brown. Let cool on racks. *(Rounds can be prepared up to 1 day ahead.)*

● LEMON CREAM: In bowl, whip cream; beat in sugar, mint and lemon rind.

● ASSEMBLY: Using spoon or piping bag fitted with 1/2-inch (1 cm) tip, cover 12 of the phyllo rounds with lemon cream. Slice 4 strawberries in half lengthwise; set aside for garnish. Arrange remaining strawberries evenly in circle around edges of rounds; spoon or pipe rosette of whipped cream in center.

● Place 4 berry-filled rounds on dessert plates; top each with second berry-filled round. Pressing lightly, top with third round. Place remaining plain phyllo rounds on top; dust with icing sugar.

● SABAYON: In large bowl set in saucepan of simmering water, whisk together egg yolks, lemon juice, wine, Drambuie and sugar until thickened and smooth. Immediately spoon sauce beside phyllo rounds on plates. Garnish with reserved strawberries and mint sprigs. Serve immediately. Makes 4 servings.

Easy Rhubarb Strudel

Rhubarb has just the right tang to go with buttery crisp phyllo pastry. At Christmas, please your guests with the mincemeat version.

❏ **TIP: For release of steam and easy slicing, make vents in the strudel before baking. Using a serrated knife, cut 7 slits in top through thickness of strudel.**

6	sheets phyllo pastry	6
1/2 cup	(approx) butter, melted	125 mL
1/3 cup	fine dry bread crumbs	75 mL
	Icing sugar	
	RHUBARB FILLING	
4 cups	chopped rhubarb (1/2-inch/1 cm pieces)	1 L
1 cup	granulated sugar	250 mL
2 tbsp	quick-cooking tapioca*	25 mL
1 tsp	grated lemon rind	5 mL

● RHUBARB FILLING: In bowl, toss rhubarb with sugar, tapioca and lemon rind; set aside.

● Place 1 sheet of phyllo on damp tea towel. Cover remaining phyllo with damp tea towel. Brush sheet with some of the butter; sprinkle with 1 tbsp (15 mL) of the bread crumbs.

● Layer remaining phyllo, brushing each sheet with butter and sprinkling with remaining bread crumbs.

● About 2 inches (5 cm) from one long edge of pastry, spoon rhubarb mixture lengthwise down pastry in 3-inch (8 cm) wide strip, leaving 2-inch (5 cm) border of pastry at each short end.

● Starting at long edge nearest filling, carefully begin to roll phyllo over filling. Roll up strudel jelly roll-style, folding in edges as you roll. Roll up firmly but allow a little slack for expansion. Carefully place strudel seam side down on greased baking sheet. Brush with butter.

● Cut 7 slits in top. Bake in 400°F (200°C) oven for 30 to 35 minutes or until crisp and golden. Transfer to rack or serving platter. Just before serving warm or at room temperature, dust with icing sugar. Makes 8 servings.

*If using frozen rhubarb, increase tapioca to 3 tbsp (50 mL).

VARIATIONS

CHEESE STRUDEL: For rhubarb filling, substitute cottage cheese filling:

● In large bowl, beat together 1/4 cup (50 mL) butter, 1/4 cup (50 mL) granulated sugar, 1 egg yolk, 1 tsp (5 mL) vanilla, 2 tbsp (25 mL) sour cream and 1 cup (250 mL) pressed cottage cheese.

● Stir in 1/3 cup (75 mL) raisins and 1 tsp (5 mL) grated lemon rind. Fold in 2 stiffly beaten egg whites.

MINCEMEAT STRUDEL: For rhubarb filling, substitute 2 cups (500 mL) mincemeat and 2 chopped peeled pears or apples.

APPLE STRUDEL: For rhubarb filling, substitute 4 large peeled, quartered and sliced apples, mixed with 1/2 cup (125 mL) granulated sugar, 1/4 cup (50 mL) chopped nuts, 1/4 cup (50 mL) raisins, 1 tsp (5 mL) grated lemon rind and 1/2 tsp (2 mL) cinnamon.

PHYLLO PASTRY

One of the most impressive wrappings for a sweet filling is flaky phyllo pastry.

● *The pastry comes in 1 lb (454 g) packages, containing about 20 sheets, and is usually frozen. Transfer the package to the refrigerator the day before you plan to use it.*

● *Prepare the filling before opening the package. When possible, plan to use the whole package.*

● *Place the phyllo on work surface; cover with damp, but not wet, tea towel. Uncover the stack to remove the sheets as you use them and recover immediately to keep the pastry from drying out.*

● *Open the first sheet and place on another damp tea towel, then proceed with the recipe.*

Apple Pecan Phyllo Crisps

Enjoy a delicious guilt-free phyllo crisp knowing that its apple filling adds fiber and vitamins to your diet.

❏ TIP: Toast pecans in small skillet over medium-low heat for 1 to 2 minutes, stirring.

2	sheets phyllo pastry	2
2 tsp	butter, melted	10 mL
1/3 cup	packed brown sugar	75 mL
1 tsp	grated lemon rind	5 mL
1 tbsp	lemon juice	15 mL
1/2 tsp	cinnamon	2 mL
3 cups	sliced peeled apples	750 mL
2 tbsp	chopped pecans, toasted	25 mL
1-1/2 tsp	icing sugar	7 mL

● Lay sheet of phyllo on work surface: brush with half of the butter. Using scissors, cut into three 5-inch (12 cm) wide strips; fold each strip crosswise into thirds. Gently mould into muffin cup. Repeat with remaining phyllo and butter to make 6 shells.

● Bake in 400°F (200°C) oven for 5 minutes or until golden. *(Shells can be stored in airtight container for up to 3 days.)*

● In heavy skillet, heat sugar, lemon rind, lemon juice and cinnamon over medium heat until bubbly; add apples and cook, stirring often, for 5 minutes or until tender. Let cool slightly.

● Spoon into prepared shells. Sprinkle with toasted pecans, then icing sugar. Makes 6 servings.

Making and Shaping Choux Pastry

Use our classic choux paste recipe to create an assortment of irresistible pastries. Just follow the shaping and baking directions below — then fill with whipped cream, fresh fruit or crème pâtissière. Or, turn to page 100 for more delicious dessert ideas using profiteroles, cream puffs and Paris-Brest rings.

1 In heavy saucepan, combine 1 cup (250 mL) water, 1/2 cup (125 mL) cubed butter and 1/4 tsp (1 mL) salt; bring to full boil. Remove from heat.

2 Add 1 cup (250 mL) all-purpose flour all at once, stirring vigorously with wooden spoon until mixture forms smooth ball that leaves side of pan.

3 Return to medium-low heat; cook, stirring constantly, for 2 minutes. Let cool for 5 minutes.

4 Using electric mixer, beat in 4 eggs, one at a time, beating well after each addition; continue beating until dough is smooth and shiny.

5 Choose one of the shaping variations below and bake as directed.

PROFITEROLES

● With spoon or pastry bag fitted with star tip, drop about 1 tbsp (15 mL) dough for each profiterole about 2 inches (5 cm) apart onto parchment paper-lined or greased baking sheets. Bake in 400°F (200°C) oven for 25 minutes or until puffed, golden and crisp. Makes about 30.

CREAM PUFFS

● With spoon or pastry bag fitted with plain tip, drop about 1 well-rounded tbsp (25 mL) dough for each puff about 3 inches (8 cm) apart onto parchment paper-lined or greased baking sheets. Bake in 400°F (200°C) oven for 25 to 30 minutes or until puffed, golden and crisp. Makes about 16.

PARIS-BREST RING

● With floured finger, trace 8-inch (20 cm) circle on each of two parchment paper-lined or greased baking sheets. Drop large spoonfuls of dough around each circle to form ring, making sure mounds touch one another.

● Glaze top of pastry (see sidebar, p. 100); sprinkle with 1/4 cup (50 mL) sliced almonds. Bake in 400°F (200°C) oven for 25 to 30 minutes or until puffed and golden. Let cool completely.

● With serrated knife, cut rings in half horizontally; pull out any moist dough inside. Replace tops and return rings to turned-off oven for 10 minutes to dry. Makes 2 rings.

Frozen Profiteroles with Chocolate Rum Sauce

Store ice cream-filled profiteroles in an airtight container in the freezer for up to one month. Add chocolate sauce just before serving.

16	profiteroles (use half Choux Pastry recipe, p. 99)	16
4 cups	coffee, vanilla or chocolate ice cream	1 L
	CHOCOLATE RUM SAUCE	
6 oz	semisweet chocolate, chopped	175 g
2/3 cup	water	150 mL
1/4 cup	butter	50 mL
1 tsp	instant coffee granules	5 mL
1 tbsp	rum	15 mL

● CHOCOLATE RUM SAUCE: In small saucepan, combine chocolate, water, butter and coffee granules; cook over low heat, stirring frequently, until chocolate is melted. Remove from heat; stir in rum.

● Slice top third from each profiterole, reserving tops. Pull out any moist dough inside. Soften ice cream in refrigerator for 15 minutes, if necessary. Fill each profiterole with scoop of ice cream. Replace tops.

● Arrange profiteroles in bowl. Drizzle with sauce and serve immediately. Makes 8 servings.

Classic Cream Puffs

Although both the puffs and the cream filling can be prepared in advance and stored separately, filled puffs should be refrigerated and served within the hour.

❏ TIP: For a summer-fresh variation on Classic Cream Puffs, add some fresh fruit flavor. Combine 2 cups (500 mL) blueberries, sliced strawberries or raspberries with 2 tbsp (25 mL) orange liqueur and let stand for 2 hours. Layer fruit between the filling when assembling the cream puffs and serve immediately.

16	glazed cream puffs (use Choux Pastry recipe, p. 99)	16
1/3 cup	icing sugar	75 mL
	FILLING	
2 cups	whipping cream	500 mL
2 tbsp	granulated sugar	25 mL
1 tsp	vanilla	5 mL

● FILLING: In deep bowl, whip together cream, sugar and vanilla.

● Slice top third from each cream puff, reserving tops. Pull out any moist dough inside. With spoon or piping bag, fill each with filling. Replace tops. Dust with icing sugar. Serve immediately or refrigerate for up to 1 hour. Makes 16.

GLAZING CHOUX PASTRY

A simple wash of egg and milk helps to smooth out rough edges on the dough and gives the cooked pastry a lustrous golden glaze.

● *Beat together 1 egg yolk and 2 tbsp (25 mL) milk. Dip finger into yolk mixture and lightly smooth top of each uncooked plain pastry. (For pastry formed with pastry bag star tip, use pastry brush.) Don't let yolk mixture dribble down sides of pastries onto baking sheet because it will prevent pastries from rising.*

Crème Pâtissière

Choux pastry and this heavenly filling were made for each other! Use it to fill profiteroles, cream puffs or éclairs. For an elegant finish, dust filled pastries with icing sugar or drizzle with melted chocolate.

3	egg yolks	3
1/2 cup	granulated sugar	125 mL
2 tbsp	all-purpose flour	25 mL
1-1/2 cups	hot milk	375 mL
1 tbsp	butter	15 mL
1 tsp	vanilla	5 mL

● In heavy saucepan, beat egg yolks; gradually beat in sugar. Using whisk, blend in flour. Gradually stir in milk and bring to boil, whisking constantly.

● Reduce heat to low and cook for 2 minutes, stirring constantly. Stir in butter and vanilla. Pour into bowl and cover surface with waxed paper; let cool. Makes about 2 cups (500 mL).

Paris-Brest

Filled with praline-whipped cream and dusted with icing sugar, this delectable choux pastry ring makes an impressive sweet ending to any special occasion. Since the Choux Pastry recipe makes two rings, bake and fill one and freeze the second.

1	Paris-Brest Ring (use Choux Pastry recipe, p. 99)	1
	Icing sugar	
	PRALINE POWDER	
1/3 cup	whole unblanched almonds	75 mL
1/4 cup	granulated sugar	50 mL
	FILLING	
2 cups	whipping cream	500 mL
1 tbsp	granulated sugar	15 mL
1 tsp	vanilla	5 mL

● PRALINE POWDER: In small heavy saucepan, stir almonds with sugar over medium heat until sugar melts. Reduce heat to medium-low; cook for 3 to 5 minutes, without stirring, until syrup is rich golden brown. Immediately pour onto greased baking sheet; let cool until crisp, about 10 minutes.

● Transfer to plastic bag; pound with rolling pin into chunks. Crush to powder with rolling pin or in food processor. *(Powder can be stored in airtight container for up to 1 month.)*

● FILLING: In bowl, whip together cream, sugar and vanilla; blend in praline powder.

● Remove top of Paris-Brest ring; spoon filling into bottom of ring, reserving some for garnish, if desired. Replace top. Pipe rosettes of remaining cream around center of edge, if desired. Dust with icing sugar. Serve immediately or refrigerate for up to 1 hour. Makes 6 servings.

Chocolate Chestnut Éclairs

Chestnuts and chocolate give a European pastry flair to these spectacular éclairs.

❏ TIP: Chestnuts grow in prickly husks, which split when ripe to reveal shiny brown nuts. Chestnuts sold in supermarkets already have these husks removed. When buying chestnuts, avoid ones that are already bagged; instead, select your own from open bins. Pick firm nuts that feel heavy for their size and discard any that seem dry or shrivelled.

	Icing sugar	

CHOCOLATE CHOUX PASTRY

1 cup	all-purpose flour	250 mL
2 tbsp	unsweetened cocoa powder	25 mL
1 cup	water	250 mL
1/2 cup	butter	125 mL
1/4 tsp	salt	1 mL
5	(approx) eggs	5

CHESTNUT FILLING

3/4 lb	chestnuts	375 g
1-1/2 cups	(approx) milk	375 mL
1/4 cup	granulated sugar	50 mL
1/2 tsp	vanilla	2 mL
1/2 cup	whipping cream	125 mL
1/2 cup	pine nuts	125 mL
1/2 cup	mixed candied peel	125 mL
2 tbsp	kirsch or rum	25 mL

CUSTARD SAUCE

2 cups	milk	500 mL
4	egg yolks	4
1/3 cup	granulated sugar	75 mL
1/4 tsp	salt	1 mL
1/2 tsp	vanilla	2 mL

● CHOCOLATE CHOUX PASTRY: Combine flour with cocoa. In saucepan, bring water, butter and salt to boil; remove from heat. Add flour mixture all at once, vigorously stirring with wooden spoon until dough comes away from side of pan. Return to medium heat and cook, stirring constantly, for 2 minutes. Let cool for 5 minutes.

● Beat in 3 of the eggs, one at a time, beating vigorously after each addition. Lightly beat remaining eggs; gradually beat in enough of the eggs, 1 tbsp (15 mL) at a time, just until dough is smooth and flows when spoon is lifted.

● Using pastry bag fitted with 3/4-inch (2 cm) star tip, pipe fingers about 4 inches (10 cm) long and 1 inch (2.5 cm) wide onto parchment paper-lined or greased baking sheets. Bake in 400°F (200°C) oven for 15 minutes. Reduce heat to 350°F (180°C); bake for 15 to 20 minutes longer or until firm to the touch. Let cool on rack.

● CHESTNUT FILLING: Meanwhile, using knife, score cross on flat side of each chestnut. In saucepan of boiling water, blanch 4 or 5 at a time for 3 minutes; peel away shells and inner brown skins.

● In separate saucepan, combine chestnuts, 1-1/2 cups (375 mL) milk and sugar; bring to boil. Reduce heat; cover and simmer, stirring occasionally, for 45 to 60 minutes or until chestnuts are very tender, adding more milk if necessary to keep chestnuts covered. Drain and reserve milk.

● Purée chestnuts and vanilla in food processor, adding enough reserved milk if necessary to make smooth thick purée. Transfer to large bowl and let cool completely. Beat in enough milk (about 2 tbsp/25 mL) to make creamy consistency. Whip cream; fold into chestnut purée along with nuts, candied peel and kirsch.

● CUSTARD SAUCE: In heavy saucepan, heat milk just until bubbles appear around edge. In large bowl, whisk together egg yolks, sugar and salt; gradually whisk in milk.

● Return to saucepan; cook over medium-low heat, stirring constantly with wooden spoon, for 3 to 5 minutes or until mixture thickens enough to coat spoon. Do not boil. Immediately remove from heat; strain through fine sieve into bowl. Add vanilla; let cool completely. Cover and refrigerate until chilled or overnight.

● ASSEMBLY: Halve éclairs lengthwise; remove any soft dough inside. Spoon filling into éclairs. Replace tops; dust with icing sugar. Spoon some custard sauce onto plates and top with éclairs. Makes about 10 éclairs.

Cool Desserts

*Whether the choice is a silky Crème Caramel, an elegant Mandarin Trifle,
refreshing Peach Mousse Parfait or the new and glamorous Almond Praline Semifreddo, these luscious
cool-on-a-spoon desserts are an easy yet memorable finale to any meal. Best of all, most of our chilled or
frozen desserts are make-ahead — royal desserts-in-waiting, if you will! — and that's especially important for
busy people who love to entertain. You'll also find the scoop on superlative homemade ice cream plus the
makings for some of the most sublime sundaes you'll ever sink your spoon into!*

Classic Crème Caramel

*This crème caramel is so
smooth and silky that you'll
want to linger over each
delicious spoonful.*

❏ TIP: If some of the caramel
sticks to the custard cups
when unmoulding custards,
set cups in pan with enough
boiling water to come halfway
up sides for a few minutes to
melt caramel. Spoon caramel
over custards.

2/3 cup	granulated sugar	150 mL
1/3 cup	water	75 mL
4	egg yolks	4
2	eggs	2
2 cups	hot milk	500 mL
1 tsp	vanilla	5 mL

● In heavy saucepan, combine half of the
sugar with water; bring to boil over
medium-high heat, stirring occasionally.

● Boil, without stirring, for 5 to 8 minutes
or just until syrup turns amber in color.
(Watch carefully because caramel burns
quickly.) Remove immediately from heat.

● Pour caramel evenly into six 6-ounce
(175 mL) custard cups or one 6-cup (1.5 L)
soufflé dish. Lift each cup and swirl caramel
evenly over bottom. (Caramel will harden in
the cups, but will soften again when custard
is baked.) Set aside.

● In large bowl, whisk together egg yolks,
eggs and remaining sugar; gradually stir in
milk and vanilla. Skim off froth.

● Pour egg mixture evenly over caramel in
custard cups.

● Place custard cups in large baking pan;
pour in enough boiling water to come
halfway up sides of cups.

● Bake in 350°F (180°C) oven for about
40 minutes for custard cups, or 50 minutes
for soufflé dish, or until knife inserted into
custard centers comes out clean. Remove
cups from water; let cool completely.
Cover and refrigerate until chilled or for
up to 2 days.

● To unmould, run knife around edge of
custard and invert onto dessert plates or
serving dish. Makes 6 servings.

VARIATION

ORANGE CARAMEL CUSTARD: Substitute
1 tbsp (15 mL) grated orange rind for
vanilla. Add 2 tbsp (25 mL) orange liqueur
or orange juice to the egg mixture.

Watch syrup carefully when boiling because it burns quickly. Remove from heat when amber in color.

To cover bottoms evenly with caramel, lift cups and swirl gently.

Custards are baked when knife inserted into centers comes out clean.

105

Floating Islands on Lemon Cream

This pretty citrus dessert has the soft-textured, tangy taste of lemon meringue pie.

❏ TIP: To get the most juice from lemons, roll them on the counter first to break the membranes.

4	egg yolks	4
1 cup	granulated sugar	250 mL
1 tbsp	cornstarch	15 mL
2 cups	light cream	500 mL
1/2 cup	lemon juice	125 mL
	Shreds of lemon rind	
	MERINGUES	
4	egg whites	4
1/4 tsp	cream of tartar	1 mL
1/2 cup	granulated sugar	125 mL

● In heavy saucepan, whisk egg yolks lightly. Whisk in sugar and cornstarch; whisk in cream and lemon juice. Bring slowly to boil over medium heat, stirring almost constantly; boil gently for 1 minute. Let cool to room temperature, stirring 2 or 3 times (mixture thickens as it cools). Cover with plastic wrap and refrigerate until cold.

● MERINGUES: In bowl, beat egg whites with cream of tartar until soft peaks form. Gradually beat in sugar until stiff glossy peaks form.

● Fill wide saucepan half-full with water; heat until barely simmering. Using large spoon, scoop meringue into rounded egg shapes and drop into saucepan, being careful not to let them touch one another. Poach, in batches, for 2 minutes; gently turn meringues over and poach for 2 to 3 minutes longer or just until set. Remove with slotted spoon onto tea towel.

● Spoon lemon cream mixture onto dessert plates; top each with 3 meringues. Sprinkle with lemon rind. Makes 4 servings.

Cappuccino Cream

This creamy dessert combines velvety smoothness with a deeply satisfying coffee flavor. Almost coffee and dessert in one, it's a delightful finale to a special dinner for four.

3/4 tsp	unflavored gelatin	4 mL
2 tbsp	cold water	25 mL
2	egg yolks	2
1/3 cup	granulated sugar	75 mL
1/2 cup	milk	125 mL
1 tbsp	instant coffee granules	15 mL
1 tbsp	coffee liqueur (optional)	15 mL
1 tsp	vanilla	5 mL
1/2 cup	whipping cream	125 mL
1 oz	semisweet chocolate, grated	30 g

● In small bowl, sprinkle gelatin over cold water; let stand for 5 minutes or until softened. In separate bowl, whisk egg yolks with sugar for 2 to 3 minutes or until pale and thickened. Set aside.

● In small saucepan, bring milk to gentle simmer over medium-low heat; stir in gelatin mixture and coffee granules until dissolved. Gradually add to egg mixture, whisking constantly.

● Return to saucepan; cook over medium-low heat for 3 to 5 minutes or until thick enough to coat back of spoon. Strain through fine sieve into bowl; stir in coffee liqueur (if using) and vanilla. Refrigerate for 15 to 20 minutes or until cool.

● Whip cream. Whisk one-third into coffee mixture; fold in remaining whipped cream. Pour half of the mixture into wine glasses or small parfait glasses; sprinkle with half of the chocolate. Top with remaining coffee mixture. Chill for at least 3 hours or up to 2 days. Just before serving, sprinkle with remaining chocolate. Makes 4 servings.

Strawberry Creamy Hearts

The mould for this heart-shaped dessert is pierced to drain off excess liquid.

❑ TIP: Quark is a cultured fresh cheese which is not as sweet as cottage cheese or as sharp as yogurt. It's available in supermarket dairy cases and delicatessens. Like yogurt, it's often paired with fruit and can replace cream cheese in cheesecakes (see Warm Rhubarb Cheesecake Pie, p. 76).

3/4 lb	quark or light cream cheese	375 g
2 tbsp	granulated sugar	25 mL
1/2 tsp	vanilla	2 mL
1/3 cup	whipping cream	75 mL
	Strawberry Purée (recipe follows)	
	Strawberries	

● Line one 6-inch (15 cm) or four 3-inch (8 cm) porcelain heart moulds with dampened cheesecloth, leaving overhang; set aside.

● In bowl and using wooden spoon (or electric mixer if using cream cheese), beat quark with sugar and vanilla until fluffy. In separate bowl, whip cream; stir about one-third into quark mixture. Fold in remaining whipped cream.

● Spoon into prepared mould; fold overhanging cheesecloth over top. Cover with plastic wrap; set on dish in refrigerator to drain for at least 6 hours or overnight.

● Unmould onto dessert plate. Surround with strawberry purée; garnish with berries. Makes 4 servings.

STRAWBERRY PURÉE

2 cups	strawberries	500 mL
1/3 cup	granulated sugar	75 mL
1/3 cup	water	75 mL
	Orange liqueur (optional)	

● In blender or food processor, process strawberries, sugar and water until smooth. Pass through sieve to remove seeds. Stir in liqueur (if using). Makes 1-1/2 cups (375 mL).

Fruited Ricotta Charlotte

Choose sliced kiwifruit, peach halves, raspberries and blueberries — or any combination of your favorite fresh fruit — to garnish this luscious summer dessert. Serve with raspberry sauce, if desired (recipe, p. 112).

❏ TIP: For a show-stopping presentation, tie with a pretty satin ribbon and dust with icing sugar.

	LADYFINGERS	
4	eggs, separated	4
2/3 cup	granulated sugar	150 mL
1 tsp	vanilla	5 mL
2/3 cup	all-purpose flour	150 mL
Pinch	salt	Pinch
	Icing sugar	
	FILLING	
2 tbsp	lemon juice	25 mL
2 tbsp	water	25 mL
2	pkg unflavored gelatin	2
1-1/2 cups	ricotta cheese	375 mL
3/4 cup	icing sugar	175 mL
1/3 cup	amaretto	75 mL
1 tbsp	grated lemon rind	15 mL
1-1/2 cups	whipping cream	375 mL
3/4 cup	chopped toasted almonds (see p. 51)	175 mL
	GARNISH	
	Assorted fresh fruit	
1/4 cup	apricot jam, heated	50 mL

● LADYFINGERS: Line two baking sheets with parchment paper; draw 12-1/2- x 3-1/4-inch (31 x 8 cm) rectangle on each.

● In bowl, beat egg yolks with half of the sugar for 5 minutes or until thickened. Add vanilla.

● In separate bowl, beat egg whites until soft peaks form; gradually beat in remaining sugar until stiff peaks form. Whisk one-third into yolk mixture. Combine flour and salt; sift half over yolk mixture and fold in. Fold in half of the remaining whites, then remaining flour mixture, then remaining whites until blended.

● Spoon batter into piping bag fitted with 3/4-inch (2 cm) plain tip. Pipe 3-1/4-inch (8 cm) ladyfingers, just touching each other, to fill in rectangles on baking sheets. Pipe remaining batter into individual fingers 3-1/4 inches (8 cm) long and 1 inch (2.5 cm) apart. Sift icing sugar generously over tops.

● Bake in 300°F (150°C) oven for 25 to 30 minutes or until light golden but still soft. Let cool on baking sheets for 5 minutes; loosen with spatula. Line edge of 8-inch (2 L) springform pan with ladyfinger rectangles, bending and trimming to fit. Place half of the individual ladyfingers in bottom of pan.

● FILLING: In small saucepan, combine lemon juice with water; sprinkle with gelatin and let stand for 1 minute. Heat over low heat until dissolved.

● In bowl, beat ricotta with sugar until smooth; blend in gelatin mixture, 1 tbsp (15 mL) of the amaretto and lemon rind. Whip cream; fold into ricotta mixture along with almonds.

● Brush half of the remaining amaretto over ladyfingers in pan. Spoon in half of the ricotta mixture. Top with remaining ladyfingers; brush with remaining amaretto. Top with remaining ricotta mixture. Cover and refrigerate until set, at least 4 hours or overnight.

● GARNISH: Remove side of pan. Arrange fruit over filling. Brush fruit with jam. Makes about 8 servings.

Amaretto Almond Charlotte

A charlotte is a mousse surrounded by ladyfingers. When set, unmould this pretty one and turn upside down onto serving platter to display the attractive pattern of the ladyfingers.

20	soft ladyfingers	20
1	pkg unflavored gelatin	1
1/4 cup	cold water	50 mL
3	egg yolks	3
1/2 cup	granulated sugar	125 mL
1 tbsp	instant coffee granules	15 mL
1 cup	hot milk	250 mL
1/2 cup	amaretto (or extra-strong coffee)	125 mL
1-1/2 cups	whipping cream	375 mL
1/2 cup	chopped toasted almonds (see p. 51)	125 mL
1/2 cup	chopped semisweet chocolate	125 mL
	Whipped cream (optional)	

● Line bottom of 8-cup (2 L) round soufflé dish with waxed paper. Cut enough of the ladyfingers in half diagonally lengthwise to arrange on bottom of dish like spokes of wheel. Arrange remaining ladyfingers around side of dish.

● In saucepan, sprinkle gelatin over cold water. Meanwhile, in bowl, beat egg yolks with sugar until pale. Dissolve coffee granules in hot milk; whisk into egg yolk mixture.

● Heat gelatin mixture gently just until dissolved; stir in egg yolk mixture. Cook over medium heat, stirring constantly, until thickened slightly, about 5 minutes. Stir in amaretto.

● Transfer to bowl; set in another bowl of water and ice. Let cool until room temperature, stirring occasionally so mixture does not set around edge.

● Whip cream; fold into cooled custard along with almonds and chocolate. Spoon into prepared soufflé dish and smooth surface. Trim ladyfingers to top of mousse mixture. Cover with plastic wrap and refrigerate for 3 hours or until set.

● To unmould, run knife around edge of ladyfingers and invert onto serving platter; remove waxed paper. Serve with whipped cream (if using). Makes 8 to 10 servings.

Four-Berry Summer Pudding

This refreshing pudding is delicious any time of the year. When fresh berries are not available, use frozen (thawed) raspberries, blackberries and blueberries.

❏ **TIP:** Wild low-bush blueberries are smaller than cultivated berries but their great flavor is worth the price — and the picking!

2 cups	blueberries	500 mL
1/2 cup	granulated sugar	125 mL
2-1/2 cups	each raspberries, blackberries and sliced strawberries	625 mL
2 tbsp	frozen raspberry juice concentrate or liqueur (optional)	25 mL
16	slices (approx) country-style white bread or egg bread	16
1 cup	whipping cream, whipped	250 mL

● In heavy saucepan, cook blueberries with sugar over low heat until juicy and sugar has dissolved. Remove from heat; combine with raspberries, blackberries and strawberries.

Stir in raspberry juice concentrate (if using). Set aside.

● Trim crusts from bread. Line bottom and sides of 8-cup (2 L) dome-shaped bowl with bread, trimming to fit where necessary and reserving remaining bread.

● Spoon in half of the fruit mixture; cover with layer of bread, trimmed to fit. Spoon in remaining fruit and cover with remaining bread, trimmed to fit.

● Cover with plastic wrap. Set small plate over top and weigh down with heavy can; refrigerate for 8 hours or overnight.

● To serve, unmould onto serving plate. Serve with whipped cream. Makes 8 servings.

Raspberry Custard Squares

Serve this make-ahead layered refrigerator dessert with whole fresh raspberries. In winter, purée and strain thawed frozen raspberries to serve as a sauce.

CRUST

2 cups	crushed vanilla wafer crumbs	500 mL
1/2 cup	toasted chopped almonds or walnuts	125 mL
1 tbsp	granulated sugar	15 mL
1/3 cup	butter, melted	75 mL

CUSTARD LAYER

2/3 cup	granulated sugar	150 mL
2 tbsp	cornstarch	25 mL
2 cups	milk	500 mL
3	egg yolks	3
1/2 tsp	vanilla	2 mL
1-1/2	pkg unflavored gelatin	1-1/2
1/3 cup	cold water	75 mL

RASPBERRY LAYER

2	pkg (each 300 g) frozen unsweetened raspberries, thawed (3 cups/750 mL)	2
1/2 cup	granulated sugar	125 mL
1 tbsp	lemon juice	15 mL
1 cup	whipping cream	250 mL

● CRUST: In bowl, combine crumbs, almonds and sugar; mix in butter. Pat into 8-inch (2 L) square glass baking dish. Bake in 350°F (180°C) oven for 10 to 15 minutes or until fragrant and lightly browned. Let cool on rack.

● CUSTARD LAYER: Meanwhile, in heavy saucepan, stir sugar with cornstarch; whisk in milk and cook over medium-low heat, stirring constantly, for 5 to 10 minutes or until slightly thickened and smooth.

● In bowl, whisk egg yolks; stir in half of the hot milk mixture. Return egg yolk mixture to pan; cook, stirring constantly, for about 3 minutes or until thickened. Remove from heat; stir in vanilla.

● Stir gelatin into cold water; let stand for 1 minute, then stir half into custard. Cover and set remaining gelatin mixture aside for raspberry layer. Lay waxed paper directly on surface of custard; let cool. Pour over crust; refrigerate until set, about 2 hours.

● RASPBERRY LAYER: Press raspberries through food mill or fine sieve to remove seeds and make about 1 cup (250 mL). Transfer to small saucepan; add sugar and cook over medium heat for 2 minutes, stirring to dissolve sugar. Remove from heat; stir in lemon juice and reserved gelatin mixture until gelatin is dissolved. Chill until consistency of raw egg whites.

● Whip cream; fold in raspberry mixture. Spread over custard; cover and refrigerate until set, about 4 hours. *(Dessert can be covered and refrigerated for up to 2 days.)* Cut into squares to serve with forks. Makes 8 servings.

Simply the Best Vanilla Ice Cream

This superb French vanilla ice cream is made with a creamy custard. For a continental touch, use a vanilla bean when making the custard. Its tiny seeds fleck the frozen ice cream with real vanilla. You'll get much the same flavor with vanilla extract, but not the flecks.

2 cups	light cream	500 mL
1	vanilla bean, split lengthwise (or 1 tbsp/15 mL vanilla)	1
6	egg yolks	6
2/3 cup	granulated sugar	150 mL
1 cup	whipping cream	250 mL

● Scrape out seeds from vanilla bean. In heavy saucepan, heat light cream and vanilla bean and seeds (vanilla extract is added later) just until tiny bubbles form around edge of pan. Remove from heat; cover and let stand for 10 minutes.

● In large bowl, whisk together egg yolks and sugar; gradually pour in warm cream, whisking constantly to break up seeds. Transfer to saucepan; cook over medium-low heat, stirring constantly, for about 5 minutes or until mixture thickens enough to coat back of spoon. Do not boil.

● Immediately remove from heat. Add vanilla extract if you did not use vanilla bean. Blend in whipping cream.

● Let cool to room temperature; cover and refrigerate until thoroughly chilled. Freeze in ice-cream maker following manufacturer's instructions. Makes about 4 cups (1 L).

SENSATIONAL SUNDAE SCOOPS

Whatever the season, no dessert is as irresistible as ice cream. Even pure and simple, one scoop of Bittersweet Chocolate Orange (p. 114), Peach (P. 116) or any of the Fruity Frozen Yogurts (p. 118) is sheer bliss!

But if you're an ice-cream lover who can't resist a decadent sundae and wants to share the pleasure, why not make your next get-together with friends a Cookies 'n' Sundae Bar. Dip into our COOKIES chapter for a delicious selection to arrange on plates — then set out bowls of chopped fruit (berries are best), toasted nuts, crunchy brittle (p. 178) and sauces. The three "musts" in the sauce department originated with the late Lanny Salsberg whose Metropolitan Ice Cream Company started a revolution in ice-cream eating in Toronto.

Gooey Caramel Sauce

● *Place bowl of cold water and pastry brush by stove. In large heavy saucepan, stir together 1-1/2 cups (375 mL) sugar and 2 tbsp (25 mL) water; cook over medium heat, without stirring, for 6 to 8 minutes or until light amber color.*

● *With brush dipped in cold water, brush down side of pan as sugar starts to caramelize; cook, stirring with wooden spoon, for about 1-1/2 minutes or until caramel is rich amber color. Add 1/2 cup (125 mL) sugar; cook, stirring, until sugar has dissolved. Remove from heat.*

● *Meanwhile, heat 1 cup (250 mL) whipping cream just until small bubbles form around edge. Carefully stir warm cream into sugar mixture (sauce will bubble up) until well combined. Makes about 1-1/2 cups (375 mL).*

Dark Chocolate Sauce

● *In small heavy saucepan, stir together 1/2 cup (125 mL) each granulated sugar, water and corn syrup; bring to boil and cook for 1 minute.*

● *Meanwhile, in separate saucepan, heat 1/2 cup (125 mL) whipping cream just until small bubbles form around edge; remove from heat and let stand for 1 minute. Stir in 8 oz (250 g) coarsely chopped semisweet chocolate until melted. Stir in sugar syrup until well combined. Makes about 2 cups (500 mL).*

Raspberry Sauce

● *In food processor, purée 2 pkg (each 300 g) partially thawed frozen raspberries; strain through sieve into bowl to remove seeds. Stir in 1-3/4 cups (425 mL) sifted icing sugar and 1/4 cup (50 mL) lemon juice until well combined. Makes about 2 cups (500 mL).*

Chocolate and caramel sauces *keep for up to two weeks in the refrigerator but become quite thick when cold. Reheat gently until smooth and warmed through.* ***Raspberry sauce*** *keeps for up to 3 days in the refrigerator. Stir before serving.*

Bittersweet Chocolate Orange Ice Cream

Chocolate and orange combine to create an exciting and refreshing taste that's impossible to resist.

❏ TIP: Serve ice cream in chocolate cups or in chocolate-drizzled tulip cookie shells (p. 116).

4	oranges	4
1-1/4 cups	granulated sugar	300 mL
1/2 cup	water	125 mL
6	egg yolks	6
2 cups	milk	500 mL
1/4 cup	skim milk powder	50 mL
5 oz	cold bittersweet or semisweet chocolate	150 g
1 cup	whipping cream	250 mL
2 tbsp	orange liqueur	25 mL

● Score rind of each orange into eighths; cut thin slice from top and bottom. Carefully remove thin outer rind (orange part only); cut into very thin julienne strips to make about 1 cup (250 mL) rind. (Reserve fruit from orange for another use.)

● In saucepan, cover orange rind with water and bring to boil; reduce heat and simmer for 1 minute. Drain and rinse under cold water; drain again and set aside.

● In saucepan, combine 1/2 cup (125 mL) of the sugar with 1/2 cup (125 mL) water and bring to boil; reduce heat and simmer for 5 minutes. Add orange rind and simmer for 10 minutes or until tender. Drain and let cool. Dice half of the rind and set aside; reserve remaining rind.

● In large bowl, whisk together egg yolks and remaining sugar. In heavy saucepan, combine milk and milk powder; cook over medium-high heat for about 3 minutes or until tiny bubbles appear around edge of pan. Gradually pour into egg yolk mixture, whisking constantly.

● Return to saucepan and cook over medium-low heat, stirring constantly, for about 5 minutes or until custard is thick enough to coat back of spoon. Do not boil. Strain through fine sieve into bowl. Let cool to room temperature.

● Meanwhile, break chocolate into chunks. In food processor fitted with steel blade, process chocolate until finely ground. Stir into custard. Stir in cream, reserved diced rind and orange liqueur. Cover and refrigerate until thoroughly chilled. Freeze in ice-cream maker following manufacturer's instructions. Garnish each serving with reserved rind. Makes about 4 cups (1 L).

Easy Rhubarb and Strawberry Ice

Rhubarb and strawberries make an absolutely delicious sorbet, or ice — and you don't need any special equipment to turn out this refreshing frozen confection.

2 cups	granulated sugar	500 mL
1 cup	water	250 mL
4 cups	chopped rhubarb	1 L
3 cups	strawberries, sliced	750 mL

● In stainless steel or enamel saucepan, combine sugar with water; bring to boil, whisking to dissolve sugar.

● Add rhubarb and return to boil. Cover and reduce heat to low; simmer for about 15 minutes or until rhubarb is softened.

● Let cool; add strawberries and purée. Cover and refrigerate until thoroughly chilled. Transfer to 9-inch (2.5 L) square baking dish. Cover with plastic wrap and freeze until almost solid, about 3 hours.

● Break into large chunks and purée in food processor or blender. Transfer to airtight container and freeze for about 3 hours or until firm but not solid. *(Ice can be frozen for up to 4 days; purée again 3 hours before serving.)*

● Transfer to refrigerator for about 10 minutes or until softened slightly. Serve in scoops on frosted plates and garnish with extra sliced strawberries. Makes 8 cups (2 L).

Almond Praline Semifreddo

In Italian, semifreddo *means partially frozen. In the language of the dessert world, it translates into an easy and glamorous make-ahead dessert. Layered with chocolate and almond brittle (praline), this semifreddo has all the velvety, satisfying creaminess of homemade ice cream without the bother of an ice-cream machine.*

❑ **TIP: Praline can be stored at room temperature in airtight container for up to 5 days.**

3/4 cup	whole blanched almonds	175 mL
1-1/4 cups	granulated sugar	300 mL
6 oz	semisweet chocolate, chopped	175 g
2-3/4 cups	whipping cream	675 mL
1/3 cup	amaretto	75 mL
6	egg yolks	6
1/3 cup	strong cold coffee	75 mL
8	soft ladyfingers	8

● Arrange almonds close together on lightly greased baking sheet; set aside.

● In small heavy saucepan, combine 3/4 cup (175 mL) of the sugar and 1/4 cup (50 mL) water; cook over medium heat until sugar dissolves. Increase heat to medium-high; boil for 5 to 8 minutes, without stirring, or until rich caramel color. Immediately pour over almonds; let cool completely. Break praline into pieces. In food processor and using steel blade, chop coarsely.

● Place chocolate in bowl. In small saucepan, bring 3/4 cup (175 mL) of the cream to boil; pour over chocolate and whisk until melted and smooth. Stir in 2 tbsp (25 mL) of the liqueur. Set 1 cup (250 mL) aside to serve separately.

● In top of double boiler over hot, not boiling, water, beat yolks with remaining 1/2 cup (125 mL) sugar for 3 minutes or until pale. Beat in 2 tbsp (25 mL) each of the coffee and liqueur. Cook, stirring, for 5 to 8 minutes or until thick enough to coat back of spoon. Let cool to room temperature.

● Line 8-1/2-inch (2.25 L) springform pan with ladyfingers; brush with remaining coffee and liqueur. Whip remaining 2 cups (500 mL) cream; fold in yolk mixture and all but 1/3 cup (75 mL) of the praline. Spread one-quarter over ladyfingers. Drizzle with 2 tbsp (25 mL) of the chocolate sauce. Repeat three more times. Freeze for at least 8 hours or up to 5 days.

● Remove from freezer 30 minutes before serving. Sprinkle reserved praline around edge. Serve with reserved chocolate sauce. Makes 8 to 12 servings.

Peach Ice Cream

Enjoy this summer-sweet ice cream when peaches are plentiful.

1 lb	ripe peaches (about 4)	500 g
1/2 cup	granulated sugar	125 mL
1 tbsp	lemon juice	15 mL
1/2 tsp	almond extract	2 mL
1 cup	light cream	250 mL
1 cup	whipping cream	250 mL
1/4 cup	skim milk powder	50 mL

● In pot of boiling water, blanch peaches for 30 seconds; peel and cut into quarters. In food processor or blender, purée peaches, sugar, lemon juice and almond extract to make about 2 cups (500 mL).

● Transfer purée to large bowl; blend in light cream, whipping cream and milk powder. Cover and refrigerate until thoroughly chilled. Freeze in ice-cream maker following manufacturer's instructions. Makes about 4 cups (1 L).

Tulip Cookie Shells

Make these elegant cookie shells the bases for showstopper desserts. Fill the edible fluted containers with ice cream or sorbet and serve them with the fruit sauce of your choice.

❏ **TIP: It's important to work quickly when shaping tulip shells because they're easiest to handle while still warm. If possible, line baking sheets with parchment paper for easy removal of the cookies.**

2	egg whites	2
1/2 cup	granulated sugar	125 mL
1/3 cup	all-purpose flour	75 mL
1/4 cup	unsalted butter, melted	50 mL
2 tsp	water	10 mL
1 tsp	vanilla	5 mL
	Ice cream or sorbet	
	Fruit sauce	

● Line three baking sheets with parchment paper or grease and flour sheets. Using 6-inch (15 cm) plate, trace two circles on each sheet, leaving 1 inch (2.5 cm) between each circle.

● In large bowl, whisk together egg whites, sugar, flour, butter, water and vanilla just until blended.

● Using 3 tbsp (50 mL) batter for each cookie, drop onto circles on prepared baking sheet. With metal spatula, gently spread batter as thinly as possible to fill circles.

● Bake one sheet at a time in upper half of 400°F (200°C) oven for 6 to 8 minutes or until edges are just beginning to brown. Remove baking sheet from oven and place on rack.

● Using metal spatula, immediately lift one cookie and place onto lightly greased inverted tall glass about 1-1/2 inches (4 cm) in diameter.

● Working quickly, lightly shape warm cookie with fingers to create fluted effect. Let cool completely on glass. Repeat with remaining cookie. If cookie is too firm to mould, return to oven for 15 to 30 seconds or until softened. *(Cookie shells can be stored in airtight container for up to 2 days. Recrisp in 275°F/140°C oven for 1 minute.)*

● Fill cookie shells with ice cream or sorbet and serve with fresh fruit sauce. Makes six 6-inch (15 cm) shells.

VARIATIONS
ALMOND COOKIE SHELLS: Substitute 1/2 tsp (2 mL) almond extract for vanilla. Stir 1/4 cup (50 mL) ground almonds into batter.

CHOCOLATE-DRIZZLED COOKIE SHELLS: Melt 2 oz (60 g) semisweet chocolate. Dip fork or spoon into chocolate and drizzle over inside of cookie shells for splattered effect. *(Do not store cookie shells with chocolate on them.)*

ORANGE-BLOSSOM COOKIE SHELLS: Substitute 1/2 tsp (2 mL) almond extract for vanilla. Add 2 tsp (10 mL) grated orange rind to batter.

Gently spread batter as thinly as possible to fill circles traced on parchment paper.

Using metal spatula, lift baked cookie and place onto inverted glass.

Working quickly, shape warm cookie with fingers to create fluted effect.

Fruity Frozen Yogurt

Scoop this icy summer treat into chilled glasses and add more fresh fruit.

❏ TIP: To pan-freeze, pour mixture into shallow metal baking pan, cover and freeze for 3 to 4 hours or until almost firm. Break up mixture and process in food processor, in batches if necessary, until smooth and creamy. Place in chilled airtight container and freeze for 1 hour or until firm.

3 cups	cubed peeled cantaloupe	750 mL
1/2 cup	plain yogurt	125 mL
1/3 cup	instant dissolving (fruit/berry) sugar	75 mL
1 tbsp	orange juice	15 mL

● In food processor, process cantaloupe until smooth. Blend in yogurt, sugar and orange juice; freeze in ice-cream maker following manufacturer's instructions. Or, pan-freeze (see Tip, this page).

● Serve immediately or transfer to airtight container and freeze for up to 1 day. If making ahead, process in food processor before serving for smoother texture. Makes 5 servings.

FROZEN FRUIT METHOD: At least 5 hours before serving, cover and freeze fruit in single layer on baking sheet until solid. In food processor, process fruit with sugar until coarsely chopped. Stir together yogurt and orange juice. With machine running, gradually pour yogurt mixture through feed tube. Process until smooth and creamy. Serve immediately.

VARIATIONS

PEACH FROZEN YOGURT: Substitute sliced peaches for the cantaloupe.

STRAWBERRY FROZEN YOGURT: Substitute sliced strawberries for the cantaloupe.

RASPBERRY FROZEN YOGURT: Purée 3 cups (750 mL) raspberries; strain through sieve into bowl to remove seeds. Increase sugar to 1/2 cup (125 mL).

Peach Mousse Parfait with Berries

Layered with berries and cookies, this mousse is a wonderful way to indulge in summer's bounty of tree-ripened peaches.

❑ TIP: To peel peaches, plunge into boiling water for 30 to 60 seconds; slip off skins and sprinkle with fresh lemon juice to prevent discoloration.

3 cups	sliced peeled peaches	750 mL
1/2 cup	granulated sugar	125 mL
1 tbsp	lemon juice	15 mL
2 tbsp	kirsch, peach nectar or orange juice	25 mL
4 tsp	unflavored gelatin	20 mL
1/4 cup	cold water	50 mL
2 cups	whipping cream	500 mL
1 cup	crumbled macaroons	250 mL
1 cup	raspberries	250 mL
	GARNISH	
8	raspberries	8
8	peach slices	8

● In large saucepan, combine peaches with sugar; bring to boil over medium heat. Reduce heat to medium-low and simmer for 10 minutes or until tender. Transfer to food processor and process until smooth; pour into large bowl. Stir in lemon juice; let cool to room temperature. Stir in kirsch.

● In saucepan, sprinkle gelatin over cold water; let stand for 1 minute to soften. Heat over low heat until gelatin is dissolved; whisk in 1/2 cup (125 mL) of the peach purée. Whisk gelatin mixture back into purée. Whip cream; whisk one-quarter into purée. Fold in remaining whipped cream.

● Fill eight 1-cup (250 mL) parfait or wine glasses with one-third of the mousse. Sprinkle each with 2 tbsp (25 mL) macaroons; top with half of the remaining mousse. Top each with raspberries; spoon remaining mousse over top. Garnish each with raspberry and peach slice. Makes 8 servings.

CHOOSING A SPIRIT

A splash of brandy, cognac, rum or a flavored liqueur adds a wonderfully concentrated taste to many desserts. The following are the most popular liqueurs or fruit spirits, with descriptions and substitutions where appropriate.

Nut Liqueurs
● *Of the nut liqueurs, amaretto, an almond liqueur, is the most widely used. Use a few drops of almond extract as a substitute. Frangelico is the hazelnut equivalent. Replace with a dash of vanilla.*

Coffee and Chocolate Liqueurs
● *There are several brands of coffee liqueur, of which Kahlua and Tia Maria are well known. Crème de cacao, a chocolate liqueur, is widely sold.*

Fruit Spirits
● *Apples: Calvados, a fruit spirit distilled from hard cider, is the best, or use apple schnapps.*
● *Apricots: Apricot brandy is brandy with apricot flavoring added.*
● *Berries and Cherries: Black currant liqueur is often called cassis. For intense raspberry flavor, framboise, raspberry liqueur and raspberry schnapps are available. Kirsch is the classic cherry fruit spirit, but cherry brandy and whisky can be substituted.*
● *Oranges: Orange flavors come as triple sec, Grand Marnier, orange schnapps, Cointreau and orange brandy.*
● *Peaches and Pears: Peach flavor shines in peach liqueur or peach schnapps, and pears in poire William, pear liqueur or schnapps.*
● *In a pinch, brandy, fruit juices or fruit juice concentrates can be substituted for fruit liqueurs, brandies or spirits.*

Black Currant Mousse

Cool and creamy mousses are one of the most delicious ways to savor the fruits of summer. Enjoy this black currant version in high summer — or try our rhubarb, strawberry or raspberry variations.

❏ **TIP: For a sensational presentation, pipe whipped cream around the base of the unmoulded mousse. Garnish with scented geranium, mint sprigs or whole currants.**

4 cups	black currants	1 L
1-1/4 cups	granulated sugar	300 mL
2/3 cup	water	150 mL
2 tbsp	cassis (optional)	25 mL
1 tbsp	lemon juice	15 mL
1-1/2	pkg unflavored gelatin	1-1/2
1-1/2 cups	whipping cream	375 mL

● In saucepan, combine black currants, 1 cup (250 mL) of the sugar and 2 tbsp (25 mL) of the water. Bring to boil; reduce heat and simmer, covered, for 2 to 5 minutes or until tender. In food processor or blender, process currant mixture until smooth. Press through sieve into bowl to remove skins and make about 2 cups (500 mL) purée. Stir in cassis (if using) and lemon juice.

● Meanwhile, in small saucepan, sprinkle gelatin over remaining water; let stand for 5 minutes to soften. Warm over low heat until dissolved; stir into currant mixture. Place in large bowl of ice and water to chill, stirring frequently, for 20 to 30 minutes or until consistency of raw egg whites. Remove from ice water.

● Whip cream with remaining sugar; whisk about one-quarter into chilled currant mixture. Fold in remaining whipped cream. Pour into rinsed 6-cup (1.5 L) stainless steel, glass or plastic mould. Cover and refrigerate for at least 6 hours or up to 2 days.

● To unmould, wrap hot damp tea towel around mould for 1 minute. Using knife, loosen top edge of mousse from mould. Tilt or gently shake mould to loosen mousse. Invert rinsed serving platter on top of mould. Grasp platter and mould; quickly turn over. Shake, using quick downward motion, to release mousse from mould. Lift off mould. (If mousse sticks, repeat procedure.) Makes 6 to 8 servings.

VARIATIONS

RHUBARB MOUSSE: Substitute rhubarb, cut into 1-inch (2.5 cm) pieces, for the black currants, orange juice for the lemon juice, and orange liqueur for the cassis. Use 3/4 cup (175 mL) sugar and 2/3 cup (150 mL) water.

● In nonaluminum saucepan, combine rhubarb, 1/2 cup (125 mL) of the sugar and 2 tbsp (25 mL) of the water. Bring to boil; reduce heat and simmer, covered, for about 10 minutes or until tender. In food processor or blender, process until smooth to make about 2 cups (500 mL). Transfer to bowl.

● Complete mousse as directed, dissolving gelatin in remaining water and beating remaining sugar with whipping cream.

RASPBERRY OR STRAWBERRY MOUSSE: Substitute raspberries or hulled strawberries for the black currants. Instead of cassis, use raspberry liqueur for raspberry mousse or orange liqueur for strawberry mousse.

● Purée berries and press through sieve to make 2 cups (500 mL). In saucepan, combine purée with 1/2 cup (125 mL) sugar; cook over low heat, stirring, for about 5 minutes or until sugar has dissolved.

● Complete mousse as directed, dissolving gelatin in 1/2 cup (125 mL) water and whipping cream with 1/4 cup (50 mL) sugar.

SETTING AND MOULDING MOUSSES

● *Most fruit mixtures can be set with gelatin. However, fresh figs, kiwifruit, papaya, pineapple and prickly pears contain enzymes that prevent gelatin from setting properly. With the exception of kiwifruit, these fruits can be set with gelatin if the chopped fruit is first boiled for 5 minutes.*

● *Before adding whipped cream to a gelatin mixture, the mixture should be chilled until slightly thickened to ensure a fluffy, even texture. To chill, place bowl (preferably metal) of gelatin mixture over a larger bowl of ice and water. Stir occasionally at first to prevent lumps, then more frequently once the mixture is cold. If gelatin mixture becomes too firm before*

adding additional ingredients, gently warm it by placing over a pan of barely simmering water and stirring until softened.

● *Choose any decorative mould of the same capacity as the one specified in the recipe. To prepare mould, rinse with cold water, then invert to drain off excess, leaving mould damp.*

● *Use stainless steel, glass or plastic moulds, or line smooth round or ring moulds of tin or aluminum with plastic wrap. Mixtures containing red, purple or blue fruits (for example, strawberries, raspberries, rhubarb, blueberries, black currants) may become discolored in tin or aluminum moulds.*

Lemon and Lime Soufflé

This spectacular citrus dessert can be made, and then refrigerated, up to two days ahead of time.

❏ **TIP:** To grate rind, use a hand grater. Try to avoid using the white pith, which is slightly bitter.

8	eggs, separated	8
1-1/4 cups	granulated sugar	300 mL
1 tbsp	grated lemon rind	15 mL
1 tbsp	grated lime rind	15 mL
1/2 cup	lemon juice	125 mL
1/2 cup	lime juice	125 mL
2	pkg unflavored gelatin	2
1-1/2 cups	whipping cream	375 mL
1	lime, sliced	1
	GARNISH	
1/4 cup	toasted sliced almonds (see p. 51)	50 mL
1/2 cup	whipping cream	125 mL
1	lime, thinly sliced	1
	Grated lime rind	

● Cut double thickness of waxed paper 2 inches (5 cm) higher than 6-cup (1.5 L) soufflé dish or glass bowl and long enough to leave 1-inch (2.5 cm) overlap when wrapped around dish. Lightly grease top 2 inches (5 cm) of paper; tape snugly to outside of dish, greased side inside.

● In large heatproof bowl set over saucepan of gently simmering water, beat egg yolks with 3/4 cup (175 mL) of the sugar for 8 to 10 minutes or until thick, creamy and tripled in volume. Remove bowl; stir in lemon and lime rinds and juices. Set aside.

● In large separate heatproof bowl, whisk egg whites with remaining sugar. Set over saucepan of boiling water, whisking often, for 3 minutes or until white and finger can remain in mixture for 10 seconds; remove from heat. With electric mixer, beat for 8 to 10 minutes or until very cool.

● In small saucepan, sprinkle gelatin over 1/2 cup (125 mL) water; let stand for 1 minute. Heat over low heat until dissolved. Stir into egg yolk mixture.

● Whip cream; whisk about one-third into egg yolk mixture; fold in remaining cream. Repeat with egg white mixture. Press lime slices onto bottom and up side of prepared dish; pour in mixture. Refrigerate until set, about 4 hours, or up to 2 days.

● GARNISH: Just before serving, carefully peel off paper; press almonds into side of soufflé above rim. Whip cream; garnish top with lime slices, whipped cream and lime rind. Makes about 10 servings.

Tiramisu

Grano, a café bakery in north Toronto, serves a superlative version of this popular Italian dessert. Their coffee-laced mascarpone trifle is moist and creamy yet cuts beautifully into squares to serve.

1	Sponge Cake (recipe follows)	1
1 tbsp	unsweetened cocoa powder	15 mL
	Chocolate curls (see p. 27)	

COFFEE MIXTURE

1/2 cup	ground espresso beans	125 mL
3 cups	boiling water	750 mL
2 tbsp	brandy	25 mL
1 tbsp	granulated sugar	15 mL
1 tbsp	amaretto	15 mL
1 tbsp	coffee liqueur	15 mL

MASCARPONE FILLING

3	egg yolks	3
3 tbsp	granulated sugar	50 mL
1 lb	mascarpone cheese	500 g
3 cups	whipping cream, whipped	750 mL

● COFFEE MIXTURE: Combine ground espresso with water; let stand for 5 minutes, stirring occasionally. With coffee filter, strain into bowl and let cool. Stir in brandy, sugar, amaretto and coffee liqueur.

● MASCARPONE FILLING: In large heatproof bowl set over simmering water, beat egg yolks and sugar with electric mixer for 10 to 12 minutes or until tripled in volume; remove from heat. Whisk in mascarpone.

Stir in one-quarter of the whipped cream; fold in remaining whipped cream.

● ASSEMBLY: Cut sponge cake into 2 layers. Cover 13- x 9-inch (3 L) baking dish with 1 of the layers. Soak with half of the coffee mixture; spoon in half of the mascarpone mixture. Repeat with remaining cake, coffee and mascarpone. Sprinkle with cocoa; garnish with chocolate curls. Chill for 4 hours or up to 8 hours. Makes 16 servings.

SPONGE CAKE

5	eggs	5
1-1/2 cups	granulated sugar	375 mL
2-1/2 cups	sifted cake-and-pastry flour	625 mL
2 tsp	baking powder	10 mL

● In large bowl, beat eggs and sugar with electric mixer for 10 to 12 minutes or until more than doubled in volume and batter falls in ribbons when beaters are lifted. Sift flour with baking powder; gently fold into egg mixture.

● Spoon into greased or parchment- or waxed paper-lined 13- x 9-inch (3 L) cake pan. Bake in 375°F (190°C) oven for 20 to 25 minutes or until tester inserted into center comes out clean. Run knife around edges to loosen cake; let cool in pan on rack for 10 minutes. Remove from pan and let cool completely on rack.

CHOCOLATE SILHOUETTES

Chocolate garnishes transform even the simplest desserts into wonderful extravaganzas. The easiest and most popular garnish is chocolate curls (for tips on how to make foolproof curls, see p. 27). But you can also add a touch of whimsy to parfaits, trifles and other chilled desserts with chocolate silhouettes.

● Draw desired outline (for example, butterflies, hearts, Christmas bells or stars) on paper; place on back of large baking sheet. Cover with sheet of waxed paper, making sure that outline shows through; tape both papers to baking sheet.

● Melt 1 oz (30 g) chocolate over hot, not boiling, water; let cool slightly. Pipe chocolate in steady continuous flow over silhouette outlines. Chill until hard. Lift off and arrange decoratively over dessert.

Mandarin Trifle

The tang of mandarins and the creaminess of custard add up to a winner of a trifle. When fresh mandarins or clementines are available, substitute 12 peeled or sectioned mandarins for the canned variety.

1 cup	orange marmalade	250 mL
1 cup	whipping cream	250 mL
1/3 cup	orange liqueur	75 mL
3	cans (each 10 oz/284 mL) mandarin oranges, drained	3
	CUSTARD	
4	egg yolks	4
1/2 cup	granulated sugar	125 mL
1/3 cup	cornstarch	75 mL
3 cups	milk	750 mL
2 tbsp	grated orange rind	25 mL
3 tbsp	orange liqueur or concentrated orange juice	50 mL
	SPONGE CAKE	
4	eggs, separated	4
3/4 cup	granulated sugar	175 mL
1 tsp	vanilla	5 mL
1/2 cup	all-purpose flour	125 mL
Pinch	salt	Pinch
	Icing sugar	

● CUSTARD: In bowl, whisk together egg yolks, sugar, cornstarch and 1/2 cup (125 mL) of the milk; set aside.

● In heavy saucepan, heat remaining milk with orange rind over medium-high heat for 3 to 5 minutes or until bubbles form around edge; gradually whisk into yolk mixture. Return to pan and cook over medium heat, whisking constantly, for about 5 minutes or until thickened.

● Remove from heat; stir in liqueur. Transfer to bowl; place waxed paper directly on surface. Refrigerate until completely cooled, about 4 hours. *(Custard can be refrigerated for up to 2 days.)*

In photo: Mandarin Trifle (top); Christmas Pavlova (p. 46)

● SPONGE CAKE: In deep bowl, beat egg yolks with 1/2 cup (125 mL) of the granulated sugar for 3 to 5 minutes or until pale and thickened; blend in vanilla. In separate bowl, beat egg whites until soft peaks form; gradually beat in remaining sugar until stiff glossy peaks form.

● Combine flour with salt. Alternately fold egg whites and flour mixture into yolk mixture, making 3 additions of whites and 2 of flour. Spread evenly into waxed paper-lined 15- x 10-inch (40 x 25 cm) jelly roll pan. Bake in 375°F (190°C) oven for 13 to 15 minutes or until top springs back when touched.

● Dust clean tea towel with icing sugar. Run knife around edge of cake; invert onto towel. Carefully peel off paper. Beginning at long side, immediately roll up cake tightly in towel; let cool. Unroll cake and spread with marmalade; reroll tightly without towel. *(Cake can be wrapped and stored up to 3 days ahead or frozen for up to 1 week.)* Cut into 1/2-inch (1 cm) thick slices.

● ASSEMBLY: Whip cream. Whisk custard to loosen; fold in half of the whipped cream. Reserve remaining whipped cream in refrigerator.

● Line bottom of 10-cup (2.5 L) trifle bowl with cake slices. Brush with half of the orange liqueur. Top with one row of cake slices standing against side of bowl. Spoon about one-third of the custard mixture over cake. Cover with about one-third of the mandarin segments. Top with remaining cake slices; brush with remaining liqueur.

● Spoon in another third of the custard mixture; arrange another third of the mandarins attractively on top and at edge to show through glass. Cover with remaining custard mixture. Spread with reserved whipped cream. Decorate with remaining mandarins. *(Trifle can be covered and refrigerated for up to 1 day.)* Makes 10 to 12 servings.

Raspberry Truffle Trifle

You'll want a 12-cup (3 L) serving bowl — preferably clear glass — for this extravagantly delicious and impressive dessert.

❏ TIP: It's easy to drizzle the chocolate sauce over the whipped cream as we did in our photo. Simply spoon sauce into small plastic bag, snip corner and use as you would a piping bag.

1	7-inch (18 cm) sponge cake	1
1/2 cup	raspberry liqueur	125 mL
1 cup	whipping cream	250 mL
	CUSTARD	
3 cups	milk	750 mL
3/4 cup	light cream	175 mL
3	eggs	3
1/2 cup	granulated sugar	125 mL
1/4 cup	all-purpose flour	50 mL
3 tbsp	raspberry liqueur	50 mL
1-1/2 tsp	vanilla	7 mL
	RASPBERRY SAUCE	
2	pkg (each 300 g) frozen unsweetened raspberries, thawed (3 cups/750 mL)	2
1/4 cup	icing sugar	50 mL
2 tbsp	raspberry liqueur	25 mL
	CHOCOLATE TRUFFLE SAUCE	
8 oz	semisweet chocolate, coarsely chopped	250 g
3/4 cup	whipping cream	175 mL
1/4 cup	raspberry liqueur	50 mL

● RASPBERRY SAUCE: In food processor or blender, purée raspberries and icing sugar; strain. Stir in liqueur. *(Sauce can be refrigerated for up to 3 days.)*

● CUSTARD: In large saucepan, heat milk and cream until bubbles appear around edge of pan. In bowl, beat eggs with sugar until light, about 3 minutes; whisk in flour until smooth. Gradually pour in hot milk mixture, whisking constantly. Return to pan; cook, whisking constantly, until boiling. Stir in liqueur; simmer, whisking, for 2 minutes. Stir in vanilla. Pour into bowl; place plastic wrap directly on surface and let cool to room temperature. *(Custard can be refrigerated for up to 8 hours.)*

● CHOCOLATE TRUFFLE SAUCE: In top of double boiler over simmering water, heat chocolate, cream and liqueur, stirring, until chocolate is melted. Let cool to room temperature.

● ASSEMBLY: Cut cake into 3 layers. Drizzle 1/2 cup (125 mL) raspberry sauce over bottom and side of serving bowl. Place 1 cake layer on bottom; drizzle with 2 tbsp (25 mL) of the liqueur. Pour one-third of the custard over cake. Drizzle with one-third of the remaining raspberry sauce. Reserve 3 tbsp (50 mL) chocolate truffle sauce for garnish; drizzle with one-third of the remaining chocolate truffle sauce. Repeat with two more layers of cake, liqueur, custard and sauces. Refrigerate for at least 8 hours or up to 1 day.

● Whip cream; add remaining liqueur. Spread over top. Warm reserved chocolate truffle sauce slightly; drizzle over whipped cream. Makes 16 servings.

Fruity Cheesecake Trifle

The flavors of amaretto (almond-flavored liqueur) and amaretti (Italian almond biscuits) combine with ricotta and whipping cream in this luscious festive trifle. If amaretti are unavailable, substitute an 8- x 4-inch (1.5 L) pound cake, cut into 1/2-inch (1 cm) slices.

❏ **TIP:** To make frosted grapes, brush green and red seedless grapes with lightly beaten egg white. Roll immediately in granulated sugar to coat well. Place on rack to dry; refrigerate, uncovered, for up to 1 day.

40	amaretti biscuits	40
2 tbsp	amaretto or orange juice	25 mL
3 cups	fresh or individually frozen (thawed, drained) raspberries	750 mL
3	oranges, peeled and sliced	3
3	kiwifruit, peeled and sliced	3
	FILLING	
1-1/2 cups	ricotta or pressed cottage cheese	375 mL
3/4 cup	icing sugar	175 mL
2 tbsp	amaretto (or 1 tsp/5 mL vanilla)	25 mL
4 tsp	grated orange rind	20 mL
1-1/2 cups	whipping cream	375 mL
	GARNISH	
	Frosted grapes	
	Chocolate leaves (see p. 29)	
	Strawberries or raspberries (optional)	

● FILLING: In bowl, beat ricotta with icing sugar until smooth; stir in amaretto and orange rind. Whip cream; stir one-quarter into ricotta mixture. Fold in remaining whipped cream; set aside.

● Brush rounded side of amaretti biscuits with amaretto. Arrange about half of the biscuits and one-third of the raspberries, oranges and kiwifruit in bottom of 12-cup (3 L) trifle bowl. Decoratively arrange half of the remaining fruit partway up sides of bowl.

● Spoon in enough of the filling to hold fruit in place. Top with remaining biscuits; decoratively top with remaining fruit. Top with remaining filling. Refrigerate for at least 2 hours or up to 6 hours.

● Garnish with frosted grapes, chocolate leaves, and berries (if using).
Makes 10 to 12 servings.

Puddings, Crumbles, Crisps and Soufflés

There's nothing homier or more comforting than a pudding, warm and steaming in a bowl. Choose from a bounty of cold-weather puddings as well as quick and easy crumbles and crisps made from summer's sweetest fruit. But don't let their ease of preparation fool you. Puddings have class and style, too! — as you'll see with our impressive Hot Fudge Soufflé and elegant Christmas puddings.

Canary Pudding with Pear Sauce

Make the sauce for this lemony sponge pudding with firm but ripe Bosc or Anjou pears.

❏ **FOR PERFECT STEAMED PUDDINGS:**
● **Grease bowl or mould well for easy unmoulding.**
● **Fill bowl no more than two-thirds full to allow for expansion.**
● **Let pudding stand for 5 minutes before unmoulding. If pudding won't slip out easily, grasp the plate and bowl together and give plate light, firm tap on countertop.**
● **Puddings will keep warm for up to 1 hour if left in bowl in saucepan of hot water.**

1/3 cup	butter	75 mL
1/3 cup	granulated sugar	75 mL
2	eggs	2
1 tsp	grated lemon rind	5 mL
1 tsp	vanilla	5 mL
1 cup	all-purpose flour	250 mL
2 tsp	baking powder	10 mL
1/4 tsp	salt	1 mL
Pinch	each cinnamon and nutmeg	Pinch
1/4 cup	milk	50 mL

	PEAR SAUCE	
1-1/2 cups	water	375 mL
1/2 cup	dried apricots	125 mL
3	pears	3
2 tbsp	lemon juice	25 mL
1/4 cup	granulated sugar	50 mL
2 tsp	cornstarch	10 mL
1 tsp	vanilla	5 mL

● In bowl, cream butter with sugar until light and fluffy; beat in eggs until thick and creamy. Add lemon rind and vanilla. Stir together flour, baking powder, salt, cinnamon and nutmeg. Add to creamed mixture alternately with milk, beating well after each addition.

● Spoon into greased 6-cup (1.5 L) heatproof bowl or pudding mould. Cover batter with circle of greased waxed paper. Cover bowl with foil and secure with string.
● Place on rack in large deep saucepan; pour in enough boiling water to come halfway up side of bowl. Bring to brisk simmer and cover; reduce heat to low and simmer gently for 50 to 55 minutes or until tester inserted into center comes out clean. Let stand for 5 minutes before unmoulding.
● PEAR SAUCE: Meanwhile, in saucepan, combine water and apricots; bring to boil. Reduce heat and simmer for 10 minutes. Remove from heat and let stand for 30 minutes; return to simmer and cook for 15 to 20 minutes or until apricots are tender but firm.
● Peel and core pears. In food processor or blender, purée one pear with lemon juice; blend in sugar and cornstarch until smooth. Stir into apricot mixture and bring to simmer; cook, stirring, until thickened and clear. Remove from heat.
● Cut remaining pears into eighths; add to apricot mixture. Cook over medium-low heat for 5 minutes or just until pears are tender. Stir in vanilla.
● Remove foil and paper from pudding; invert onto deep-rimmed serving plate. Spoon sauce over top. Serve warm. Makes 6 to 8 servings.

Tangerine Sponge Pudding

This pudding, which forms a light cake layer on top and a tangy citrus sauce underneath, is delicious served hot or cold (photo, p. 43). Substitute oranges for tangerines, if desired.

3 tbsp	butter, softened	50 mL
3/4 cup	granulated sugar	175 mL
3	eggs, separated	3
1 tbsp	grated tangerine rind	15 mL
1/4 cup	tangerine juice	50 mL
1 tsp	grated lemon rind	5 mL
1 tbsp	lemon juice	15 mL
1/3 cup	all-purpose flour	75 mL
1 cup	hot milk	250 mL

● In bowl, cream together butter and sugar. Beat in egg yolks one at a time; beat in tangerine rind and juice, and lemon rind and juice. Stir in flour. Gradually blend in hot milk, stirring constantly.

● In bowl, beat egg whites until stiff peaks form; stir about one-quarter into batter. Fold in remaining whites. Pour into shallow ungreased 8-cup (2 L) baking dish; set in pan of hot water. Bake in 350°F (180°C) oven for 35 to 40 minutes or until browned on top and firm to the touch. Makes 6 servings.

Snow Pudding with Tropical Fruit Sauce

This baked pudding has the light texture of a sponge cake and is best served warm rather than hot.

1/2 cup	granulated sugar	125 mL
3 tbsp	vegetable oil	50 mL
2	egg yolks	2
2 tbsp	water	25 mL
2 tsp	grated lime rind	10 mL
2 tbsp	lime juice	25 mL
1-1/4 cups	sifted cake-and-pastry flour	300 mL
2 tsp	baking powder	10 mL
1/4 tsp	salt	1 mL
Pinch	mace or nutmeg	Pinch
3	egg whites	3
	TROPICAL SAUCE	
1	can (14 oz/398 mL) pineapple chunks	1
1 tsp	cornstarch	5 mL
2	tangerines	2
1	mango, peeled and cut in chunks	1

● In large bowl, blend together sugar, oil, egg yolks, water, and lime rind and juice. Stir together flour, baking powder, salt and mace; stir into bowl, blending well.

● In large bowl, beat egg whites until stiff peaks form. Stir about 1 cup (250 mL) into batter; fold in remaining egg whites.

● Pour into ungreased 6-cup (1.5 L) tube pan. Bake in 350°F (180°C) oven for 30 to 35 minutes or until top is golden and springs back when touched. Invert pan and let cake hang for 5 minutes.

● TROPICAL SAUCE: Meanwhile, drain juice from pineapple into saucepan; set fruit aside. Stir in cornstarch. Squeeze juice from one of the tangerines into pan. Finely chop 1 tsp (5 mL) tangerine rind; add to pan. Peel and section remaining tangerine, removing any membrane with sharp knife and adding any juices to pan; set sections aside.

● Bring juice mixture to simmer; cook, stirring, until thickened and clear. Cook over medium-low heat for 3 minutes longer. Reserve a few sections of tangerine for garnish; add remaining sections to pan along with pineapple and mango. Heat, stirring, just until warm.

● Spoon about 2 tbsp (25 mL) sauce around edge of pudding. Run knife around edge and invert onto deep-rimmed plate. Spoon remaining sauce in center and over top. Garnish with reserved tangerine sections. Makes about 8 servings.

Orange Fudge Pudding with Rum Sauce

Here's a moist and chocolaty pudding to cheer a winter's day.

❏ **TIP:** When tying cover on any steamed pudding, use sturdy string and allow enough to form loop and provide handle for safe and easy removal.

1/3 cup	butter	75 mL
1/2 cup	packed brown sugar	125 mL
1 tsp	grated orange rind	5 mL
1 tsp	vanilla	5 mL
1/4 cup	milk	50 mL
1/4 cup	orange juice	50 mL
1 cup	all-purpose flour	250 mL
1/4 cup	unsweetened cocoa powder	50 mL
1-1/2 tsp	baking powder	7 mL
1/2 tsp	baking soda	2 mL
1/4 tsp	salt	1 mL
3	egg whites	3

RUM SAUCE

2 tbsp	packed brown sugar	25 mL
2 tbsp	unsweetened cocoa powder	25 mL
2 tbsp	rum	25 mL
2 tbsp	butter, melted	25 mL
1/2 cup	light cream	125 mL

● In large bowl, cream butter with 1/4 cup (50 mL) of the sugar until light and fluffy. Stir in orange rind and vanilla.

● Combine milk with orange juice. Sift together flour, cocoa, baking powder, baking soda and salt; add to creamed mixture alternately with milk mixture, beating well after each addition.

● In large bowl and using clean beaters, beat egg whites until soft peaks form; beat in remaining sugar until stiff peaks form. Stir about 1 cup (250 mL) into batter; fold in remaining egg whites.

● Pour into greased 6-cup (1.5 L) heatproof bowl or pudding mould. Cover batter with circle of greased waxed paper; cover bowl with foil and secure with string.

● Place in roasting pan; pour in enough boiling water to come halfway up side of bowl. Bake in 350°F (180°C) oven for 45 to 50 minutes or until pudding is firm and comes away from edge of bowl.

● RUM SAUCE: In small heavy saucepan, stir together sugar, cocoa, rum and butter until smooth. Bring to boil, stirring constantly; reduce heat to medium and cook for 2 minutes. Add cream in thin steady stream, stirring constantly until heated through.

● Remove foil and waxed paper from pudding; invert onto deep-rimmed serving plate. Pour sauce over top. Serve warm. Makes 6 to 8 servings.

JUST FOR KIDS!

Hot Chocolate Pudding

This smooth, creamy and downright chocolaty stovetop pudding makes a perfect weekday family dessert. Garnish with orange section and twist of orange rind.

● In heavy saucepan, mix 1/2 cup (125 mL) granulated sugar, 1/4 cup (50 mL) sifted unsweetened cocoa powder, 3 tbsp (50 mL) all-purpose flour and 1/2 tsp (2 mL) salt; gradually whisk in 2 cups (500 mL) hot milk until smooth. Cook, whisking constantly, over medium-high heat for about 5 minutes or until boiling and thickened.

● Remove from heat; whisk in 1 tsp (5 mL) vanilla. Divide among custard cups or dessert dishes. Let cool to lukewarm or serve chilled. Makes 4 servings.

Warm Saskatoon Pudding

Each serving of this old-fashioned comfort pudding includes a scoop of the light cake topping with a big spoonful of the juicy deep-red berry bottom. A splash of cream is a must!

3 cups	saskatoon berries	750 mL
1 cup	chopped rhubarb	250 mL
3 tbsp	water	50 mL
1 tbsp	lemon juice	15 mL
1-1/4 cups	granulated sugar	300 mL
1/4 tsp	cinnamon	1 mL
1 tbsp	cornstarch	15 mL
1/4 cup	butter, softened	50 mL
1	egg	1
1 tsp	grated orange rind	5 mL
1 cup	sifted cake-and-pastry flour	250 mL
1 tsp	baking powder	5 mL
1/4 tsp	salt	1 mL
1/3 cup	milk	75 mL

● In saucepan, cook berries, rhubarb, 2 tbsp (25 mL) of the water and lemon juice over medium heat, stirring occasionally, for 15 minutes without boiling. Stir in 3/4 cup (175 mL) of the sugar and cinnamon; simmer for 5 minutes, stirring often, or until fruit is tender.

● Dissolve cornstarch in remaining water. Stir into fruit mixture and bring to boil; reduce heat and simmer, stirring, for 2 to 3 minutes or until thickened. Spoon into greased 8-inch (2 L) cake pan.

● In large bowl, cream butter with remaining sugar until fluffy; beat in egg and orange rind.

● Stir together flour, baking powder and salt; stir about half into batter. Blend in milk; stir in remaining flour mixture. Spread evenly over berry mixture. Bake in 375°F (190°C) oven for about 45 minutes or until tester inserted into center comes out clean. Makes about 8 servings.

Cherry Clafouti

This custardy fruit pudding is equally delicious served hot, warm or cold.

❏ TIP: Instead of cherries, you can use fresh or frozen blueberries, plums, apricots or a combination of these fruits.

3 cups	pitted cherries	750 mL
2	eggs	2
1/2 cup	all-purpose flour	125 mL
1 cup	hot milk	250 mL
1/3 cup	granulated sugar	75 mL
1 tbsp	butter, melted	15 mL
1 tbsp	kirsch (or 1 tsp/5 mL vanilla)	15 mL
Pinch	salt	Pinch
	Icing sugar	

● Arrange cherries evenly over bottom of greased shallow 9- or 10-inch (23 or 25 cm) pie plate or 6- or 8-cup (1.5 or 2 L) oval baking dish; set aside.

● In bowl, beat eggs lightly; gradually beat in flour until smooth. Blend in milk, sugar, butter, kirsch and salt; pour over cherries.

● Bake in 400°F (200°C) oven for 30 to 35 minutes or until puffed and golden. Sprinkle with icing sugar. Makes 4 to 6 servings.

Apple Meringue Pudding

Instead of a traditional two-crust apple pie, try this lighter meringue-topped variation. The sweet meringue marries beautifully with the tart cranberry-apple filling, for a delicious low-fat dessert that's easy to prepare.

5	apples, peeled and chopped (about 6 cups/1.5 L)	5
1 cup	cranberries	250 mL
1/2 cup	packed brown sugar	125 mL
2 tbsp	all-purpose flour	25 mL
2 tsp	cinnamon	10 mL
4	egg whites	4
1/2 tsp	cream of tartar	2 mL
2/3 cup	granulated sugar	150 mL
1 tsp	vanilla	5 mL

● In bowl, combine apples, cranberries, brown sugar, flour and cinnamon; spoon into 10-inch (25 cm) pie plate. Cover with foil and bake in 325°F (160°C) oven for 20 minutes. *(Recipe can be prepared to this point and refrigerated for up to 1 day; bring to room temperature before proceeding.)*

● In bowl, beat egg whites with cream of tartar until soft peaks form. Gradually beat in granulated sugar until stiff peaks form. Fold in vanilla.

● Spread meringue over baked fruit, covering completely. Bake in 325°F (160°C) oven for 35 to 40 minutes or until golden brown. Serve immediately. Makes 8 servings.

Pear and Raspberry Cobbler

For a summer-fresh dessert all year round, use partially thawed, individually quick-frozen raspberries. If using frozen blocks or clumps of unsweetened raspberries, partially thaw and add 2 tsp (10 mL) cornstarch to fruit mixture, tossing well.

❏ **TIP: If you don't have any buttermilk on hand, or only need a small amount, you can substitute soured milk that you prepare yourself. Pour 3/4 tsp (4 mL) lemon juice or vinegar into a measuring cup. Add enough milk to make 1/3 cup (75 mL); let stand for 10 minutes, then stir.**

4 cups	chopped peeled pears (about 5)	1 L
1 cup	raspberries	250 mL
1/4 cup	granulated sugar	50 mL
1 tsp	grated lemon rind	5 mL
4 tsp	lemon juice	20 mL
1/2 tsp	cardamom or nutmeg	2 mL
	TOPPING	
1 cup	all-purpose flour	250 mL
2 tbsp	granulated sugar	25 mL
4 tsp	baking powder	20 mL
1/4 tsp	baking soda	1 mL
Pinch	salt	Pinch
1/4 cup	butter	50 mL
1/3 cup	buttermilk	75 mL
	GLAZE	
	Milk	
	Granulated sugar	

● In bowl, combine pears, raspberries, sugar, lemon rind and juice, and cardamom; toss well. Arrange in 6-cup (1.5 L) baking dish or divide among six 3/4-cup (175 mL) custard cups. Set aside.

● TOPPING: In bowl, stir together flour, sugar, baking powder, baking soda and salt; cut in butter until mixture resembles coarse crumbs. Add buttermilk all at once, stirring with fork to make soft, slightly sticky dough; gather into ball.

● On lightly floured surface, knead dough about 8 times or until smooth. Roll out into circle about 1/2 inch (1 cm) thick. Using 3-inch (8 cm) fluted cookie cutter, cut out 6 rounds; arrange evenly over fruit.

● GLAZE: Brush dough lightly with milk; sprinkle with sugar. Bake in 400°F (200°C) oven for 20 to 25 minutes or until fruit is tender and topping is golden brown. Serve warm. Makes 6 servings.

French Toast Pudding

This easy bread pudding makes a satisfying weekday dessert or a leisurely Sunday breakfast. Older children can make it themselves.

● Tear 8 slices crusty bread into small pieces and place in greased 8-cup (2 L) baking dish. Sprinkle with 1 tbsp (15 mL) cinnamon; pour in 3 cups (750 mL) hot milk.

● In small bowl, beat together 2/3 cup (150 mL) maple syrup, 2 lightly beaten eggs and 1 tsp (5 mL) salt until blended; stir into bread mixture. Bake in 350°F (180°C) oven for 1 hour or until pudding is set and lightly browned. Makes 6 servings.

Bread Pudding with Rye Whisky Sauce

This bread pudding is not too rich or sweet, but moist, custardy and easy to prepare. You can substitute rum or brandy for the rye whisky. The sauce is a syrupy consistency; for a thicker sauce, increase cornstarch to 2 tsp (10 mL).

6	eggs, lightly beaten	6
2 cups	milk	500 mL
2 cups	light cream	500 mL
1 cup	granulated sugar	250 mL
1 cup	raisins	250 mL
1 cup	chopped toasted walnuts (see p. 51)	250 mL
1/2 cup	butter, melted	125 mL
1 tsp	vanilla	5 mL
1/2 tsp	cinnamon	2 mL
1/4 tsp	nutmeg	1 mL
8 cups	cubed day-old French bread	2 L

RYE WHISKY SAUCE		
1 cup	granulated sugar	250 mL
1 cup	whipping cream	250 mL
2 tbsp	unsalted butter	25 mL
1 tsp	cornstarch	5 mL
2 tbsp	cold water	25 mL
3 tbsp	rye whisky	50 mL

● In large bowl, combine eggs, milk, cream, sugar, raisins, walnuts, butter, vanilla, cinnamon and nutmeg. Stir in bread; let stand for about 20 minutes or until well moistened.

● Pour into greased 12-cup (3 L) baking dish. Bake in 350°F (180°C) oven for 1-1/4 hours or until well browned and slightly puffy.

● RYE WHISKY SAUCE: In heavy saucepan, combine sugar and cream. Bring to boil; cook over medium-high heat for 1 minute. Stir in butter. Blend cornstarch with water; stir into sauce and cook for 30 seconds. Remove from heat; stir in whisky. Serve warm with pudding. Makes 8 servings.

Three-Fruit Pudding

Figs, apricots and dates star in this light Christmas pudding. For a memorable finish, serve it warm with Orange Custard Sauce.

❏ TIP: To microwave the pudding, follow instructions but use microwave ring mould and substitute lid or plastic wrap for foil. Microwave at High for 6 to 8 minutes, rotating once, or until pudding comes away from side of mould but is still slightly damp on surface. Let stand for 10 minutes.

1/2 cup	butter, softened	125 mL
2/3 cup	packed brown sugar	150 mL
1	egg	1
1 tsp	vanilla	5 mL
1-1/2 cups	all-purpose flour	375 mL
1 tsp	nutmeg	5 mL
1/2 tsp	cinnamon	2 mL
1/2 tsp	salt	2 mL
1/2 tsp	baking powder	2 mL
1/2 cup	orange juice	125 mL
3/4 cup	slivered dried apricots	175 mL
3/4 cup	slivered pitted dates	175 mL
3/4 cup	chopped figs	175 mL
1/4 cup	slivered almonds	50 mL
	Granulated sugar	
	Orange Custard Sauce (recipe follows)	

● In large bowl, cream butter with sugar until light; beat in egg and vanilla.

● Stir together flour, nutmeg, cinnamon, salt and baking powder. Stir one-third into batter, then half of the orange juice; repeat additions. Toss remaining flour mixture with apricots, dates, figs and almonds; stir into batter.

● Grease 8-cup (2 L) pudding bowl or ring mould; sprinkle with granulated sugar. Spoon batter into bowl; cover with circle of greased waxed paper. Cover bowl with foil and secure with string.

● Place on rack in large saucepan; pour in enough boiling water to come two-thirds up side of bowl. Cover and bring to boil; reduce heat and simmer for about 1-1/4 hours for ring mould, 2-1/2 hours for pudding bowl, or until tester inserted into center comes out clean.

● Let stand for 5 minutes. Remove foil and paper; invert onto serving plate. Serve immediately with Orange Custard Sauce. Makes 8 servings.

ORANGE CUSTARD SAUCE

1/2 cup	granulated sugar	125 mL
3	egg yolks	3
1 tsp	grated orange rind	5 mL
1/2 cup	orange juice	125 mL
1 tbsp	orange liqueur (optional)	15 mL
3/4 cup	whipping cream	175 mL

● In heavy saucepan over low heat or in top of double boiler over barely simmering water, beat together sugar, egg yolks and orange rind until creamy, about 3 minutes. Gradually beat in orange juice, and liqueur (if using); beat for about 8 minutes or until fluffy and doubled in volume. Let cool to room temperature. Whip cream; fold into sauce. *(Sauce can be covered and refrigerated for up to 8 hours.)* Makes about 4 cups (1 L).

MICROWAVE SHORTCUTS FOR CHRISTMAS PUDDINGS

To plump up raisins or currants *before steaming or baking, add 1 tsp (5 mL) water, juice or brandy to each cup (250 mL) dried fruit; cover and microwave at High for 15 seconds.*

To warm brandy or liqueurs for flaming, *microwave 1/4 cup (50 mL) at High for about 20 seconds.*
To reheat steamed puddings, *place on plate and cover with bowl. Microwave at Medium-Low to*

Medium (30% to 50%) just until warmed through.
To get more juice from oranges, *lemons and limes, microwave whole fruit at High for 20 to 30 seconds. Cut and squeeze.*

Christmas Plum Pudding

There are some dishes you eat only once a year. Steamed Christmas pudding is one of them. Its glorious spicy fragrance and the lusciousness of the Orange Hard Sauce melting over the rum-soaked, fruit-filled pudding make it worth the wait!

❏ **TIP:** To make the pudding ahead of time, let cool before removing from mould. Overwrap and refrigerate for up to 4 weeks or freeze for up to 3 months. To reheat, return the pudding to mould and steam, or reheat in microwave (see p. 135).

1/2 cup	butter, softened	125 mL
3/4 cup	packed brown sugar	175 mL
2	eggs	2
1 tbsp	grated orange rind	15 mL
1 cup	all-purpose flour	250 mL
1 cup	fine stale (not dry) bread crumbs	250 mL
1 tsp	baking soda	5 mL
1/2 tsp	each salt, cinnamon and nutmeg	2 mL
1/4 tsp	each cloves and ginger	1 mL
1 cup	chopped candied mixed peel	250 mL
1 cup	seeded raisins (Lexia)	250 mL
3/4 cup	halved candied cherries	175 mL
1/2 cup	golden raisins	125 mL
1/2 cup	slivered almonds	125 mL
1/3 cup	rum, brandy or orange juice	75 mL
1/4 cup	rum or brandy (for flaming)	50 mL
	Orange Hard Sauce (recipe follows)	

● In large bowl, cream butter with sugar until fluffy. Beat in eggs, one at a time, beating well after each addition; add orange rind.

● In separate bowl, combine flour, bread crumbs, baking soda, salt, cinnamon, nutmeg, cloves and ginger; stir in candied peel, seeded raisins, cherries, golden raisins and almonds. With wooden spoon, stir half of the dry ingredients into creamed mixture; stir in 1/3 cup (75 mL) rum, then remaining dry ingredients.

● Line bottom of greased 8-cup (2 L) pudding ring mould or 6-cup (1.5 L) pudding bowl with circle of greased waxed paper, pressing into any patterns of mould. Pack batter in evenly.

● Cover batter with circle of greased waxed paper; cover mould with lid. To cover bowl, make 1-inch (2.5 cm) pleat across middle of large piece of foil and place over bowl. Press sides down; trim edge, leaving 2-inch (5 cm) overhang. Tie string securely around top of bowl; fold foil overhang up over string.

● Place mould on rack in large saucepan; pour in enough boiling water to come two-thirds up side of mould.

● Cover and simmer over medium-low heat, adding water as needed to maintain level, for 1-1/2 to 2 hours for ring mould, 2-1/2 to 3 hours for pudding bowl, or until tester inserted into center comes out clean. Let stand for 5 minutes. Remove paper and unmould onto serving plate.

● In saucepan, warm 1/4 cup (50 mL) rum over medium-low heat just until heated through but not boiling. Remove from heat. Using long match, carefully ignite rum; pour over pudding. Serve with Orange Hard Sauce. Makes 10 to 12 servings.

ORANGE HARD SAUCE		
1/2 cup	butter, softened	125 mL
1-1/2 cups	sifted icing sugar	375 mL
3 tbsp	grated orange rind	50 mL
2 tbsp	orange juice	25 mL
1 tsp	lemon juice	5 mL

● In bowl, cream together butter and sugar; beat in orange rind and juice and lemon juice until fluffy. Roll into log shape or pipe into rosettes. Refrigerate until firm. Cut log into 1-inch (2.5 cm) thick slices. Makes 1-1/2 cups (375 mL).

Peach Crumble with Ginger

A crispy almond topping over juicy gingered peaches gives new meaning to old-fashioned comfort food. This dessert is wonderful with thickened yogurt or vanilla ice cream.

4 cups	sliced peeled peaches	1 L
1/4 cup	chopped crystallized ginger	50 mL
1 tbsp	all-purpose flour	15 mL
3/4 cup	rolled oats	175 mL
1/2 cup	packed brown sugar	125 mL
1/4 cup	all-purpose flour	50 mL
1 tsp	cinnamon	5 mL
1/2 cup	cold butter, cubed	125 mL
1/2 cup	slivered almonds, toasted	125 mL

● In bowl, toss together peaches, ginger and flour; set aside.

● In separate bowl, combine rolled oats, sugar, flour and cinnamon; cut in butter until mixture resembles coarse crumbs. Stir in almonds.

● Divide peach mixture among six greased 1-cup (250 mL) baking dishes; top evenly with oats mixture. Place on baking sheet and bake in 375°F (190°C) oven for 35 to 40 minutes or until bubbly and golden brown on top. Serve warm. Makes 6 servings.

Apple and Mincemeat Crumble

Mincemeat and a few Brazil nuts turn an ordinary dessert into a festive finale. This crumble is so delicious you won't want to save it just for Christmas!

4 cups	sliced peeled apples (about 5)	1 L
1-1/2 cups	mincemeat	375 mL
2 tbsp	lemon juice	25 mL
1/2 cup	all-purpose flour	125 mL
1/3 cup	packed brown sugar	75 mL
1/3 cup	rolled oats	75 mL
1/3 cup	butter	75 mL
1/2 cup	chopped Brazil nuts	125 mL

● In 9-inch (2.5 L) square baking dish, combine apples, mincemeat and lemon juice.

● In bowl, stir together flour, sugar and rolled oats; cut in butter until mixture resembles coarse crumbs. Stir in nuts. Sprinkle evenly over apple mixture. Bake in 375°F (190°C) oven for 45 minutes or until apples are tender. Makes 6 servings.

Rhubarb Crisp

This family-favorite pudding is a great way to enjoy rhubarb.

❏ **TIP: Instead of baking this crisp in the oven, microwave at High for 4 minutes; rotate dish. Microwave at High for 3 to 4 minutes longer or until fruit is tender. Let stand for 5 minutes.**

4 cups	sliced rhubarb (about 1-1/2 lb/750 g)	1 L
2 tbsp	granulated sugar	25 mL
2/3 cup	packed brown sugar	150 mL
1/2 cup	rolled oats	125 mL
1/2 cup	coarsely chopped pecans	125 mL
1/4 cup	all-purpose flour	50 mL
1/4 cup	wheat germ	50 mL
1/4 cup	sweetened flaked coconut	50 mL
1/2 tsp	cinnamon	2 mL
1/4 tsp	ginger	1 mL
1/4 cup	butter, softened	50 mL

● Arrange rhubarb evenly in 8-cup (2 L) shallow baking dish; sprinkle with granulated sugar.
● In large bowl, mix together brown sugar, rolled oats, pecans, flour, wheat germ, coconut, cinnamon and ginger. With pastry blender or fingertips, work in butter until crumbly. Sprinkle over rhubarb; press lightly.
● Bake in 350°F (180°C) oven for 40 to 45 minutes or until browned and fruit is fork-tender. Makes 4 to 6 servings.

Mixed Berry Crisp

If you use frozen berries, be sure to bake for 10 to 15 minutes longer.

8 cups	berries	2 L
2 tbsp	granulated sugar	25 mL
2 tbsp	all-purpose flour	25 mL
	TOPPING	
1 cup	all-purpose flour	250 mL
3/4 cup	rolled oats	175 mL
1/2 cup	chopped toasted pecans	125 mL
1/2 cup	granulated sugar	125 mL
1/2 cup	packed brown sugar	125 mL
2 tbsp	cinnamon	25 mL
1 tbsp	grated orange rind	15 mL
2/3 cup	butter	150 mL

● Toss together berries, sugar and flour; arrange evenly in greased 13- x 9-inch (3.5 L) baking dish.
● TOPPING: In bowl, combine flour, oats, pecans, granulated and brown sugars, cinnamon and orange rind; cut in butter until crumbly. Sprinkle evenly over berries.
● Bake in 350°F (180°C) oven for 30 to 35 minutes or until bubbly and top is golden. Let stand for 20 minutes before serving. Makes 12 servings.

Cranberry Apple Crisp

Pleasing sweet and tart flavors are perfectly balanced in this easy, satisfying dessert.

6 cups	sliced peeled cored apples	1.5 L
1 cup	cranberries, cut in half	250 mL
2 tbsp	packed brown sugar	25 mL
	TOPPING	
1/2 cup	packed brown sugar	125 mL
1/2 cup	all-purpose flour	125 mL
1/2 cup	rolled oats	125 mL
1 tsp	cinnamon	5 mL
1/4 cup	butter, softened	50 mL
1/3 cup	sliced almonds	75 mL

● In 8-inch (2 L) square shallow baking dish, toss together apples, cranberries and sugar; set aside.
● TOPPING: In bowl, combine sugar, flour, rolled oats and cinnamon. With pastry blender or fingertips, work in butter until crumbly; sprinkle over fruit. Sprinkle with almonds. Bake in 350°F (180°C) oven for 40 to 45 minutes or until browned and fruit is fork-tender. Makes 4 to 6 servings.

Vanilla Soufflés with Strawberry Coulis

Creamy, light and irresistibly delicious, this gorgeous dessert is the perfect ending to any special-occasion dinner.

1/4 cup	granulated sugar	50 mL
1	pkg (4 oz/125 g) cream cheese, softened	1
3 tbsp	packed brown sugar	50 mL
2	eggs, separated	2
1 tsp	vanilla	5 mL
	STRAWBERRY COULIS	
2 cups	hulled strawberries	500 mL
2 tbsp	instant dissolving (fruit/berry) sugar	25 mL
1 tbsp	lemon juice	15 mL
	GARNISH	
	Icing sugar	
	Fresh mint sprigs	

● Grease four 3/4-cup (175 mL) custard cups; sprinkle with 2 tbsp (25 mL) of the granulated sugar. Set aside.

● In mixing bowl, beat together cream cheese, brown sugar, egg yolks and vanilla until smooth.

● In separate bowl, beat egg whites until soft peaks form. Gradually beat in remaining granulated sugar until stiff peaks form; whisk one-quarter into cheese mixture. Fold in remaining egg whites. Divide evenly among prepared custard cups.

● Place custard cups in baking dish; pour in enough boiling water to come halfway up sides of cups. Bake in 325°F (160°C) oven for 20 to 25 minutes or until tops are golden and puffed and knife inserted near centers comes out clean.

● STRAWBERRY COULIS: Meanwhile, mash strawberries and press through fine sieve into saucepan. Stir in sugar and lemon juice; heat just until boiling.

● To serve, run knife around custards to loosen; invert onto plates. Spoon sauce around custards. Dust each serving with icing sugar. Garnish with mint. Serve immediately. Makes 4 servings.

HOW TO GET THE MOST OUT OF EGGS

Storing Eggs

● *Eggs are perishable. Store them in your refrigerator, large ends up, in the container in which you bought them rather than on the refrigerator door where temperature changes and vibrations can affect them. Store eggs away from strong-smelling foods because they can absorb odors.*

● *Shelled eggs can be frozen for up to four months. Freeze them in an airtight container, allowing room for expansion. Egg whites can be frozen alone. To freeze yolks or whole eggs, break them into a bowl, mixing very lightly. To prevent lumpiness in the yolks, add salt, granulated sugar or corn syrup (depending on their intended use) in these amounts: 1/2 tsp (2 mL) salt or 1 tbsp (15 mL) sugar or corn syrup for every 1 cup (250 mL) of eggs. Freeze eggs in small quantities so you thaw only what you need.*

What to do with Half an Egg

● *Egg yolks: Use in scrambled eggs, omelettes, white sauce, cream soups, Hollandaise sauce, custard or custard sauce.*

● *Egg whites: Use in scrambled eggs, omelettes, meringues or soufflés. In many baking recipes, you can substitute two egg whites for a whole egg.*

Beating Egg Whites

● *The secret to extra-high meringues and soufflés is a stable white foam.*

● *Start with eggs at room temperature. If they're cold from the refrigerator, cover with warm water for a few minutes.*

● *Always use a glass or metal mixing bowl, not a plastic one. Make sure that there's no yolk in the whites and that the beaters are clean and grease-free.*

● *To beat egg whites, whisk or beat with an electric mixer until stiff and glossy. Do not overbeat because egg whites get lumpy and begin to lose volume.*

Hot Fudge Soufflé

Go ahead, indulge! Light and delicate, smooth and sensuous, a chocolate soufflé is the quintessential impressive dessert and — best of all — it's easy to make. For a spectacular contrast, serve the hot soufflé with vanilla ice cream.

2 oz	unsweetened chocolate	60 g
2 tbsp	butter	25 mL
4	eggs, separated	4
2/3 cup	granulated sugar	150 mL
2 tbsp	cool coffee	25 mL
1 tbsp	coffee liqueur or rum	15 mL
1/4 tsp	cream of tartar	1 mL
	icing sugar	

● Grease 6-cup (1.5 L) soufflé dish; sprinkle with granulated sugar and set aside.

● In bowl over hot, not boiling, water, melt chocolate with butter.

● In mixing bowl, combine egg yolks, half of the granulated sugar, and the coffee.

Using electric mixer, beat for about 5 minutes or until thickened and mixture falls in ribbons when beaters are lifted. Mix in chocolate mixture and liqueur until blended.

● In separate bowl, beat egg whites with cream of tartar until soft peaks form; gradually beat in remaining sugar until stiff peaks form. Whisk about one-quarter into chocolate mixture until blended. Fold in remaining egg whites.

● Pour into prepared dish. Bake on baking sheet in 375°F (190°C) oven for 35 minutes or until puffed and almost firm to the touch. Dust with icing sugar. Serve immediately. Makes 4 to 6 servings.

❏ **TIP:** The secret to successful soufflés is proper beating of the eggs. In this recipe, egg yolks beaten with sugar form the soufflé base. Beat until mixture leaves a ribbon trail when beaters are lifted.

❏ **TIP:** For maximum volume, first whisk in about one-quarter of egg whites, then fold in remainder.

141

Wonderful Fruit

*Fruit makes an easy and tasty dessert all year long — from the first rhubarb
and strawberries in spring to all the glorious fruit of summer (raspberries, peaches, blueberries,
saskatoons, plums — the list is endless!) and the cold-storage apples and pears, citrus and bananas that
see us through the winter. Serve fruit fresh in a Margarita Salad, drizzle it with Citrus Curd Sauce or dip it
in Chocolate Fondue for the ultimate no-effort dessert. Or dress it up, like Saucy Poached Pears or
Chocolate Crêpes with Banana Filling, and you have a dazzling finale to any elegant occasion.*

Caramel Peaches with Mascarpone

This delicious dessert takes only minutes to prepare. You can substitute brandy, Grand Marnier, orange juice or peach nectar for the peach schnapps.

1 cup	mascarpone or cream cheese	250 mL
2 tbsp	sifted icing sugar	25 mL
1 tbsp	peach schnapps	15 mL
1/2 tsp	vanilla	2 mL
	CARAMEL PEACHES	
4 cups	thinly sliced peeled peaches	1 L
2 tbsp	lemon juice	25 mL
1/3 cup	butter	75 mL
1 cup	packed brown sugar	250 mL
2 tbsp	peach schnapps	25 mL
1/4 cup	whipping cream	50 mL

● In bowl, cream together mascarpone cheese, sugar, schnapps and vanilla just until smooth; set aside.

● CARAMEL PEACHES: In large bowl, combine peaches and lemon juice; set aside.

● In saucepan, melt butter over high heat; add sugar and peach schnapps. Bring to boil; boil for 2 minutes. Stir in cream until smooth. Pour over peaches and stir to mix.

● To serve, spoon caramel peaches onto each serving plate. Decoratively pipe or spoon mascarpone mixture onto center of each. Serve immediately. Makes 6 servings.

Cointreau Coffee Custard

Spoon this refreshing sauce over berries, orange segments, sliced peaches or any other favorite fruit — or serve it as a dip with fruit.

1/3 cup	packed brown sugar	75 mL
1/4 cup	all-purpose flour	50 mL
1 tsp	instant coffee granules	5 mL
3/4 cup	milk	175 mL
1	egg yolk	1
1/4 cup	butter	50 mL
2 tsp	Cointreau or orange liqueur	10 mL
1 cup	whipping cream	250 mL

● In heavy saucepan, combine sugar, flour and coffee granules. Over medium heat, gradually whisk in milk; cook, whisking, until thickened, about 5 minutes.

● In bowl, lightly beat egg yolk; stir in one-quarter of the hot mixture. Return to saucepan; cook, stirring, for 1 minute. Remove from heat; stir in butter and liqueur.

● Transfer to bowl and cover surface with waxed paper; refrigerate until chilled or for up to 8 hours.

● Just before serving, whip cream; fold into coffee mixture. Makes 3-1/2 cups (875 mL).

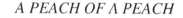

A PEACH OF A PEACH

Buying: Since peaches are very perishable and bruise easily when fully ripe, they are picked for the market in the early stages of maturity. Choose firm peaches with no blemishes or bruises. Select them for a good "ground" color (yellow) rather than for the amount of "blush" (red). Those with any green tinge will not ripen properly. Most of the midseason and late varieties are freestones — good for eating fresh, cooking or preserving.

Storing: Keep peaches in a cool dry place, then refrigerate in a single layer when fully ripe. They should keep for a few days at this stage.

Peeling: To peel, plunge peaches into boiling water for 30 to 60 seconds; slip off skins and sprinkle with fresh lemon juice to prevent discoloration.

Beaujolais Baked Apples

The familiar baked apple becomes a sophisticated yet easy dessert when cooked in a honey-wine sauce.

8	baking apples	8
2/3 cup	chopped walnuts	150 mL
1/3 cup	packed brown sugar	75 mL
3 tbsp	butter, melted	50 mL
1/2 tsp	nutmeg	2 mL
1 cup	Beaujolais or other dry red wine	250 mL
1/4 cup	liquid honey	50 mL
	Whipped cream (optional)	

● Core apples and peel thin strip around top of each; arrange in 13- x 9-inch (3.5 L) baking dish.

● Combine walnuts, sugar, butter and nutmeg; spoon into apple cavities. Stir together wine and honey; pour over apples.

● Bake apples in 400°F (200°C) oven for 35 to 45 minutes or until tender, basting every 10 minutes.

● To serve, spoon sauce over apples; top with dollop of whipped cream (if using). Makes 8 servings.

Winter Fruit Bowl

Lichees and apricots add a delightful taste surprise to this sunny fruit dessert. Serve with crème fraîche or yogurt.

❑ TIP: To make crème fraîche, whisk together 1 cup (250 mL) each sour cream and whipping cream. Put in container and refrigerate for 24 hours or until thickened. Makes 2 cups (500 mL).

1	can (19 oz/540 mL) lichees	1
1 cup	dried apricots	250 mL
1/4 cup	golden raisins	50 mL
6	grapefruit	6
1	honeydew or cantaloupe melon	1
2 cups	cubed pineapple (fresh or canned)	500 mL
1 tbsp	chopped crystallized ginger	15 mL
	Liquid honey	

● Drain lichees, reserving juice in small nonaluminum saucepan; cover and refrigerate lichees.

● Add apricots and raisins to saucepan; cover and soak for 1 hour or refrigerate overnight. Bring to boil, reduce heat and simmer for about 10 minutes or until apricots are tender. Let cool.

● Peel grapefruit; with sharp knife, pare off outer membrane. Holding fruit over large bowl, cut away sections from inner membranes; squeeze out juice from membranes.

● Halve, peel and seed honeydew; cut into bite-size cubes. Add honeydew, pineapple, ginger, lichees and apricot mixture to bowl. Toss and add honey to taste. Chill for up to 4 hours. Makes about 8 servings.

WHAT'S NEW IN DRIED FRUIT

There was a day when the choice of dried fruit was limited to raisins, dates, figs, prunes and apricots, with an occasional stretch to peaches and pears. New from the dehydrator are dried cherries, blueberries and cranberries. Add them to a fresh fruit salad or use them in quick breads and baking.

Margarita Fruit Salad

For an elegant presentation, rub the rims of glass dessert dishes or cocktail glasses with lime juice and dip into sugar.

1	each small cantaloupe and honeydew melon, cut into chunks or balls	1
2	each oranges and grapefruit, peeled and sectioned	2
1	mango, peeled and diced	1
2 cups	hulled strawberries, halved	500 mL
1/2 cup	granulated sugar	125 mL
1/3 cup	orange juice	75 mL
3 tbsp	tequila	50 mL
3 tbsp	orange liqueur	50 mL
3 tbsp	lime juice	50 mL
1 cup	coarsely grated fresh coconut (or dried unsweetened flaked), toasted (see p. 84)	250 mL

● In large bowl, combine cantaloupe, honeydew, oranges, grapefruit, mango and strawberries; set aside.

● In small saucepan, cook sugar and orange juice over medium-high heat, stirring, for 3 minutes or until sugar dissolves. Stir in tequila, liqueur and lime juice. Let cool to room temperature.

● Pour juice mixture over fruit and gently stir to mix well. Cover and refrigerate for at least 2 hours or overnight. Just before serving, sprinkle with coconut. Makes 8 servings.

Saucy Poached Pears

Cranberry and orange sauces combine for fabulous taste and a spectacular presentation. If you like, garnish platter or each serving with fresh mint.

8 cups	water	2 L
2 cups	granulated sugar	500 mL
	Rind and juice of 2 lemons	
6	firm pears, peeled and cored	6

ORANGE CUSTARD SAUCE

5	egg yolks	5
1/3 cup	granulated sugar	75 mL
1 cup	milk	250 mL
1 cup	whipping cream	250 mL
1 tbsp	grated orange rind	15 mL

CRANBERRY SAUCE

2-1/3 cups	cranberries	575 mL
1/2 cup	granulated sugar	125 mL
2 tsp	grated orange rind	10 mL
1/2 cup	orange juice	125 mL

● ORANGE CUSTARD SAUCE: In bowl, whisk yolks with sugar. In heavy saucepan, heat milk, cream and orange rind over medium-high heat just until bubbles form around edge of pan; gradually whisk into yolk mixture. Return to saucepan; cook, stirring, over medium-low heat, without boiling, for 5 to 8 minutes or until thick enough to coat back of spoon.

● Immediately strain through fine sieve into bowl; place waxed paper directly on surface. Refrigerate for at least 3 hours or until chilled. *(Custard can be refrigerated for up to 3 days.)*

● CRANBERRY SAUCE: Meanwhile, in saucepan, bring cranberries, sugar, orange rind and juice to boil, stirring. Reduce heat to medium-low; simmer for 4 to 6 minutes or until berries begin to pop. Purée in blender. Press through fine sieve. Cover and refrigerate until chilled. *(Sauce can be refrigerated for up to 5 days or frozen for up to 1 month.)*

● Meanwhile, in large saucepan, combine water, sugar, lemon rind and juice; bring to boil and boil for 5 minutes. Reduce heat to medium-low and add pears; simmer for about 30 minutes or until tender. Let cool completely in syrup to prevent discoloration. Drain pears; reserve syrup for another use.

● Arrange pears on serving platter or 6 individual plates. Spoon some cranberry sauce around pears; surround with some orange custard sauce. With tip of pointed knife, swirl sauces together. Serve extra sauces separately. Makes 6 servings.

In photo: Saucy Poached Pears; chocolate truffles

PEAR-FECTION!

One of the most popular fruits for cool-weather eating is the juicy pear. It's delicious fresh, poached or baked in pies, tarts, crumbles and cakes. The three most common and readily available varieties are Bartlett, Bosc and Anjou, although you may find other types, such as Clapp and Seckel, in season at some fruit markets.

● *Delicious all-purpose **Bartlett pears** can be eaten fresh, cooked or canned. Bell-shaped, with green-yellow skin when ripe, they are generally available in early autumn.*

● *Crisp, juicy **Bosc pears** store well. You can identify them by their unique long necks and russet-yellow color. Available from early October, they're also good for cooking.*

● ***Anjou pears*** *are a late-harvest pear and store well, making them available during the winter months. They are squatter in shape than the other types and have a light green skin.*

Whatever variety you choose, be sure to let pears ripen before using them for cooking; otherwise, the finished dish may taste flat. To ripen pears quickly, seal in a plastic bag and keep at room temperature. To keep longer, store ripe pears in the refrigerator.

Poached Pears with Brandied Cheese

You can prepare the different parts of this dessert ahead, cover and refrigerate them separately for up to 8 hours, then assemble the dessert just before dinner. Use pears that are firm but ripe, preferably Bartlett.

8	pears	8
3 cups	dry white wine	750 mL
1/2 cup	granulated sugar	125 mL
4	whole cloves	4
4	whole allspice	4
1	stick cinnamon	1
2 cups	vanilla ice cream, softened	500 mL
8	amaretti biscuits or macaroons	8
	CHEESE FILLING	
1/2 lb	cream cheese	250 g
1/4 cup	icing sugar	50 mL
1 tbsp	brandy (or 1 tsp/5 mL vanilla)	15 mL

● Peel pears; cut in half lengthwise. Using melon baller, remove core; cut out stem. In large stainless steel or ceramic-lined Dutch oven, stir together wine, sugar, cloves, all-spice and cinnamon until sugar is dissolved.

● Add pears; pour in just enough water to cover pears and bring to boil. Reduce heat and simmer gently for 10 to 25 minutes, depending on ripeness of pears, or until pears are tender. With slotted spoon, remove pears to shallow dish and let cool.

● Return liquid to high heat and cook, uncovered, until reduced to about 1 cup (250 mL); strain and set aside to let cool.

● Stir ice cream until sauce consistency; stir in cooled poaching liquid. Crush biscuits coarsely.

● CHEESE FILLING: In bowl, beat together cream cheese, sugar and brandy.

● To serve, spoon some of the ice cream sauce onto each dessert plate; top with two pear halves, cut sides up. Mound tablespoonful (15 mL) cheese filling in center of each pear. Sprinkle with biscuit crumbs. Makes 8 servings.

VARIATION

FRUIT-POACHED PEARS: Substitute 3/4 cup (175 mL) each apple juice, orange juice and water for wine; omit sugar.

Gratin of Red Fruits with Honey Ice Cream

For the easy honey ice cream, stir a big spoonful of flavorful wildflower honey into softened vanilla ice cream and refreeze before scooping.

8 cups	hulled strawberries	2 L
2 cups	raspberries	500 mL
1 cup	granulated sugar	250 mL
6	egg yolks	6
1/4 tsp	grated orange rind	1 mL
1 cup	port or white wine	250 mL
	Honey ice cream	

● Slice strawberries; set aside at room temperature for up to 1 hour.

● Just before serving, using slotted spoon, divide strawberries equally among 8 very shallow heatproof bowls. Top each evenly with raspberries.

● In heavy saucepan over low heat or in top of double boiler over barely simmering water, beat sugar, egg yolks and orange rind until creamy and sugar has dissolved, about 3 minutes. Gradually pour in port, beating constantly; cook, beating, until thickened and doubled in volume, about 8 minutes.

● Spoon sauce over fruit; broil for 1-1/2 to 3 minutes or until fruit is warmed and sauce browns and crisps. Nestle a scoop of ice cream in center of each bowl. Makes 8 servings.

Orange Stewed Rhubarb

Orange enhances the tang of rhubarb in this easy springtime dessert.

3/4 cup	granulated sugar	175 mL
2/3 cup	water	150 mL
7 cups	coarsely chopped rhubarb (1-1/2 lb/750 g)	1.75 L
2 tbsp	finely grated orange rind	25 mL
1/4 cup	orange juice	50 mL

● In large saucepan, dissolve sugar in water over low heat; bring to boil. Add rhubarb; cover and return to boil.

● Reduce heat to medium-low; simmer for 10 to 15 minutes or until softened but not stringy. Stir in orange rind and juice. Let cool. Makes 4 servings.

Citrus Curd Sauce

For a jiffy dessert with style, whisk lemony orange curd into a tangy smooth sauce and spoon it over goblets of fresh fruit — as we did for our cover photo.

2	eggs	2
3/4 cup	granulated sugar	175 mL
3 tbsp	cornstarch	45 mL
1 tsp	grated orange rind	5 mL
1 cup	boiling water	250 mL
1/4 cup	orange juice	50 mL
1/4 cup	lemon juice	50 mL
1 cup	sour cream	250 mL

● In large heatproof glass bowl, lightly beat together eggs, sugar, cornstarch and orange rind; pour in water, orange juice and lemon juice. Set bowl over pot of lightly boiling water; cook, whisking often, for 20 to 30 minutes or until thickened.

● Transfer to clean bowl; place waxed paper directly on surface of curd and refrigerate until completely chilled. (*Curd can be refrigerated for up to 3 days.*) Whisk to gently loosen; stir in sour cream. Makes about 3 cups (750 mL).

Chocolate Fondue

This leisurely dessert is still a favorite, especially for entertaining guests of all ages. Serve with a platter of fruit dippers — banana chunks, pear wedges, clementine sections, strawberries, grapes, starfruit slices and cubes of pound or light fruitcake. Buy a bar of milk chocolate for this fondue.

6 oz	bittersweet chocolate, chopped	175 g
4 oz	milk chocolate, chopped	125 g
3/4 cup	whipping cream	175 mL
2 tbsp	amaretto, brandy or rum	25 mL

● Place chopped bittersweet and milk chocolates in fondue pot.

● Heat cream until boiling; pour over chocolate, whisking until melted. Add brandy. Set over warmer. Makes 2 cups (500 mL).

CHOCOLATE-DIPPED STRAWBERRIES

Nothing makes a more dazzling impression than a tray of chocolate-dipped strawberries.

● *In heatproof bowls set over hot, not boiling, water, melt a variety of chocolates: bittersweet or semisweet and white are a good combination. Allow*

4 oz (125 g) per 4 cups (1 L) berries.

● *Make sure your strawberries are plump, red, firm, perfectly dry and still have the green caps to hold while dunking them into the chocolate.*

● *Let excess chocolate drip back into bowl and arrange berries on waxed paper to cool and firm. Refrigerate for up to 3 hours before serving.*

Nectarine and Orange Compote

When poaching, make sure the fruit is completely covered in syrup; if not, poach it in batches.

4 cups	water	1 L
3/4 cup	granulated sugar	175 mL
6	nectarines or peaches	6
2	oranges	2
2 tbsp	lemon or lime juice	25 mL
1/4 cup	white rum (optional)	50 mL

● In saucepan, bring water and sugar to boil, stirring until sugar dissolves.

● Meanwhile, blanch nectarines in boiling water for 30 to 60 seconds; plunge into cold water to cool. Peel, halve and pit.

● Cut thin strips of rind from one of the oranges and add to pan; squeeze juice into pan. Add lemon juice. Add nectarines and return to boil; reduce heat and simmer for 5 to 8 minutes or until fruit is tender when pierced.

● Place nectarines in bowl; pour in syrup. Let cool. Slice remaining orange; halve each slice and add to bowl. Add rum (if using). Makes 6 servings.

Dessert Crêpes

Versatile, delectable crêpes are a perfect dessert for any special occasion. Serve them stuffed with a sweet apple filling — as Bield House in apple-growing Collingwood, Ontario does — or choose other fruits. Or, roll them around ice cream and sauce with fruit compote or chocolate.

❏ TIP: Cooked crêpes can be stacked between sheets of waxed paper, wrapped and refrigerated for up to 3 days or frozen for up to 2 months.

1 cup	all-purpose flour	250 mL
1/4 tsp	salt	1 mL
3	eggs	3
1-1/4 cups	milk	300 mL
3 tbsp	(approx) butter, melted	50 mL
	Apple Filling (recipe follows)	

● In bowl, combine flour and salt; make well in center. Whisk together eggs, milk and 2 tbsp (25 mL) of the butter; gradually pour into well, whisking to draw in flour until smooth. Cover and refrigerate for 1 hour. Strain to give smooth, whipping-cream consistency.

● Heat 8-inch (20 cm) crêpe pan over medium heat until drop of water sprinkled on pan spatters briskly. Brush with some of the remaining butter.

● Stir batter to reblend; pour 2 tbsp (25 mL) into center of pan. Quickly tilt and rotate pan to form thin crêpe. Cook for 40 seconds or until bottom is golden and top no longer shiny.

● With spatula, loosen and turn crêpe over, using fingers to assist. Cook for 30 seconds or until golden. Transfer to plate. Repeat with remaining batter, brushing pan with butter as necessary and stacking crêpes on plate.

● Spread each crêpe with apple filling and fold into quarters or roll up. Makes about 10 servings.

APPLE FILLING		
6	apples, peeled, cored and thickly sliced	6
1 tbsp	lemon juice	15 mL
1/4 cup	butter	50 mL
1/3 cup	packed brown sugar	75 mL
2 tbsp	raisins	25 mL
2 tbsp	chopped walnuts, toasted	25 mL
1/2 tsp	grated lemon rind	2 mL
1/4 tsp	cinnamon	1 mL
1/3 cup	apple juice	75 mL

● Toss apples with lemon juice. In large skillet, melt butter; cook apples, covered, over medium heat for 8 to 10 minutes or until tender but still holding shape. Gently stir in brown sugar, raisins, walnuts, lemon rind and cinnamon; cook for about 2 minutes or until sugar melts. Stir in apple juice; let bubble for about 3 minutes or until juices thicken slightly and don't fill in when spoon is drawn across bottom of skillet. Makes about 3 cups (750 mL).

Chocolate Crêpes with Banana Filling

This luscious dessert is surprisingly low in fat! It has two egg whites instead of a whole egg, and cocoa powder instead of chocolate.

CHOCOLATE CRÊPES

1/3 cup	all-purpose flour	75 mL
2 tbsp	unsweetened cocoa powder	25 mL
1 tbsp	granulated sugar	15 mL
Pinch	salt	Pinch
2	egg whites, lightly beaten	2
1/3 cup	milk	75 mL
1/4 cup	water	50 mL
1 tsp	butter	5 mL

FILLING

1/3 cup	whipping cream	75 mL
2 tbsp	granulated sugar	25 mL
1/3 cup	plain yogurt	75 mL
1/2 tsp	vanilla	2 mL
3	bananas, sliced	3

CHOCOLATE SAUCE

1/4 cup	unsweetened cocoa powder	50 mL
3 tbsp	granulated sugar	45 mL
3 tbsp	water	45 mL
3 tbsp	corn syrup	45 mL
1/2 tsp	vanilla	2 mL

● CHOCOLATE CRÊPES: In bowl, combine flour, cocoa, sugar and salt. Make well in center; whisk in egg whites. Gradually whisk in milk and water until smooth.

● Heat small nonstick skillet or crêpe pan over medium heat; brush pan with some of the butter. Add 2 tbsp (25 mL) batter, swirling to cover pan. Cook for about 40 seconds or until edge curls and crêpe no longer sticks. Turn and cook for 30 seconds; remove and set aside. Repeat with remaining batter, brushing pan with remaining butter as necessary.

● CHOCOLATE SAUCE: In saucepan, combine cocoa with sugar; whisk in water and corn syrup. Bring to boil over medium-high heat; boil for 1 minute, whisking constantly. Remove from heat; stir in vanilla. Let cool until thickened.

● FILLING: In bowl, whip cream with sugar; stir in yogurt and vanilla.

● ASSEMBLY: Spread about 2 tbsp (25 mL) filling over each crêpe. Arrange overlapping banana slices on one-quarter of crêpe; fold in half, then in half again. Arrange 2 filled crêpes on each of 4 dessert plates; drizzle with chocolate sauce. Makes 4 servings.

Cookies, Squares and Tiny Delights

Here's the best of the cookie batches! From the very first bite, our cookies say satisfaction pure and simple — whether it's Extra-Peanutty Peanut Butter Cookies, Divine Chocolate Brownies or sophisticated Florentines. We've included cookies and tiny delights for the holidays, too — from kid-pleasing Fat Teddies to old-fashioned Ginger Tree Ornaments and buttery shortbread. Plus melt-in-your-mouth truffles that are extra-easy to make — and even easier to eat!

Layered Wedding Diamonds

A delicious chocolate filling is sandwiched between thin cookie layers. For more dazzle, garnish with edible gold glitter instead of pastry crumbs.

1 cup	butter, softened	250 mL
1 cup	granulated sugar	250 mL
3	egg yolks	3
1 cup	sour cream	250 mL
3-3/4 cups	all-purpose flour	925 mL
1/2 tsp	baking soda	2 mL
	FILLING	
2 cups	milk	500 mL
5	egg yolks	5
1 cup	granulated sugar	250 mL
5 oz	semisweet chocolate, melted	150 g
1/4 cup	unsweetened cocoa powder	50 mL

● FILLING: In heavy saucepan, heat milk over medium heat until bubbles form around edge. Meanwhile, in large bowl, beat egg yolks; gradually beat in sugar until thickened. Gradually whisk in milk until blended. Whisk in chocolate and cocoa.

● Return to saucepan; cook over medium-low heat, stirring, for 20 to 25 minutes or until mixture thickly coats back of spoon. Transfer to bowl; place waxed paper directly on surface and refrigerate overnight.

● In bowl, cream butter with sugar. Beat in egg yolks, one at a time; beat in sour cream. Stir together flour and baking soda; blend into sour cream mixture until well blended. Divide into six portions. Cover and refrigerate for 1 hour.

● On lightly floured surface, roll out each portion into 15- x 9-inch (40 x 23 cm) rectangle. Place on inverted baking sheet; bake in 375°F (190°C) oven for 8 to 12 minutes or until golden. Let cool slightly; transfer to rack.

● Set 1/2 cup (125 mL) filling aside. Spread each layer with about 1/3 cup (75 mL) filling, leaving 1/2-inch (1 cm) border uncovered; stack layers on inverted baking sheet. Spread reserved filling on top, leaving border. Trim off enough uncovered border to crumble into 2 tbsp (25 mL) crumbs; sprinkle over top. Refrigerate for about 2 hours or until set. *(Recipe can be prepared to this point, covered and refrigerated overnight or frozen for up to 1 week.)*

● Trim borders to form straight edges (use trimmings for snacks). Score lengthwise at 1-inch (2.5 cm) intervals. Holding knife at 45° angle to first marks, score into diamonds; cut. Makes about 4 dozen.

Layered Wedding Diamonds (in center of plate); True Love Hearts (p. 154); White Chocolate Petits Fours (p. 41)

True Love Hearts

This nutty, crispy cookie is delicious made in any shape, but hearts are perfect for a wedding, shower or Valentine's Day — or for your true love any time at all!

1-3/4 cups	hazelnuts	425 mL
3-1/2 cups	all-purpose flour	875 mL
2 tsp	grated lemon rind	10 mL
2 tsp	cinnamon	10 mL
1/4 tsp	cloves	1 mL
2 cups	butter, softened	500 mL
1-1/3 cups	granulated sugar	325 mL
2 tsp	vanilla	10 mL
1/2 cup	raspberry or strawberry jam	125 mL
	Icing sugar	

● On baking sheet, toast hazelnuts in 350°F (180°C) oven for 8 to 10 minutes or until fragrant. Transfer to clean tea towel; rub to remove skins. In food processor, grind nuts to make 2 cups (500 mL); combine with flour, lemon rind, cinnamon and cloves.

● In bowl, cream butter with sugar until fluffy; stir in vanilla and flour mixture, mixing until ball forms. Divide into 4 portions; wrap and chill for 30 minutes.

● Between sheets of waxed paper, roll out each portion to 1/8-inch (3 mm) thickness. Chill for 10 minutes. Using 2-3/4-inch (7 cm) floured heart-shaped cookie cutter, cut out cookies. Using 1-3/4-inch (4.5 cm) heart-shaped cookie cutter, cut out centers from half of cookies to form "frames." Reroll centers and scraps to cut out more pairs of hearts and frames, to make about 30 of each.

● Bake on greased baking sheets in 375°F (190°C) oven for 8 to 10 minutes or until golden. Let cool slightly; remove to rack and let cool completely. *(Cookies can be stored in airtight container for up to 5 days.)*

● Spread about 1 tsp (5 mL) jam over each heart. Dust frames with icing sugar. Place over jam. *(Once sandwiched, cookies can be stored in airtight container for up to 1 day.)* Makes about 2-1/2 dozen.

Greek Shortbread

Sweet tables in Greece always boast this fragrant buttery shortbread, known as kourabiéthes.

❏ **TIP: Rose water is available at Middle Eastern or specialty food shops.**

2 cups	butter, softened	500 mL
3/4 cup	granulated sugar	175 mL
2	egg yolks	2
2 tbsp	brandy	25 mL
1 tsp	vanilla	5 mL
4 cups	all-purpose flour	1 L
1 tsp	baking powder	5 mL
	Whole cloves	
1/4 cup	rose water	50 mL
1-1/2 cups	icing sugar	375 mL

● In large bowl, cream butter with sugar until fluffy. Beat in egg yolks, brandy and vanilla. Stir together flour and baking powder; blend into creamed mixture, using hands to bring dough together.

● Form dough into 1-inch (2.5 cm) balls. Place 1 inch (2.5 cm) apart on ungreased baking sheets. Stud each with clove. Bake in 350°F (180°C) oven for 20 to 25 minutes or until bottoms are light golden but not brown. Remove to rack set over rimmed baking sheet.

● Sprinkle cookies with a few drops rose water; dust with icing sugar to coat. Repeat sprinkling with rose water and dusting with icing sugar. Let cool completely. *(Shortbread can be stored in airtight container for up to 5 days or frozen for up to 1 month.)* Makes about 5 dozen.

A SWEET TABLE

One of the most delightful customs in recent years is the wedding sweet table. Around midnight, when dinner has been well digested, speeches have immortalized the bride and groom and guests need a break from dancing, a table of delectable sweets magically appears, along with coffee, tea and, sometimes, liqueurs. The "table," or really the desserts on the table, can be as fancy or as simple as the wedding itself, but one thing must hold true — the sweets must be beautiful, absolutely delicious and easy to pick up.

● *Our dessert table suggestions include White Chocolate Petits Fours (p. 41), Tiny Tangerine Cheesecakes (p. 10), Caramel Pecan Squares (p. 175), Layered Wedding Diamonds (p. 152), True Love Hearts and Greek Shortbread, and Strawberry Meringue Kisses (this page). You can also include slices of larger cheesecakes and iced layer or buttercream cakes (see the CAKES chapter for a luscious selection).*

● *Finish off with an array of truffles (p. 176) and, of course, a bounty of fresh fruit to enjoy on plates — melon fingers, strawberries, pineapple wedges, a tumble of blueberries and raspberries, peaches and nectarines. For an extra-lavish touch, splash fruit with cognac!*

Strawberry Meringue Kisses

Add a dollop of Creamy Filling or whipped cream to hold the berry.

4	egg whites	4
Pinch	cream of tartar	Pinch
1 cup	granulated sugar	250 mL
1 tsp	vanilla	5 mL
32	strawberries	32
	CREAMY FILLING	
3/4 cup	cream cheese	175 mL
4 tsp	icing sugar	20 mL
1/3 cup	whipping cream	75 mL
1/2 tsp	vanilla	2 mL

● In large bowl, beat egg whites with cream of tartar until soft peaks form; gradually beat in sugar and vanilla until stiff glossy peaks form.

● With spoon or piping bag fitted with 1/4-inch (5 mm) star tip, form "nests" 1-1/2 inches (4 cm) in diameter on two foil or parchment paper-lined baking sheets.

● Bake in 225°F (110°C) oven for 1 to 1-1/4 hours or until crisp but not browned. If not completely dry inside, loosen meringues with lifter and return to oven; turn off heat and let dry until oven is cool, about 1 hour. Let meringues cool completely.

● CREAMY FILLING: Meanwhile, in bowl, blend together cream cheese and sugar; gradually beat in cream until smooth. Stir in vanilla. Refrigerate for at least 30 minutes or until chilled. Spoon into cooled meringues. Top each with strawberry. Makes about 32.

Honey Spice Cookies

Chock-full of nuts, honey and cinnamon, these extra-moist and fragrant Greek cookies are a perfect sweet ending for any special occasion. Although the cookies take a bit of time to assemble, they keep well and are actually better the next day.

❏ **TIP: For an impressive presentation, stack cookies in a multi-tiered mound on an attractive serving platter.**

2	eggs, separated	2
2/3 cup	butter, softened	150 mL
2/3 cup	shortening	150 mL
2/3 cup	granulated sugar	150 mL
1 tsp	each grated orange and lemon rind	5 mL
1 tbsp	brandy	15 mL
1 tsp	vanilla	5 mL
3-1/2 cups	sifted cake-and-pastry flour	875 mL
2 tsp	baking powder	10 mL
1-1/2 tsp	cinnamon	7 mL
1/2 tsp	cloves	2 mL

SYRUP		
1-1/2 cups	mild liquid honey	375 mL
1 cup	water	250 mL
1/2 cup	granulated sugar	125 mL
1	each strip orange and lemon rind	1

GARNISH		
1 cup	(approx) liquid honey	250 mL
1-1/2 cups	finely chopped walnuts	375 mL
	Whole cloves (optional)	

● In bowl, beat egg whites until stiff peaks form; set aside.

● In separate bowl, cream together butter, shortening and sugar until light and fluffy. Beat in egg yolks, one at a time. Blend in orange and lemon rind, brandy and vanilla. Fold in beaten whites.

● Stir together flour, baking powder, cinnamon and cloves; gradually blend into egg mixture until incorporated. Turn out dough onto well-floured surface (dough will be sticky); knead lightly 10 times. Form into disc; wrap and refrigerate for 1 hour.

● With floured fingertips, roll 1 tbsp (15 mL) dough at a time into 2-inch (5 cm) long cigar shapes; place 2 inches (5 cm) apart on greased baking sheets. Bake in 350°F (180°C) oven for 25 to 30 minutes or until golden. Let cool on racks.

● SYRUP: In small saucepan, bring honey, water, sugar, and orange and lemon rind to boil, stirring frequently to dissolve sugar. Reduce heat to medium; simmer, without stirring, for 10 minutes or until slightly thickened. Keep warm over low heat.

● Slide baking sheets under racks with cookies to catch any drips. Immerse about 6 cookies at a time into warm syrup for 30 seconds. Using slotted spoon, return cookies to rack.

● GARNISH: Spoon about 1 tsp (5 mL) honey over each cookie; sprinkle immediately with walnuts. Stud center of each with whole clove (if using). Sprinkle with any remaining honey and nuts. Store in airtight container for at least 1 day or up to 1 week. Makes about 4-1/2 dozen.

Spice Crispies

The call went out for family-favorite cookies in our recent Cookie Caper Contest. Jane Speer of Duncan, B.C. responded with this winner, an old-fashioned favorite of her mother's.

1 cup	shortening	250 mL
1 cup	granulated sugar	250 mL
1/2 cup	packed brown sugar	125 mL
1	egg	1
2 tbsp	fancy molasses	25 mL
1 tsp	vanilla	5 mL
1-1/2 cups	all-purpose flour	375 mL
1-1/2 tsp	cinnamon	7 mL
1 tsp	baking powder	5 mL
1 tsp	baking soda	5 mL
1 tsp	each allspice and nutmeg	5 mL
1 cup	rolled oats	250 mL
1/2 cup	unsweetened desiccated coconut	125 mL
2 oz	semisweet chocolate, melted (optional)	60 g

● In bowl, cream shortening with granulated and brown sugars until fluffy; beat in egg, molasses and vanilla.

● Stir together flour, cinnamon, baking powder and soda, allspice and nutmeg; stir into creamed mixture along with oats and coconut, mixing well.

● Drop by rounded teaspoonfuls (5 mL), 2 inches (5 cm) apart, onto greased baking sheets. Bake in 350°F (180°C) oven for 9 to 11 minutes or until golden. Let cool on racks. Dip fork into chocolate (if using); drizzle over cookies. Makes 6 dozen.

Coffee Drops with Mocha Glaze

These easy-to-make drop cookies are lightly flavored with coffee.

1/2 cup	butter, softened	125 mL
3/4 cup	packed brown sugar	175 mL
1	egg, beaten	1
1 tsp	vanilla	5 mL
1-1/2 cups	all-purpose flour	375 mL
1/2 tsp	baking powder	2 mL
1/2 tsp	baking soda	2 mL
1/4 tsp	salt	1 mL
1/3 cup	hot strong coffee	75 mL
1/2 cup	chopped pecans or walnuts	125 mL
	GLAZE	
1-1/2 cups	icing sugar	375 mL
3 tbsp	cold strong coffee	45 mL
1/4 cup	butter, softened	50 mL
1 tbsp	unsweetened cocoa powder	15 mL

● In large bowl, cream butter; beat in sugar until light and fluffy. Beat in egg and vanilla.

● Stir together flour, baking powder, baking soda and salt; add to creamed mixture alternately with hot coffee, stirring just until mixed. Stir in nuts. *(Dough can be wrapped and frozen for up to 1 month. Thaw in refrigerator; let stand at room temperature for 30 minutes before continuing.)*

● Drop heaping teaspoonfuls (5 mL) of dough 2 inches (5 cm) apart onto lightly greased baking sheets. Bake in 375°F (190°C) oven for 8 to 10 minutes or until lightly browned. Remove to racks and let cool.

● GLAZE: In small bowl, alternately add icing sugar and cold coffee to butter, stirring until smooth. Stir in cocoa. Spread on cooled cookies; let stand for 3 to 4 hours or until glaze sets. Makes 4 dozen.

Best-Ever Chocolate Chip Cookies

This recipe makes enough chocolaty cookies to satisfy even the hungriest chocoholic!

❏ TIP: To make Reverse Chocolate Chip Cookies, replace 1/3 cup (75 mL) of the flour with unsweetened cocoa powder and use white chocolate chips instead of dark chocolate chips.

1/2 cup	butter	125 mL
1/2 cup	shortening	125 mL
1 cup	granulated sugar	250 mL
1/2 cup	packed brown sugar	125 mL
2	eggs	2
2 tsp	vanilla	10 mL
2 cups	all-purpose flour	500 mL
1 tsp	baking soda	5 mL
1/2 tsp	salt	2 mL
1 cup	chopped walnuts	250 mL
2 cups	chocolate chips	500 mL

● In bowl, cream together butter and shortening; gradually beat in granulated and brown sugars, creaming thoroughly. Beat in eggs and vanilla.

● Stir together flour, baking soda and salt; blend into creamed mixture. Stir in nuts and chocolate chips. Chill dough for a few minutes or let stand at room temperature for 30 minutes.

● Drop dough by rounded teaspoonfuls (5 to 7 mL) onto lightly greased baking sheets. Flatten slightly to even thickness of about 1/2 inch (1 cm). Bake in 375°F (190°C) oven for 8 to 9 minutes or until golden brown around edges and still slightly underbaked in center. Let stand on baking sheets for 5 minutes; remove to racks and let cool completely. Makes about 4 dozen.

Extra-Peanutty Peanut Butter Cookies

Whole nuts double the peanuttiness in this cookie-jar favorite.

1/2 cup	butter, softened	125 mL
1/2 cup	granulated sugar	125 mL
1/2 cup	packed brown sugar	125 mL
1	egg	1
1 cup	smooth peanut butter	250 mL
1/2 tsp	vanilla	2 mL
1-1/2 cups	all-purpose flour	375 mL
1/2 tsp	salt	2 mL
1/2 tsp	baking soda	2 mL
1 cup	unsalted peanuts	250 mL

● In bowl, cream together butter and granulated and brown sugars until fluffy. Beat in egg, peanut butter and vanilla.

● Combine flour, salt and baking soda; add peanuts. Stir into peanut butter mixture.

● Using 1 tbsp (15 mL) at a time, roll into balls. Place balls 1 inch (2.5 cm) apart on lightly greased baking sheets; gently flatten with fork.

● Bake in 375°F (190°C) oven for 10 minutes or until light golden brown. Let cool on rack. Makes 3-1/2 dozen.

COOKIE BAKING TIPS

Baking Sheets

● *Use baking sheets or cookie sheets, not jelly roll pans, which have sides that deflect the heat.*

● *Nonstick baking sheets with not too dark a finish are generally a good choice for baking cookies. Shiny aluminum sheets will tend to produce soft-bottomed crusts with more even browning. Dark carbon-steel sheets absorb heat and yield crisp crusts.*

● *Choose thick baking sheets since thin ones buckle or cookies burn.*

● *Grease sheets only when called for in recipe. Cool and wipe sheets clean with paper towel between batches, if necessary.*

Ingredients

● *Butter is the best fat for flavor and appearance and should be softened to room temperature.*

● *Chop or dice candied or dried fruit with kitchen shears dipped in granulated sugar. A food processor often makes dried fruit gummy, but if you prefer to use one, combine fruit with some of the recipe's flour and use an on/off pulse motion just until chopped.*

● *Cream butter, sugar, eggs and flavorings with an electric mixer. Use low speed or wooden spoon to stir in dry ingredients. For tender cookies, fold in the last of the flour and don't overbeat.*

Dough

● *When rolling out dough for cookies, work in as little extra flour from the surface and rolling pin as possible.*

● *Use a pastry cloth and stockinette-covered rolling pin, or roll out between two sheets of waxed paper.*

● *Roll out only part of the dough at a time, keeping the rest refrigerated.*

● *If using cutters, flour and cut out as many cookies as possible in the first rolling, rerolling scraps only once for best results.*

● *Chilling cut-out cookies before baking them helps cookies keep their shape while baking and ensures tender results.*

● *Place unbaked cookies on cool baking sheets. Unless otherwise indicated, space about 1-1/2 inches (4 cm) apart to allow for spreading when baking; thin doughs spread more than thick.*

Baking

● *Bake cookies in middle of preheated oven. Be sure oven is accurate and at the correct temperature.*

● *When baking in batches, bake one sheet of cookies while you prepare the next.*

● *If you have only one baking sheet, line it with foil before baking the cookies. After baking, slide the foil off the pan and set the cookies aside to cool. Rinse the pan under cold running water, pat dry and slide the next batch of cookies on foil onto the baking sheet.*

● *Check cookies often near end of baking time since even a minute can make a great difference.*

● *Let cookies cool for a few minutes on the baking sheet before transferring to a wire rack, without overlapping, to cool completely.*

Storing

● *Let cookies cool to room temperature before storing.*

● *Store crisp and soft cookies in separate containers. Store crisp cookies between sheets of waxed paper in a loosely covered container. Store soft cookies in an airtight one so they stay moist and chewy.*

Freezing

● *You can freeze almost any cookie except meringues, or glazed or iced cookies unless specified in recipe.*

● *To package cookies for freezing, line airtight container with plastic wrap, then layer cookies in container between sheets of waxed paper. Place waxed paper on top so cookies avoid contact with ice crystals, then seal with tight-fitting lid.*

● *Most baked cookies can be frozen for up to 6 months.*

● *Most unbaked doughs can be frozen for up to 1 month. Label and date the package, including baking instructions.*

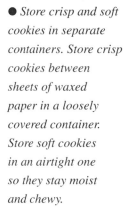

Carefully place layer of chocolate dough on top of plain dough and trim edges to make neat rectangle.

Using the waxed paper as a guide, tightly roll up two layers to form roll.

Use a very sharp knife and try not to press down when you cut roll of dough into slices.

Chocolate Peppermint Pinwheels

The dough for these two-tone cookies can be stored in the refrigerator for up to 10 days or in the freezer for up to one month.

2 oz	unsweetened chocolate	60 g
1/2 cup	butter, softened	125 mL
1 cup	granulated sugar	250 mL
1	egg	1
2 tbsp	lemon juice	25 mL
2 cups	all-purpose flour	500 mL
1/2 tsp	baking soda	2 mL
1/2 tsp	salt	2 mL
1/2 tsp	peppermint extract	2 mL
1	egg white, lightly beaten	1

● In top of double boiler over hot, not boiling, water, melt chocolate; set aside to let cool.

● In large bowl, cream butter; beat in sugar until light and fluffy. Beat in egg; stir in lemon juice. Stir together flour, baking soda and salt; gradually add to creamed mixture, stirring just until blended.

● Divide dough in half; add cooled chocolate and peppermint extract to one half. Between two sheets of waxed paper, roll out each half to 16- x 10-inch (40 x 25 cm) rectangle. Remove top sheet of waxed paper. Brush plain dough with some of the egg white; carefully invert chocolate layer on top. Roll very lightly with rolling pin; remove top sheet of waxed paper.

● With sharp knife, carefully trim edges to make neat rectangle; brush chocolate layer with remaining egg white. Using bottom sheet of waxed paper as guide and starting at long edge, tightly roll up dough jelly roll-style. Wrap in plastic wrap and refrigerate for at least 2 hours or until chilled, rolling dough occasionally on counter to maintain round shape.

● Place roll seam side down; with very sharp knife, cut into 1/8- to 1/4-inch (3 to 5 mm) thick slices. Arrange slightly apart on lightly greased baking sheets; bake in 375°F (190°C) oven for about 10 minutes or until firm to the touch. Remove to racks and let cool. Makes 5 dozen.

Florentines

These delicious cookies, flavored with ginger and lemon, are iced upside down with melted chocolate. They can be stored in an airtight container in the refrigerator for up to one week.

❏ **TIP: For a change of taste, substitute sliced almonds for the hazelnuts, and chopped candied cherries for the lemon peel — as we did for our photo.**

2/3 cup	granulated sugar	150 mL
1/2 cup	whipping cream	125 mL
3 tbsp	unsalted butter	50 mL
3/4 cup	finely chopped toasted hazelnuts	175 mL
2/3 cup	chopped crystallized lemon peel	150 mL
1/3 cup	all-purpose flour	75 mL
1/4 cup	chopped crystallized ginger	50 mL
1/2 lb	bittersweet or semisweet chocolate, melted	250 g

● In saucepan, combine sugar, cream and butter; bring to boil. Remove from heat and stir in hazelnuts, lemon peel, flour and ginger.

● Drop batter by teaspoonfuls (5 mL) onto greased and floured baking sheets, leaving enough room for cookies to spread. Pat batter thin with tines of wet fork.

● Bake in 350°F (180°C) oven for 10 minutes; remove from sheets and let cool on racks. Spread chocolate over bottoms of cooled cookies; let stand on racks, chocolate side up, until set. Makes about 2 dozen.

Sugar Cookie Cutouts

With this easy sugar cookie recipe and an assortment of cookie cutters, you can create festive cookies for every special occasion throughout the year. Decorate with Fluffy Icing, if desired.

❏ **JUST FOR KIDS! Use this recipe to make gaily colored oval eggs at Easter; owls, bats, pumpkins and witches at Halloween; bells, stars and angels at Christmas; and maple leaves for a Canada Day Picnic on July 1st.**

1 cup	butter, softened	250 mL
1/2 cup	each granulated sugar and packed brown sugar	125 mL
1	egg	1
2 tsp	vanilla	10 mL
2 cups	all-purpose flour	500 mL
1-1/2 tsp	baking powder	7 mL
1/2 tsp	nutmeg	2 mL
1/4 tsp	salt	1 mL
	Fluffy Icing (recipe follows)	

● In bowl, cream together butter and granulated and brown sugars until fluffy. Beat in egg and vanilla. Stir together flour, baking powder, nutmeg and salt; stir into creamed mixture until smooth. Form into disc; wrap and chill for at least 1 hour or up to 3 days. Bring to room temperature before rolling.

● On lightly floured pastry cloth and using stockinette-covered rolling pin, roll out dough to slightly less than 1/4-inch (5 mm) thickness. Using floured cookie cutter, cut out desired shapes.

● Transfer to parchment paper-lined or lightly greased baking sheets, leaving about 1 inch (2.5 cm) between cookies. Bake in 350°F (180°C) oven for 6 to 8 minutes or until light golden underneath. Let cool on racks. Decorate with icing, if desired. Makes about 3 dozen.

	FLUFFY ICING	
1/4 cup	butter	50 mL
1/4 cup	shortening	50 mL
2 cups	icing sugar	500 mL
1/2 tsp	vanilla	2 mL
2 tbsp	(approx) milk	25 mL
	Red, green, blue and yellow food coloring	

● In bowl, cream together butter and shortening. Beat in icing sugar, vanilla and enough milk to make smooth fluffy icing; beat for 2 minutes. Divide among 4 bowls. Mix different food coloring into each bowl, one drop at a time, until desired color. Transfer to cake-decorating tubes. Makes about 1-1/2 cups (375 mL).

Mocha Shortbread Bars

These slice-and-bake shortbreads are year-round favorites of Monica Gray of Toronto and her daughters, Rhomney and Shauna.

1 cup	butter, softened	250 mL
1/2 cup	icing sugar	125 mL
2 tsp	strong coffee	10 mL
2 tsp	vanilla	10 mL
1/4 tsp	almond extract	1 mL
2-1/3 cups	all-purpose flour	575 mL
1 tbsp	unsweetened cocoa powder	15 mL
1 tbsp	ground coffee beans	15 mL
1/4 tsp	salt	1 mL
1/4 cup	granulated sugar	50 mL

● In bowl, cream butter with icing sugar until fluffy; beat in liquid coffee, vanilla and almond extract. Stir together flour, cocoa, ground coffee and salt; blend into butter mixture, using hands if necessary.

● On waxed paper, shape dough into rectangle about 2 inches (5 cm) wide and 1 inch (2.5 cm) high. Cut into 1/2-inch (1 cm) thick slices. Bake on ungreased baking sheets in 350°F (180°C) oven for 20 to 22 minutes or until firm and lightly browned on bottom. Press lightly into granulated sugar. Let cool on racks. *(Bars can be stored in airtight containers for up to 2 weeks.)*

Spritz Cookies

By changing the discs in a cookie press, you can make many different cookies from one batch of this rich, tender dough.

1 cup	butter, softened	250 mL
1/2 cup	granulated sugar	125 mL
1	egg	1
1/2 tsp	almond extract (or 1 tsp/5 mL vanilla)	2 mL
2-1/3 cups	all-purpose flour	575 mL
1/4 tsp	salt	1 mL
	GARNISH (optional)	
	Colored sugar, candies or chopped candied fruit	

● Refrigerate baking sheets until baking time.
● In large bowl, cream butter with sugar until light and fluffy. Beat in egg, then almond extract. Stir together flour and salt; gradually stir into creamed mixture. Fill cookie press with batches of dough and press out desired shapes onto ungreased baking sheet, leaving a little space between each cookie.

● GARNISH: Decorate cookies, if desired, with sugar, candies or fruit. Bake in 375°F (190°C) oven for about 8 minutes or until light golden. Remove to racks and let cool. Makes 7 dozen.

Shortbread

Here are three different looks for butter-good shortbread. You can pat the dough into a pan to cut into bars, roll it out and cut with cookie cutters, or press into a pretty circular pattern with a Scottish shortbread mould.

❏ **TIP: Although the shortbread can be frozen for up to six months, it is at its melt-in-your-mouth best if baked and enjoyed within two weeks.**

FOR MOULDED SHORTBREAD:

Press dough into mould to completely fill pattern. Insert tip of sharp knife and gently loosen dough from mould all around edges.

Invert moulded dough onto ungreased baking sheet and remove mould.

2 cups	unsalted butter, softened	500 mL
1 cup	icing sugar	250 mL
4 cups	all-purpose flour	1 L
1/2 tsp	salt	2 mL

● In large bowl, cream butter thoroughly; beat in sugar until light and fluffy. With wooden spoon, gradually add flour and salt, mixing well. Knead dough very gently until smooth and soft but not oily. Shape and bake as directed below.

PAN SHORTBREAD BARS: Pat dough into ungreased 15- x 10-inch (40 x 25 cm) jelly roll pan; smooth surface with back of spoon. Score into 2-1/2- x 1-inch (6 x 2.5 cm) rectangles; prick each 3 times. Cover lightly and refrigerate until firm, about 2 hours.
● Cut out rectangles and place 1/2 inch (1 cm) apart on ungreased baking sheets. Place in 325°F (160°C) oven and immediately reduce temperature to 275°F (140°C). Bake for 30 minutes; turn baking sheets and bake for 5 to 10 minutes longer or until firm and golden on bottom and sand-colored on top. Remove to racks and let cool. Makes about 5 dozen.

ROLLED SHORTBREAD COOKIES: Form dough into ball; wrap in waxed paper and refrigerate overnight.
● Working with small portion of dough, roll out between two sheets of waxed paper to 1/4-inch (5 mm) thickness.

With floured cookie cutter, cut into desired shapes and place 1/2 inch (1 cm) apart on ungreased baking sheets. Decorate with candied fruit or candies. Place in 325°F (160°C) oven and immediately reduce temperature to 275°F (140°C). Bake for 20 to 25 minutes or until firm and golden on bottom and sand-colored on top. Remove to racks and let cool. Makes 5 to 6 dozen.

MOULDED SHORTBREAD: Lightly butter pattern on 6-1/2-inch (16 cm) shortbread mould; dust with flour. Divide dough into three parts. Pat each portion into mould; invert onto ungreased baking sheet and remove mould. Cover lightly and refrigerate for at least 2 hours to set design.
● Place in 325°F (160°C) oven and immediately reduce temperature to 275°F (140°C). Bake for 20 minutes; turn baking sheets and bake for 10 to 15 minutes longer or until firm and golden on bottom and sand-colored on top. Remove to racks and let cool. Makes 3 moulds.

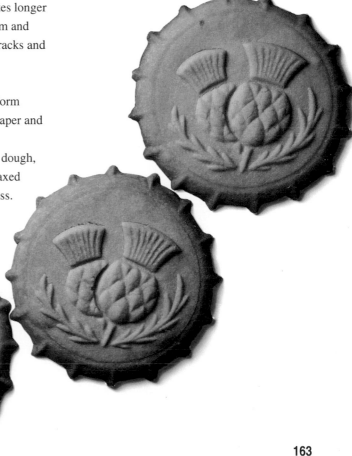

Lemon Cookies

Poppyseeds add an extra crunch to these easy-to-make cookies. Serve them with Nectarine and Orange Compote (p. 150).

1 cup	butter, softened	250 mL
1/2 cup	granulated sugar	125 mL
2 tbsp	grated lemon rind	25 mL
1 tsp	vanilla	5 mL
2 cups	all-purpose flour	500 mL
2 tbsp	poppyseeds (optional)	25 mL

● In bowl, cream butter with sugar until fluffy; mix in lemon rind and vanilla. Gradually stir in flour, and poppyseeds (if using), until mixture holds together.

● On lightly floured surface, knead dough gently until smooth. Form into disc; wrap and refrigerate for at least 20 minutes or up to 3 days. Let soften slightly at room temperature before rolling, if necessary.

● On lightly floured surface or between waxed paper, roll out dough to 1/8-inch (3 mm) thickness. Using floured 2-inch (5 cm) cookie cutter, cut out cookies and place on lightly greased baking sheets.

● Bake in 350°F (180°C) oven for 12 to 14 minutes or just until firm to the touch and lightly browned around edges. Transfer to racks and let cool. Makes about 3 dozen.

Spicy Orange Ginger Cookies

Grated gingerroot adds fresh zest to these moist cookies, the grand winner in our recent Cookie Caper Contest. Congratulations to Laurel Kreuger of Mortlach, Saskatchewan!

3/4 cup	butter, softened	175 mL
3/4 cup	granulated sugar	175 mL
1/4 cup	packed brown sugar	50 mL
1	egg	1
1/4 cup	fancy molasses	50 mL
4 tsp	grated orange rind	20 mL
1 tbsp	grated gingerroot	15 mL
2 cups	all-purpose flour	500 mL
1 tsp	baking soda	5 mL
1 tsp	cinnamon	5 mL
1/2 tsp	cloves	2 mL
1/2 tsp	cardamom	2 mL
1/4 tsp	salt	1 mL
1/4 cup	chopped crystallized ginger	50 mL

● In bowl, cream butter with granulated and brown sugars until fluffy; beat in egg, molasses, orange rind and gingerroot.

● Stir together flour, baking soda, cinnamon, cloves, cardamom and salt; stir into creamed mixture until well blended. Cover and chill for 15 minutes or until firm.

● Shape into 1-inch (2.5 cm) balls; place piece of ginger in center of each. Bake 2 inches (5 cm) apart on greased baking sheets in 325°F (160°C) oven for 12 to 15 minutes or until edges are firm. Remove to racks and let cool. Makes about 4 dozen.

Fat Teddies

These peanut butter-and-chocolate-flavored cookies are definitely as much fun to make as they are to eat!

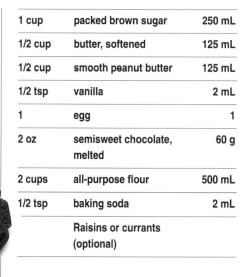

1 cup	packed brown sugar	250 mL
1/2 cup	butter, softened	125 mL
1/2 cup	smooth peanut butter	125 mL
1/2 tsp	vanilla	2 mL
1	egg	1
2 oz	semisweet chocolate, melted	60 g
2 cups	all-purpose flour	500 mL
1/2 tsp	baking soda	2 mL
	Raisins or currants (optional)	

● In bowl, beat together sugar, butter, peanut butter and vanilla until fluffy. Blend in egg, beating well. Remove about 1 cup (250 mL) of the batter to separate bowl; combine with melted chocolate.

● Stir together 1 cup (250 mL) of the flour and 1/4 tsp (1 mL) of the baking soda; gradually add to chocolate batter, blending thoroughly. Add remaining flour and baking soda to plain batter, blending thoroughly.

● Working with small pieces of dough at a time and keeping remainder covered with plastic wrap, shape 1-inch (2.5 cm) balls for bodies and heads; press together. Place 2 inches (5 cm) apart on lightly greased baking sheets, pressing lightly to flatten. Shape and add small bits of dough for ears, arms and legs, pressing together. Add raisins (if using) or tiny bits of contrasting dough for eyes, mouth, buttons and paws. Cover with plastic wrap and refrigerate for 30 minutes.

● Bake in 350°F (180°C) oven for 12 to 15 minutes or until firm to the touch and lightly browned. Let cool on sheets for 5 minutes; transfer to racks and let cool completely. *(Cookies can be refrigerated in airtight containers for up to 1 week or frozen for up to 3 months.)* Makes about 16.

No-Bake Apricot Coconut Balls

Served with coffee, these easy-to-make fruit balls are satisfying enough to stand in for dessert at the end of even a special meal.

1 cup	chopped dried apricots	250 mL
1/2 cup	chopped prunes	125 mL
1/2 cup	raisins	125 mL
3 tbsp	orange liqueur or juice	50 mL
1 tbsp	coarsely grated orange rind	15 mL
1-1/2 cups	shredded coconut	375 mL
3/4 cup	chopped toasted pecans (see p. 51)	175 mL

● In small bowl, combine apricots, prunes, raisins, liqueur and orange rind; cover and let stand for 1 hour or up to 1 day.

● In blender or food processor, chop apricot mixture finely; mix in 1 cup (250 mL) of the coconut and pecans. Shape 1 tbsp (15 mL) at a time into balls; roll in remaining coconut. Let stand on waxed paper to dry for 8 hours or overnight. *(Balls can be stored in airtight containers, each layer separated by waxed paper, in cool dry place for up to 3 weeks.)* Makes 3 dozen.

Ginger Tree Ornaments

Tint small quantities of icing with an assortment of food coloring, then pipe designs onto these spicy ginger cutouts. Or, thin the icing with a few drops of water and brush it on with a paintbrush.

❏ TIP: Add Ginger Tree Ornaments to your next Christmas Cookie exchange — along with Meringue Christmas Wreaths, Chocolate-Dipped Bars, Coconut Thumbprints and Truffle Mice (all on the next page).

1/2 cup	butter, softened	125 mL
3/4 cup	packed brown sugar	175 mL
1/4 cup	fancy molasses	50 mL
1	egg	1
1 tbsp	grated orange rind	15 mL
2-1/2 cups	all-purpose flour	625 mL
2 tsp	ginger	10 mL
1 tsp	cinnamon	5 mL
1 tsp	baking soda	5 mL
1/2 tsp	each allspice and cloves	2 mL
1/4 tsp	each cardamom and salt	1 mL
Pinch	each cayenne and black pepper	Pinch
	Decorator Icing (recipe follows)	

● In large bowl, cream butter with sugar until fluffy; beat in molasses, egg and orange rind. Stir together flour, ginger, cinnamon, baking soda, allspice, cloves, cardamom, salt, and cayenne and black peppers; gradually stir into creamed mixture.

● Gather dough into ball and knead 6 times. Shape into disc; wrap and refrigerate for 1 hour or until chilled, or for up to 3 days. Let dough soften slightly at room temperature before rolling, if necessary.

● Between two sheets of waxed paper, roll out dough to just less than 1/4-inch (5 mm) thickness. Remove top sheet of paper. With floured cookie cutters, cut out desired shapes. With straw, poke hole in top of each shape for hanging. (Reserve dough scraps for rerolling.)

● Carefully lift paper and dough onto baking sheet; freeze for 15 to 20 minutes or until dough is firm.

● Transfer cookies to parchment paper-lined or lightly greased baking sheets; bake in 350°F (180°C) oven for 10 to 12 minutes or until edges darken slightly and tops are barely firm when gently touched. Recut holes, if necessary. Remove cookies to racks and let cool. *(Cookies can be frozen for up to 3 months; thaw completely before decorating.)* Decorate as desired with icing. *(Decorated cookies can be stored in airtight container for up to 1 week.)* Makes about 2 dozen.

DECORATOR ICING		
4 cups	sifted icing sugar	1 L
3	egg whites	3
1/2 tsp	cream of tartar	2 mL

● In large bowl and using electric mixer, beat icing sugar, egg whites and cream of tartar for 7 to 10 minutes or until thickened and very smooth. Cover icing with damp tea towel to prevent drying out. Makes about 2-1/4 cups (550 mL).

Coconut Thumbprints

Before baking, fill thumbprints with tart red jam or a green or red maraschino cherry half.

In photo: (from left) Truffle Mouse; refrigerator cookie; Meringue Christmas Wreaths; Coconut Thumbprints; Chocolate-Dipped Bars.

1/2 cup	packed brown sugar	125 mL
1	pkg (4 oz/125 g) cream cheese	1
2 tbsp	butter	25 mL
2 tbsp	milk	25 mL
3/4 cup	all-purpose flour	175 mL
1 tsp	baking powder	5 mL
1-1/2 cups	flaked coconut	375 mL
1/3 cup	finely chopped preserved or crystallized ginger	75 mL
1/3 cup	finely chopped maraschino cherries	75 mL
1 cup	lightly toasted flaked coconut	250 mL
	Jam or cherry halves	

● In bowl, cream together sugar, cream cheese, butter and milk until smooth. Stir together flour and baking powder; blend into cheese mixture. Add flaked coconut, ginger and chopped cherries; mix thoroughly. Refrigerate dough for 1 hour.

● With hands, roll dough into 3/4-inch (2 cm) balls; roll each ball in toasted coconut to coat. Make indentation in center of each with finger; spoon in about 1/4 tsp (1 mL) jam. Or, push cherry half into center of each, then mound dough up around cherry.

● Place balls 2 inches (5 cm) apart on lightly greased baking sheets. Bake in 350°F (180°C) oven for 15 to 17 minutes or until golden and firm to the touch. Let cool on rack. Makes 4 dozen.

Meringue Christmas Wreaths

Decorate wreaths before baking with maraschino cherries, colored sprinkles, nuts, coarsely crushed candy cane or edible gold glitter.

2	egg whites	2
1 tsp	lemon juice	5 mL
1/4 tsp	cream of tartar	1 mL
2/3 cup	instant dissolving (fruit/berry) sugar	150 mL

● In small deep bowl, beat egg whites with lemon juice until foamy. Add cream of tartar. Gradually beat in sugar, about 1 tbsp (15 mL) at a time, beating well after each addition, until stiff shiny peaks form. (A small amount rubbed between fingers should not feel gritty — sugar should be dissolved.)
● Pipe small 1-1/2-inch (4 cm) rings onto parchment paper- or foil-lined baking sheets or drop batter by teaspoonfuls (5 mL). Bake in 250°F (120°C) oven for 1 to 1-1/4 hours or until firm. Turn off oven; leave meringues in oven for 1 hour longer. *(Meringues can be stored for up to 2 weeks in airtight container.)* Makes 2 dozen.

Truffle Mice

For variety, roll some of the mice in finely ground nuts or colorful sugar sprinkles.

4 oz	semisweet chocolate, melted	125 g
1/3 cup	sour cream	75 mL
1 cup	fine chocolate wafer crumbs (about 24)	250 mL
1/3 cup	icing sugar or fine chocolate wafer crumbs	75 mL
	GARNISH	
	Gold or silver dragées	
	Slivered almonds	
	Licorice	

● In bowl, combine chocolate and sour cream. Stir in 1 cup (250 mL) chocolate wafer crumbs; mix well. Cover and refrigerate until firm, about 1 hour. Roll scant tablespoonfuls (15 mL) of chocolate mixture into small balls slightly pointed at 1 end. Roll lightly in icing sugar. Place on waxed paper-lined tray.
● GARNISH: Insert dragées for eyes, almond slivers for ears and small bits of licorice for tails. Refrigerate until firm, about 2 hours. *(Truffles can be stored in airtight container in refrigerator for up to 1 week.)* Makes about 2 dozen.

Chocolate-Dipped Bars

This cookie dough works well with any cookie press tip. You can substitute chopped nuts or desiccated coconut for the candy canes.

1	pkg (4 oz/125 g) cream cheese	1
1/2 cup	butter	125 mL
1/2 cup	shortening	125 mL
1 tsp	vanilla	5 mL
1/2 tsp	salt	2 mL
1 cup	granulated sugar	250 mL
1	egg yolk	1
2 cups	all-purpose flour	500 mL
	GARNISH	
1 cup	semisweet chocolate chips	250 mL
1 tsp	shortening	5 mL
1/3 cup	crushed candy canes	75 mL

● Refrigerate baking sheets until baking time.
● In bowl, cream together cream cheese, butter, shortening, vanilla and salt. Add sugar, mixing well; blend in egg yolk. With wooden spoon, gradually stir in flour until smooth.
● Using cookie press with 1-inch (2.5 cm) bar tip, press out long lines of dough onto ungreased baking sheets; score at 2-1/2-inch (6 cm) intervals. Bake in 350°F (180°C) oven for 10 minutes or until cookies are firm and just starting to brown at edges. Break into bars at score lines. Let cool completely on rack.
● GARNISH: In saucepan over hot, not boiling, water, melt chocolate with shortening, stirring until smooth. Dip cookies into chocolate; sprinkle with crushed candy canes. Refrigerate on racks until set. Makes about 6 dozen.

Divine Chocolate Brownies

For a fudgier version, decrease the flour to 3/4 cup (175 mL). And for an extra hit of chocolate, ice with your favorite fudge icing.

4 oz	unsweetened chocolate, coarsely chopped	125 g
4 oz	semisweet chocolate, coarsely chopped	125 g
1 cup	butter	250 mL
2 cups	granulated sugar	500 mL
4	eggs	4
2 tsp	vanilla	10 mL
1 cup	all-purpose flour	250 mL
1/2 tsp	salt	2 mL

● In top of double boiler, over hot, not boiling, water, melt unsweetened and semisweet chocolates until softened. Let cool.

● In bowl, cream butter with sugar until light and fluffy. Add eggs, one at a time, beating well after each addition. Stir in vanilla. Stir together flour and salt; blend into butter mixture. Stir in chocolate.

● Pour batter into greased 13- x 9-inch (3.5 L) baking dish. Bake in 350°F (180°C) oven for 35 minutes or until tester inserted into center comes out slightly moist. Let cool on rack.

Grand Marnier Nanaimo Bars

Bliss at first bite! That's the only way to describe the incredible taste of these ultimate Nanaimo bars.

2 cups	graham cracker crumbs	500 mL
1 cup	unsweetened flaked coconut	250 mL
1/2 cup	toasted chopped pecans (see p. 51)	125 mL
2/3 cup	butter	150 mL
1/3 cup	sifted unsweetened cocoa powder	75 mL
1/4 cup	granulated sugar	50 mL
1	egg, beaten	1
	GRAND MARNIER LAYER	
2 cups	icing sugar	500 mL
1/4 cup	butter, softened	50 mL
1/4 cup	Grand Marnier or orange liqueur	50 mL
1 tbsp	coarsely grated orange rind	15 mL
	CHOCOLATE TOPPING	
1 tbsp	butter	15 mL
4 oz	semisweet chocolate, melted	125 g

● In bowl, stir together crumbs, coconut and pecans. In small saucepan, gently heat butter, cocoa and sugar until butter melts. Remove from heat; whisk in egg. Blend into crumb mixture. Press into greased 9-inch (2.5 L) square cake pan. Bake in 350°F (180°C) oven for 10 minutes. Let cool on rack.

● GRAND MARNIER LAYER: In bowl, blend half of the icing sugar with butter; mix in Grand Marnier, remaining icing sugar and orange rind. Spread over base.

● CHOCOLATE TOPPING: Stir butter into chocolate until melted; spread evenly over Grand Marnier layer. Let cool for 20 minutes in refrigerator; cut into bars. *(Bars can be covered and refrigerated for up to 2 weeks or frozen for up to 2 months. Let soften slightly before serving.)*

VARIATION

CLASSIC NANAIMO BARS: Make base and Chocolate Topping as above. In layer, substitute milk for Grand Marnier; add 1/2 tsp (2 mL) vanilla. Substitute 2 tsp (10 mL) grated lemon rind for orange rind.

Chocolate Pecan Bars

These chewy chocolaty squares are great bazaar sellers, and satisfy that afternoon urge for something sweet.

1-1/4 cups	all-purpose flour	300 mL
1/3 cup	packed brown sugar	75 mL
1/4 cup	unsweetened cocoa powder	50 mL
1/2 tsp	salt	2 mL
1/4 tsp	baking powder	1 mL
1/2 cup	butter	125 mL
1 cup	pecan halves	250 mL
	TOPPING	
1/2 cup	corn syrup	125 mL
1/3 cup	granulated sugar	75 mL
1/4 cup	butter, melted	50 mL
2	eggs	2
1 tbsp	all-purpose flour	15 mL

1 tsp	vanilla	5 mL
1/4 tsp	salt	1 mL
2 oz	semisweet chocolate, melted	60 g

● In bowl, stir together flour, sugar, cocoa, salt and baking powder. Using pastry blender, cut in butter until crumbly.

● Press into greased 8-inch (2 L) square cake pan. Arrange pecans, flat side down, on top.

● TOPPING: In bowl, whisk together corn syrup, sugar and butter until smooth; whisk in eggs. Stir in flour, vanilla and salt; pour over base.

● Bake in 350°F (180°C) oven for 35 to 40 minutes or until golden brown. Let cool in pan. Drizzle chocolate over top. Let chocolate set before cutting into bars.

Plenty of Applesauce Bars

These delicious bars — with their wonderful spiciness, crunchy nuts and sheer moist appleness — are a perfect lunchbox dessert.

1 cup	butter, softened	250 mL
1 cup	packed brown sugar	250 mL
1/2 cup	fancy molasses	125 mL
2	eggs	2
1/2 cup	unsweetened applesauce	125 mL
1/2 cup	sour cream	125 mL
1-1/2 cups	all-purpose flour	375 mL
1-1/2 cups	whole wheat flour	375 mL
1 cup	chopped pecans	250 mL
2 tsp	baking powder	10 mL
1/2 tsp	each baking soda, salt and cinnamon	2 mL
	DRIZZLE ICING	
3/4 cup	icing sugar	175 mL
2 tbsp	orange juice	25 mL

● In bowl, cream together butter, sugar and molasses until fluffy; beat in eggs, one at a time. Stir in applesauce and sour cream.

● Combine all-purpose and whole wheat flours, pecans, baking powder, baking soda, salt and cinnamon; stir into butter mixture.

● Spread into greased 15- x 10-inch (40 x 25 cm) jelly roll pan. Bake in 350°F (180°C) oven for 25 to 30 minutes or until cake tester inserted into center comes out clean. Let cool on rack. Cut into bars.

● DRIZZLE ICING: Whisk together icing sugar and juice. Drizzle over cooled bars.

Lunchbox Granola Bars

Old-fashioned large-flake rolled oats give these bars a chewy texture, but any rolled oats will do.

2/3 cup	butter, softened	150 mL
1/2 cup	packed brown sugar	125 mL
1/2 cup	corn syrup	125 mL
2 tsp	vanilla	10 mL
3 cups	rolled oats	750 mL
1/2 cup	flaked coconut	125 mL
1/2 cup	sunflower seeds	125 mL
1/2 cup	chopped pecans	125 mL
1/4 cup	sesame seeds	50 mL
1/4 cup	wheat germ	50 mL
1/2 cup	semisweet chocolate chips or raisins	125 mL

● In bowl, cream butter, sugar, corn syrup and vanilla until smooth; stir in oats, coconut, sunflower seeds, pecans, sesame seeds and wheat germ, mixing well. Stir in chocolate chips.

● Firmly pat into well-greased and floured 13- x 9-inch (3.5 L) cake pan; bake in 350°F (180°C) oven for 30 to 35 minutes or until golden brown. Let cool completely in pan on rack before cutting into bars.

Raisin-Date Squares

Decidedly old-fashioned, these squares have remained popular for generations. For pure date squares, replace the raisins with more dates.

3/4 cup	butter, softened	175 mL
3/4 cup	packed brown sugar	175 mL
1 tsp	vanilla	5 mL
2-1/2 cups	rolled oats	625 mL
1 cup	all-purpose flour	250 mL
1/2 tsp	baking soda	2 mL
1/2 tsp	salt	2 mL
	FILLING	
1-1/2 cups	chopped dates	375 mL
1-1/2 cups	seeded raisins	375 mL
1-1/2 cups	boiling water	375 mL
1/3 cup	granulated sugar	75 mL
1 tsp	grated lemon rind	5 mL
2 tbsp	lemon juice	25 mL
Pinch	nutmeg	Pinch

● FILLING: In heavy saucepan, combine dates, raisins, boiling water, sugar, lemon rind, lemon juice and nutmeg; simmer, covered, for about 10 minutes or until thickened and liquid is absorbed. Let cool.

● In bowl, beat together butter and sugar until fluffy. Add vanilla. Combine rolled oats, flour, baking soda and salt; mix into bowl until crumbly.

● Press half of the oats mixture evenly over bottom of greased 9-inch (2.5 L) square cake pan. Spread with filling. Sprinkle with remaining oats mixture.

● Bake in 350°F (180°C) oven for 40 to 45 minutes or until golden. Let cool until warm. Cut into squares; let cool completely.

FOR BETTER BARS AND SQUARES

● ***Mix dough just until blended;*** *over-mixing will give tough bars with hard tops.*

● ***Use correct pan size.*** *If pan is larger, dough will bake faster and become tough and dry. If pan is smaller, bars will be thicker with doughy centers.*

● ***Spread batter evenly*** *in pan for uniform baking, thickness and texture.*

● ***Check bars often*** *as they cook. Overbaked bars will be hard and dry; underbaked ones will be doughy.*

Apricot Squares

These flavorful squares are easy to make yet special enough to serve at any elegant occasion.

1/2 cup	butter, softened	125 mL
1 cup	all-purpose flour	250 mL
1/4 cup	granulated sugar	50 mL
	FILLING	
2/3 cup	dried apricots	150 mL
1 cup	water	250 mL
2	egg yolks	2
3/4 cup	packed brown sugar	175 mL
1/2 cup	all-purpose flour	125 mL
1/2 tsp	baking powder	2 mL
1/4 tsp	salt	1 mL
	ICING	
1-3/4 cups	(approx) icing sugar	425 mL
1/4 cup	butter, softened	50 mL
1-1/2 tsp	grated lemon rind	7 mL
1 tbsp	lemon juice	15 mL

● In bowl, cream butter; blend in flour and sugar, mixing well.

Press onto bottom of 9-inch (2.5 L) square cake pan; bake in 325°F (160°C) oven for about 20 minutes or until golden.

● FILLING: Meanwhile, cut apricots into small pieces. In heavy saucepan, bring apricots and water to boil; reduce heat and simmer, uncovered, for about 20 minutes or until most of the water is absorbed and apricots are tender. Set aside.

● In bowl and using electric mixer, beat egg yolks for 1 minute; add brown sugar and beat for 1 minute. Stir in flour, baking powder and salt; mix well. Blend in apricot mixture; spread over warm base. Bake in 325°F (160°C) oven for 30 to 40 minutes or until top is golden and springs back when lightly touched. Let cool.

● ICING: In small bowl, gradually beat enough of the icing sugar into butter to make smooth spreadable consistency. Blend in lemon rind and juice. Spread over apricot filling. Cut into squares.

Fresh Plum Macaroon Squares

These delicious cake-like squares are best baked and enjoyed the same day. For summer picnics or family gatherings, take them right in the cake pan. Be sure to use firm but ripe red or purple plums.

3/4 cup	butter	175 mL
1 tbsp	grated orange rind	15 mL
3/4 cup	packed brown sugar	175 mL
1/2 cup	ground almonds	125 mL
1-1/2 cups	all-purpose flour	375 mL
	TOPPING	
1/4 cup	butter, softened	50 mL
1 cup	granulated sugar	250 mL
3/4 cup	all-purpose flour	175 mL
1/2 cup	sliced almonds	125 mL
3	eggs	3
1 tbsp	grated orange rind	15 mL
1/2 cup	ground almonds	125 mL
1/2 tsp	baking powder	2 mL
4 cups	sliced plums	1 L

● In bowl, beat butter with orange rind until creamy. Stir in sugar, then ground almonds. Gradually blend in flour, using fingertips when mixture becomes stiff.

● Grease sides of 13- x 9-inch (3.5 L) cake pan; press mixture into pan. Bake in 375°F (190°C) oven for 12 to 15 minutes or until lightly browned and firm to the touch.

● TOPPING: Meanwhile, in small bowl, combine butter and 1/4 cup (50 mL) each of the sugar and flour; mix in sliced almonds and set aside.

● In mixing bowl, beat eggs with remaining sugar for about 5 minutes or until thickened and light in color; stir in orange rind.

● Combine remaining flour, ground almonds and baking powder; stir into egg mixture.

● Arrange plums evenly over base; spread egg mixture over top. Sprinkle with sliced almond mixture. Bake in 375°F (190°C) oven for 40 to 45 minutes or until top is puffed and golden and plums are tender when pierced with fork. Run knife around edges of pan; let cool in pan on rack. Cut into squares.

Caramel Pecan Squares

If you like Turtles chocolates, you won't be able to resist these chewy, nutty caramel treats.

1 cup	butter, softened	250 mL
3/4 cup	packed brown sugar	175 mL
1 tsp	vanilla	5 mL
2 cups	all-purpose flour	500 mL

CARAMEL FILLING

1-1/3 cups	packed brown sugar	325 mL
3/4 cup	whipping cream	175 mL
3/4 cup	corn syrup	175 mL
1/3 cup	butter	75 mL
1-1/2 cups	chopped pecans	375 mL

TOPPING

10 oz	semisweet chocolate, chopped	300 g
1/4 cup	butter	50 mL
1/4 cup	whipping cream	50 mL
1 cup	pecan halves	250 mL

● In bowl, beat butter, sugar and vanilla until creamy; blend in flour, 1/2 cup (125 mL) at a time. Pat into lightly greased 15- x 10-inch (40 x 25 cm) jelly roll pan. Bake in 350°F (180°C) oven for 18 to 22 minutes or until golden. Let cool in pan on rack.

● CARAMEL FILLING: In saucepan, cook sugar, cream, corn syrup and butter over medium-high heat, stirring often, for 10 to 12 minutes or until thickened and candy thermometer registers 230°F (110°C) (thread stage). Remove from heat; stir in pecans. Spread evenly over base. Let cool completely.

● TOPPING: In top of double boiler over hot, not boiling, water, melt together chocolate, butter and cream, stirring occasionally. Spread evenly over filling. Let cool for 15 minutes. Score into 1-1/2-inch (4 cm) squares; press pecan half into each square. Refrigerate for 30 minutes or until set. *(Pan can be covered and refrigerated for up to 1 week.)* Cut into squares.

JUST FOR KIDS!

Crispy Squares

Children of all ages will love these delicious no-bake squares.

❑ **TIP: To make these squares in the microwave, melt butter in 8-cup (2 L) measure at High for 30 to 40 seconds. Add marshmallows, tossing to coat; microwave at High for 1 to 1-1/2 minutes or until melted, stirring once. Continue with recipe.**

3 tbsp	butter	50 mL
4 cups	marshmallows (about 30)	1 L
1/4 tsp	vanilla	1 mL
4 cups	crispy rice cereal	1 L

● In large saucepan, melt butter over medium heat; stir in marshmallows until melted. Remove from heat; stir in vanilla and cereal until coated.

● Press into lightly greased 8-inch (2 L) square cake pan. Let cool. Cut into squares.

VARIATIONS

PEANUT BUTTER SQUARES: In large saucepan, melt 2/3 cup (150 mL) corn syrup with 1/2 cup (125 mL) smooth peanut butter; stir in 4 cups (1 L) crispy rice cereal and 1/2 cup (125 mL) raisins until coated. Press into pan and refrigerate for 1 hour or until firm. Cut into squares.

ROCKY ROAD SQUARES: Add 1 cup (250 mL) chopped walnuts to Crispy Squares mixture; press into pan. Sprinkle with 1-1/2 cups (375 mL) mini marshmallows and 1/2 cup (125 mL) chocolate chips; gently press into squares. Broil for 1 minute. Let cool. Cut into squares.

Chocolate Truffles

Nothing is more special or indulgent than truffles — especially these! Dusted in cocoa, the crisp chocolate coating encloses a velvety filling that melts luxuriously in your mouth. A little bit of heaven!

❏ **TIP: Piping rather than spooning a delicate filling cuts down on handling. If you don't have a pastry bag, make your own from a small, sturdy plastic bag by snipping off a little piece of one corner.**

GANACHE FILLING		
1 cup	whipping cream	250 mL
1/2 lb	semisweet or bittersweet chocolate, chopped	250 g
2 tbsp	chocolate liqueur (or 1 tsp/5 mL vanilla)	25 mL
	Icing sugar	

COATING		
3/4 lb	semisweet or bittersweet chocolate, chopped	375 g
1 cup	unsweetened cocoa powder	250 mL

● GANACHE FILLING: In small saucepan, heat cream just until bubbles form around edge of pan; remove from heat. Stir in chocolate until smooth; stir in liqueur. Transfer to bowl; cover and refrigerate for 1 hour or until thickened and cold.

● Using whisk (not electric mixer), beat chocolate mixture just until creamy and lighter in color. Do not overbeat or mixture will separate.

● Using pastry bag fitted with 1/2-inch (1 cm) plain tip, pipe filling into 1-inch (2.5 cm) diameter rounds on two waxed paper-lined baking sheets. Cover and refrigerate for 30 minutes or until firm.

● Working with rounds of filling from one baking sheet at a time, lightly roll in icing sugar. Gently roll each round between fingertips to round off tips. Return to waxed paper-lined sheet and freeze for about 1 hour or until hard and almost frozen.

● COATING: In top of double boiler over hot, not boiling, water, melt chocolate. Remove from heat and let cool slightly. Sift cocoa into pie plate. Using two forks, dip balls from one baking sheet at a time into chocolate, letting excess drip off. (If chocolate thickens, rewarm gently over hot water.) Place balls in cocoa.

● Using two clean forks, roll truffles in cocoa; refrigerate on waxed paper-lined baking sheet until hardened. Place truffles in candy cups and store in covered container in refrigerator until just before serving. *(Truffles can be refrigerated for up to 1 week or frozen for up to 3 months.)* Makes 4 dozen.

VARIATIONS

CHOCOLATE ORANGE TRUFFLES: In filling, substitute orange-flavored liqueur or orange juice for chocolate liqueur; add 1 tbsp (15 mL) finely grated orange rind. Do not roll chocolate-coated truffles in cocoa. Garnish with strips of orange rind just before serving.

HAZELNUT TRUFFLES: In filling, substitute hazelnut liqueur for chocolate liqueur; add 1/2 cup (125 mL) ground hazelnuts. Roll chocolate-coated truffles in 2 cups (500 mL) finely chopped toasted hazelnuts instead of cocoa.

Lightly roll rounds of filling in icing sugar; gently roll each round between fingertips to round off tips.

Using two forks, dip balls into melted chocolate, letting excess drip off.

Using two clean forks, roll truffles in cocoa powder.

● Test for hard-crack stage by dropping a little syrup into very cold water. Remove syrup from water and bend; it should be brittle and snap easily.

● Stir baking soda into syrup; pour immediately onto well-greased 17-1/2- x 11-1/2-inch (45 x 29 cm) jelly roll pan. Using two wooden spoons, spread brittle as evenly and thinly as possible. Let cool until hardened.

Pecan Brittle

Irresistible nutty brittle is a delightful gift any time of the year. Wrap it decoratively or present it in a festive wicker basket.

❏ TIP: It's very important that you know when the sugar syrup has reached soft- and hard-crack stages. To take away the guesswork, use a candy thermometer as an accurate test.

2 cups	granulated sugar	500 mL
1 cup	corn syrup	250 mL
1/2 cup	water	125 mL
1-1/2 cups	pecans	375 mL
2 tbsp	butter	25 mL
1/2 tsp	salt	2 mL
1/2 tsp	baking soda	2 mL

● In heavy saucepan, combine sugar, corn syrup and water. Bring to boil over medium heat; cover and cook for 3 minutes. Uncover and stir in pecans.

● Place candy thermometer in saucepan and cook, without stirring, for about 15 minutes or until soft-crack stage of 270° to 290°F (132° to 143°C).

● Add butter and salt; cook, stirring constantly, for about 5 minutes or until hard-crack stage of 300° to 310°F (150° to 155°C).

● Using wooden rolling pin or mallet, break candy into pieces. *(Brittle can be stored in airtight container for up to 1 month.)* Makes about 1-1/4 lb (625 g).

VARIATIONS

PEANUT OR ALMOND BRITTLE: Substitute unsalted shelled peanuts or blanched almonds for pecans.

CHOCOLATE-DRIZZLED NUT BRITTLE: Drizzle melted semisweet or bittersweet chocolate over cooled pieces of brittle. Let stand at room temperature for about 2 hours or until set.

White Chocolate Almond Bark

This simple confection can also be made with semisweet chocolate.

1-1/2 lb	white chocolate, finely chopped	750 g
1 cup	unblanched whole almonds, toasted and cooled (see p. 51)	250 mL

● In bottom of double boiler, bring water to simmer; remove from heat. Add chocolate to top of double boiler and stir frequently until melted. Stir in almonds.

● Spread evenly onto waxed paper-lined 15- x 11-inch (40 x 28 cm) jelly roll pan. Refrigerate for 1 hour or until firm. Break into pieces. *(Bark can be layered between waxed paper and refrigerated in airtight container for up to 3 weeks.)* Makes 1-3/4 lb (875 g).

Peanut Butter Melts

You can refrigerate these for up to five days or freeze them for up to one month.

2/3 cup	icing sugar, sifted	150 mL
1/2 cup	crunchy peanut butter	125 mL
1/4 cup	butter, softened	50 mL
2 oz	white chocolate, melted and slightly cooled	60 g
1/2 lb	milk chocolate	250 g
1 tsp	shortening	5 mL
2 cups	crushed peanut brittle	500 mL

● In bowl and using electric mixer, beat icing sugar, peanut butter, butter and white chocolate until smooth. Cover and freeze for 25 to 30 minutes or until firm.

● With icing sugar-dusted hands, roll mounded teaspoonfuls (5 mL) at a time into balls; place on waxed paper-lined baking sheet. Cover and freeze for 25 to 30 minutes or until firm.

● In top of double boiler over hot, not boiling, water, melt milk chocolate with shortening. Working with 12 balls at a time, dip into chocolate mixture; scoop out with fork. Sprinkle immediately with crushed brittle. Cover and refrigerate for 30 minutes or until firm. Makes about 2 dozen.

Brownie Miniatures

These moist chocolaty brownies, baked in tiny paper cups, make delicious mouthfuls. A simple topping of Rosebuds, mint chocolate wafers or large chocolate chips doubles as icing.

1/3 cup	packed brown sugar	75 mL
1/4 cup	butter	50 mL
3 oz	semisweet chocolate	90 g
1/2 tsp	vanilla	2 mL
1	egg, lightly beaten	1
1/3 cup	all-purpose flour	75 mL
24	chocolate Rosebuds	24

● In saucepan, melt sugar, butter and chocolate over low heat, stirring, until chocolate is just melted.

Remove from heat and let cool for 1 minute. Blend in vanilla and egg; gently fold in flour just until blended.

● Spoon into tiny paper baking cups. Bake in 350°F (180°C) oven for 10 to 12 minutes or until set. Remove from oven; set Rosebud on top of each. Let cool. Makes about 2 dozen.

The Contributors

ELIZABETH BAIRD is food director of *Canadian Living* magazine and one of Canada's best-known food writers. Editor of *Canadian Living*'s bestselling *Country Cooking* and author of *Summer Berries*, *Classic Canadian Cooking* and *Elizabeth Baird's Favourites*, her name is synonymous with Canadian cooking at its best. Elizabeth reviewed over 500 recipes from Canada's leading food writers to select only the finest desserts for this cookbook, and has included many of her own favorites.

FRANK BALDOCK is a former wine columnist for *The Toronto Star*. He now writes about food and wine for a number of Canadian magazines, restaurants and for radio.

VICKI BURNS is a member of the *Canadian Living* Test Kitchen and a contributing food writer to the magazine.

JAMES CHATTO writes about food, wine and travel for several Canadian magazines.

JANET CORNISH is a member of the *Canadian Living* Test Kitchen and is also a trained chef.

KATHLEEN CROWLEY is a freelance writer and the author of *The New Look of Beef*. She has written about food for several Canadian magazines, including *Canadian Living*.

CAROL FERGUSON was *Canadian Living*'s first food editor and is also the editor of *The Canadian Living Entertaining Cookbook* and the first *Canadian Living Cookbook*. She is now a food writer and consultant. Together with Margaret Fraser, she has written *A Century of Canadian Home Cooking*, to be published this fall.

JEREMY FERGUSON is a well-known food, wine and travel writer. He also has a weekly column, Consuming Passions, in *The Globe and Mail.*

MARGARET FRASER, a former associate food editor of *Canadian Living,* has played a prominent role as editor of several *Canadian Living* cookbooks and is now a food consultant. Together with Carol Ferguson, she has written *A Century of Canadian Home Cooking*, to be published this fall.

HEATHER HOWE is a member of the *Canadian Living* Test Kitchen and has been involved in food articles and recipe testing for the magazine.

PATRICIA JAMIESON was manager of *Canadian Living*'s Test Kitchen for four years and is now Test Kitchen director at *Eating Well* magazine in Charlotte, Vermont.

ANNE LINDSAY is *Canadian Living*'s contributing nutrition editor and is also a food writer, consultant and author of several bestselling cookbooks, including *Lighthearted Everyday Cooking.*

JAN MAIN is a home economist and the owner of Jan Main's Kitchen, a cooking school and catering business in Toronto. She also writes about food for several magazines, including *Canadian Living*.

BETH MOFFATT is a freelance home economist, food stylist and food writer. She recently returned to Toronto from Brussels.

ROSE MURRAY is a food writer, consultant, broadcaster and author of several cookbooks, including *Rose Murray's Comfortable Kitchen Cookbook.*

MARIE NIGHTINGALE is food writer for *The Mail-Star* and *The Chronicle-Herald* in Halifax. A native Haligonian, she is also author of the bestselling *Out of Old Nova Scotia Kitchens*, a culinary history of the province.

RUTH PHELAN trained at the Cordon Bleu Cooking School in London, England and at Ballymaloe Cooking School in Ireland. A freelance food consultant and food writer, she has been with the *Canadian Living* Test Kitchen for the last five years.

DAPHNA RABINOVITCH trained at Tante Marie's Cooking School in San Francisco and taught at the Badia a Coltibuno Cooking School in Tuscany. Former senior pastry chef at the David Wood Food Shop, she has been manager of the *Canadian Living* Test Kitchen since 1990.

IRIS RAVEN is a freelance food writer and frequent contributor to *Canadian Living* magazine.

DUFFLET ROSENBERG is the owner of Dufflet Pastries in Toronto and director of the Great Cooks cooking school. Her incredible desserts started a revolution in Toronto over 15 years ago and are now featured in many restaurants and food shops throughout the city.

KAY SPICER is a home economist, food consultant and journalist. Her most recent cookbook is *From Mom With Love — Real Home Cooking.*

EDNA STAEBLER is an award-winning journalist and author of the bestselling *Food That Really Smecks, More Food That Really Smecks* and the *Smecks Appeal* cookbook series.

LINDA STEPHEN is a freelance food writer, consultant and caterer. She also teaches at The Bonnie Stern Cooking School.

BONNIE STERN is proprietor of The Bonnie Stern Cooking School in Toronto. She is also a food writer, broadcaster, columnist and the author of several popular cookbooks, including *Desserts by Bonnie Stern.*

LUCY WAVERMAN is a food writer, consultant, teacher and the author of several cookbooks including *Lucy Waverman's Fast and Fresh Cookbook.*

CAROL WHITE is a freelance writer. At one time, she was food features editor at *Canadian Living* and also created and wrote the Chefs' Showcase recipe column at *The Toronto Star.*

Canadian Living's **TEST KITCHEN** developed many of the delicious recipes included here, as well as creating many tempting new desserts for this book and updating old favorites for today's tastes and kitchens.

Photography Credits

FRED BIRD: front and back covers; front flap; back flap (bottom); title page; contents page (top, bottom left and bottom right photos); pages 8, 9, 11, 12, 15, 17, 18, 19, 21, 23, 25, 26, 29, 31, 33, 37, 39, 40, 43, 45, 47, 49, 50, 53, 61, 63, 64, 67, 69, 70, 73, 79, 81, 82, 83, 85, 87, 89, 91, 92, 93, 97, 98, 99, 101, 105, 109, 111, 113, 115, 117, 118, 121, 122, 125, 126, 127, 129, 131, 134, 136, 137, 138, 141, 147, 149, 151, 153, 155, 157, 158, 159, 160, 161, 162, 163, 164, 165, 168, 169, 173, 174, 176, 177, 178, 179.

CHRISTOPHER CAMPBELL: pages 34, 94 and 142.
FRANK GRANT: photo of Elizabeth Baird on back flap and on page 6; pages 42, 72, 75, 96, 167, 192.
JOHN STEPHENS: page 103.
MIKE VISSER: page 57.
ROBERT WIGINGTON: contents page (center photo, bottom row); page 145.
STANLEY WONG: page 106.

Special Thanks

A warm word of thanks goes out to all the people who have made DESSERTS the beautiful, workable and luscious-looking book it is. First accolades go to the contributing food writers who have created many of the fine recipes in the book. Their names and accomplishments are listed above. A very special thank-you goes to the *Canadian Living* Test Kitchen. Our manager, Daphna Rabinovitch, came to us two years ago, already well-known in Toronto as a premier pastry chef. She has lent sparkle and taste to the Test Kitchen and has streamlined techniques for the many dessert recipes that have been developed there. Besides testing all the recipes until we at *Canadian Living* are sure they'll work perfectly for you every time, Daphna and her team — Vicki Burns, Janet Cornish, Heather Howe and Ruth Phelan — have also contributed recipes to this book as food writers.

Not to be forgotten are the behind-the-scenes editors who

check and recheck, polish and repolish every word. On a regular basis, these tasks of exactitude fall to Susan Lawrence and Beverley Renahan, senior editors at *Canadian Living* magazine. For DESSERTS, Beverley Renahan has had the additional task of yet another edit and polish. Credit is due to both Carol Ferguson and Margaret Fraser who created the original *Canadian Living* recipe standards.

Wanda Nowakowska is the wizard project editor from Madison Press whose amazing perseverance, attention to detail and optimism have added much to the creation of DESSERTS. It's to her credit that she still enjoys an apple pie.

Thanks, too, go to Helen Gougeon, originator many years ago of the Bite-Size Lemon Tarts and Fresh Blueberry Tart; Monica Gray, for her fabulous Mocha Shortbread Bars; plus chefs Mark McEwan, Mark Bussieres and Lucia Ruggiero, whose desserts enhance this book.

Index

RECIPES BY CONTRIBUTOR

For your easy reference, we have included a listing of recipes by contributor — organized alphabetically, with a page reference.

ELIZABETH BAIRD

Almond and Red Currant Pie, 78
Apple Filling, 150
Berry Cream Chocolate Tarts, 95
Berry Crisp Pie, 80
Chocolate Date and Nut Loaf, 59
Chocolate-Dipped Strawberries, 149
Classic Cream Puffs, 100
Classic Nanaimo Bars, 170
Country-Style Apple Pie, 78
Down-Home Seeded Raisin Pie, 76
Easy Rhubarb and
     Strawberry Ice, 115
Fluffy Icing, 161
Four-Berry Summer Pudding, 110
Fresh Blueberry Tart, 94
Frozen Profiteroles with Chocolate
     Rum Sauce, 100
Glazed Nutty Fruitcake, 64
Grand Marnier Nanaimo Bars, 170
Gratin of Red Fruits with
     Honey Ice Cream, 148
Lemon Almond Pound Cake, 58
Lightened Lemon-Yogurt
     Coffee Cake, 54
Making and Shaping Choux
     Pastry, 99
Mocha Shortbread Bars, 162
No-Bake Apricot Coconut Balls, 165
Orange Custard Sauce, 135
Orange Pecan Cake, 57
Paris-Brest, 101
Peach Pie with Peach Coulis, 74

Perfect Pastry Every Time, 71
Plum Tart, 93
Prizewinning Sour Cherry Pie, 73
Raisin-Date Squares, 172
Raspberry Custard Squares, 111
Sponge Cake, 123
Strawberry Cream Layers, 96
Strawberry Meringue Kisses, 155
Sugar Cookie Cutouts, 161
Three-Fruit Pudding, 135
Tiramisu, 123
Winter Fruit Bowl, 144

FRANK BALDOCK

Beaujolais Baked Apples, 144

VICKI BURNS

Honey Spice Cookies, 156

JAMES CHATTO

Orange Stewed Rhubarb, 149

JANET CORNISH

Cointreau Coffee Custard, 143
Lunchbox Granola Bars, 172

KATHLEEN CROWLEY

French Toast Pudding, 134

CAROL FERGUSON

Best-Ever Chocolate Chip
     Cookies, 158
Floating Islands on Lemon
     Cream, 106
Lemon Meringue Pie, 81

JEREMY FERGUSON

Vanilla Soufflés with Strawberry
     Coulis, 140

MARGARET FRASER

Apricot Purée, 36
Brownie Miniatures, 179
Chocolate Icebox Cake, 51
Chocolate-Dipped Bars, 169
Chocolate-Flecked Angel
     Food Cake, 34
Coconut Thumbprints, 168
Dress-Up Cupcakes, 43
Fast Chocolate Sauce, 18
Fat Teddies, 165
Meringue Christmas Wreaths, 169
No-Bake Pumpkin Cream Pie, 84
Orange Gateau Breton, 58
Peach Cream Roll, 60
Strawberry Meringue Custard Pie, 86
Tangerine Sponge Pudding, 130
Truffle Mice, 169
Windblown Cake, 36

HEATHER HOWE

Cantaloupe Frozen Yogurt, 118
Crispy Squares, 175
Fruity Frozen Yogurt, 118
Peach Frozen Yogurt, 118
Peanut Butter Squares, 175
Raspberry Frozen Yogurt, 118
Rocky Road Squares, 175
Strawberry Frozen Yogurt, 118

PATRICIA JAMIESON

Bittersweet Chocolate Orange
     Ice Cream, 114
Carrot Wedding Cake, 30
Cherry Clafouti, 132
Chocolate Icing, 28
Chocolate Leaves, 29
Chocolate Roses, 28
Chocolate Wedding Cake, 28
Cream Cheese Icing, 30

Peach Ice Cream, 116
Simply the Best Vanilla
 Ice Cream, 112

ANNE LINDSAY
Apple Pecan Phyllo Crisps, 98
Apricot Squares, 173
Chocolate Crêpes with Banana
 Filling, 151
Hazelnut Mocha Torte, 52
Lemon Raisin Bundt Cake, 54
Nectarine and Orange Compote, 150

JAN MAIN
Apple Meringue Pudding, 133

BETH MOFFATT
Chocolate Cassata Cake, 24

ROSE MURRAY
Apple and Mincemeat Crumble, 138
Brandied Mincemeat Ring, 65
Chocolate Peppermint Pinwheels, 160
Coffee Drops with Mocha Glaze, 157
Dark Chocolate Sauce, 112
Gooey Caramel Sauce, 112
Pan Shortbread Bars, 163
Raspberry Sauce, 112
Rolled Shortbread Cookies, 163
Shortbread, 163
Spritz Cookies, 162
Strawberry Creamy Hearts, 107
Strawberry Purée, 107
Warm Rhubarb Cheesecake Pie, 76
White Chocolate Almond Bark, 179

MARIE NIGHTINGALE
Chocolate Chestnut Eclairs, 102

RUTH PHELAN
Decorator Icing, 166
Ginger Tree Ornaments, 166

DAPHNA RABINOVITCH
Banana Spice Cake, 35
Black Currant Mousse Cake, 13
Blueberry Cinnamon Coffee Cake, 56
Cappucino Cream, 107

Christmas Pavlova, 46
Coffee Toffee Fudge Cake, 22
Fudgy Hanukkah Cake, 26
Lemon Mousse Cheesecake, 11
Light Cranberry Cheesecake, 10
Mandarin Trifle, 124
Maple Walnut Tart, 92
Raspberry Mousse Cake, 13

IRIS RAVEN
Canary Pudding with Pear Sauce, 128
Caramel-Topped Pear Pie, 80
Chocolate Pecan Bars, 171
Fresh Plum Macaroon Squares, 174
Golden Fruit Pound Cakes, 59
Orange Fudge Pudding with Rum
 Sauce, 131
Snow Pudding with Tropical Fruit
 Sauce, 130

DUFFLET ROSENBERG
Caramel Peaches with
 Mascarpone, 143
Peach Crumble with Ginger, 138
Peach Mousse Parfait with
 Berries, 119

KAY SPICER
Warm Orange Sauce, 35

EDNA STAEBLER
Hot Chocolate Pudding, 131

LINDA STEPHEN
Banana Split Roll, 63

BONNIE STERN
Amaretto Almond Charlotte, 110
Bread Pudding with Rye Whisky
 Sauce, 134
Celebration Ice Cream Cake, 51
Chocolate Apricot Mousse Cake, 14
Chocolate Cake with Candied
 Orange and Ginger, 27
Chocolate Chestnut Torte, 16
Florentines, 161
Frozen Lemon Meringue Torte, 48
Honey Hazelnut Roulade, 62

Italian Fruited Rice Cake, 41
Margarita Fruit Salad, 145
Mixed Berry Crisp, 139
Poached Pears with Brandied
 Cheese, 148
Fruit-Poached Pears, 148
Raspberry Truffle Trifle, 126

LUCY WAVERMAN
Divine Chocolate Brownies, 170
Meringues on Apricot Coulis, 47

CAROL WHITE
Frozen Hazelnut Cream Torte, 50
Ice Cream Sundae Pie, 89

**CANADIAN LIVING TEST
KITCHEN**
Almond Brittle, 178
Almond Cookie Shells, 116
Almond Praline Semifreddo, 115
Amaretto Cream Sauce, 17
Apple Strudel, 97
Banana Cream Pie, 84
Bite-Size Lemon Tarts, 94
Black Currant Mousse, 120
Caramel Pecan Squares, 175
Cheese Strudel, 97
Chocolate Banana Layer Cake, 20
Chocolate Cream Meringue Cake, 44
Chocolate Cupcake Cones, 42
Chocolate Fondue, 149
Chocolate Orange Truffles, 176
Chocolate Truffles, 176
Chocolate-Drizzled Cookie Shells, 116
Chocolate-Drizzled Nut Brittle, 178
Christmas Plum Pudding, 136
Citrus Angel Food Cake, 34
Citrus Curd Sauce, 149
Classic Angel Food Cake, 34
Classic Crème Caramel, 104
Classic Strawberry Shortcake, 40
Coconut Cream Pie, 84
Cranberry Apple Crisp, 139
Cranberry Coffee Cake, 55
Creamy Maple Pecan Yule Log, 66
Crème Pâtissière, 101
Crunchy Pecan Pie, 68

Dessert Crêpes, 150

Double Whammy Chocolate
    Cream Pie, 88

Easy Orange Dacquoise, 44

Easy Rhubarb Strudel, 97

Extra-Peanutty Peanut Butter
    Cookies, 158

Four-Layer Chocolate Cake, 17

Fruited Ricotta Charlotte, 108

Fruity Cheesecake Trifle, 127

Greek Shortbread, 154

Harvest Pumpkin Pie, 82

Hazelnut Truffles, 176

Honey Pumpkin Pie, 82

Hot Fudge Soufflé, 141

Layered Wedding Diamonds, 152

Lemon and Lime Soufflé, 122

Lemon Cookies, 164

Microwave Chocolate Cake, 23

Mincemeat Strudel, 97

Mocha Cream Meringue Cake, 44

Mocha Marble Cheesecake, 8

No-Regrets Double Chocolate
    Cake, 19

Old-Time Butter Tarts, 95

Orange Caramel Custard, 104

Orange Hard Sauce, 136

Orange-Blossom Cookie Shells, 116

Peanut Brittle, 178

Peanut Butter Melts, 179

Pear and Raspberry Cobbler, 133

Pecan Brittle, 178

Pecan Meringue Mushrooms, 67

Perfect Double-Crust Fruit Pies, 77

Perfect Processor Pastry, 71

Plenty of Applesauce Bars, 171

Raspberry Mousse, 120

Raspberry Mousse Pie, 85

Reverse Chocolate Chip Cookies, 158

Rhubarb Crisp, 139

Rhubarb Mousse, 120

Saucy Poached Pears, 146

Snacking Honey Spice Cake, 56

Strawberry Buttercream Cake, 32

Strawberry Mousse, 120

Strawberry Rhubarb Pie, 74

Summer Berry Tart, 90

Summer Fruit Flan, 38

Tiny Tangerine Cheesecakes, 10

True Love Hearts, 154

Tulip Cookie Shells, 116

Warm Saskatoon Pudding, 132

White Chocolate Petits Fours, 41

A

Almonds

Amaretto Charlotte, 110

Amaretto Cream Sauce, 17

and Red Currant Pie, 78

Brittle, 178

Cookie Shells, 116

Lemon Pound Cake, 58

Liqueur, 119

Praline Semifreddo, 115

White Chocolate Bark, 179

Amaretto

Almond Charlotte, 110

Cream Sauce, 17

Liqueur, 119

Angel Food Cakes

Chocolate-Flecked, 34

Citrus, 34

Classic, 34

Apples

and Mincemeat Crumble, 138

Beaujolais Baked, 144

Country-Style Pie, 78

Cranberry Crisp, 139

Double-Crust Pie, 77

Filling for Crêpes, 150

for Baking, 78

Meringue Pudding, 133

Pecan Phyllo Crisps, 98

Plenty of Applesauce Bars, 171

Strudel, 97

Apricots

Brandy, 119

Chocolate Mousse Cake, 14

Meringues, on Coulis, 47

No-Bake Coconut Balls, 165

Purée, 36

Squares, 173

B

Baked Apples

Beaujolais, 144

Bananas

Banana Split Roll, 63

Chocolate Crêpes, with Filling, 151

Chocolate Layer Cake, 20

Cream Pie, 84

Make-your-own Banana Splits, 42

Selecting, 35

Spice Cake, 35

Bars and Squares

Apricot, 173

Baking, 172

Caramel Pecan, 175

Chocolate Pecan, 171

Classic Nanaimo, 170

Crispy, 175

Divine Chocolate Brownies, 170

Fresh Plum Macaroon, 174

Grand Marnier Nanaimo, 170

Lunchbox Granola, 172

Mocha, 162

Pan Shortbread, 163

Peanut Butter, 175

Plenty of Applesauce, 171

Raisin-Date, 172

Raspberry Custard, 111

Rocky Road, 175

Black Currants

Liqueur, 119

Mousse, 120

Mousse Cake, 13

Purée, 13

Blackberries

Berry Cream Chocolate Tarts, 95

Four-Berry Summer Pudding, 110

Liqueur, 119

Blueberries
Berry Crisp Pie, 80
Cinnamon Coffee Cake, 56
Double-Crust Pie, 77
Four-Berry Summer Pudding, 110
Fresh Tart, 94
Shortcake, 40
Summer Berry Tart, 90
Bread Pudding
French Toast, 134
with Rye Whisky Sauce, 134
Brittle
Almond, 178
Chocolate-Drizzled Nut, 178
Peanut, 178
Pecan, 178
Brownies
Divine, 170
Miniatures, 179
Butter Tarts
Old-Time, 95
Buttermilk
Substitution, 133

C

CAKES
Black Currant Mousse, 13
Italian Fruited Rice, 41
Lemon Raisin Bundt, 54
Orange Gateau Breton, 58
Orange Pecan, 57
Raspberry Mousse, 13
Snacking Honey Spice, 56
Sponge, 123
Strawberry Buttercream, 32
Summer Fruit Flan, 38
Sweet Table, 155
Windblown, 36
Angel Food
Chocolate-Flecked, 34
Citrus, 34
Classic, 34
Baking
Adding Ingredients, 12
Baking Powder, 55
Basics, 12

Baking Soda, 55
Foam Cakes, 36
High-Altitude Baking, 62
Lining Pans, 12, 22
Measuring, 12, 65
Meringues, 44, 47, 48
Sifting, 36
Substitutions, 46
Sugar, 60
Banana
Banana Split Roll, 63
Chocolate Layer, 20
Spice, 35
Cheesecakes
Lemon Mousse, 11
Light Cranberry, 10
Mocha Marble, 8
Tiny Tangerine, 10
Chocolate
Apricot Mousse, 14
Banana Layer, 20
Cassata, 24
Chestnut Torte, 16
Coffee Toffee Fudge, 22
Cream Meringue, 44
Cupcake Cones, 42
Date and Nut Loaf, 59
Flecked Angel Food, 34
Four-Layer, 17
Fudgy Hanukkah, 26
Icebox, 51
Microwave, 23
No-Regrets Double Chocolate, 19
Wedding, 28
White Chocolate Petits Fours, 41
with Candied Orange and Ginger, 27
Christmas
Brandied Mincemeat Ring, 65
Creamy Maple Pecan Yule Log, 66
Glazed Nutty Fruitcake, 64
Golden Fruit Pound, 59
Pavlova, 46
Coffee
Blueberry Cinnamon, 56
Cranberry, 55
Lightened Lemon-Yogurt, 54
Cupcakes
Chocolate Cones, 42

Dress-Up, 43
Easter Bunny, 43
Flowerpot, 43
Frozen
Celebration Ice Cream, 51
Hazelnut Cream Torte, 50
Lemon Meringue Torte, 48
Fruit
Brandied Mincemeat Ring, 65
Glazed Nutty Fruitcake, 64
Golden Pound, 59
Meringue
Chocolate Cream, 44
Christmas Pavlova, 46
Easy Orange Dacquoise, 44
Frozen Hazelnut Cream, 50
Frozen Lemon, 48
Mocha Cream, 44
Pound
Chocolate Date and Nut, 59
Golden Fruit, 59
Lemon Almond, 58
Rolls
Banana Split, 63
Creamy Maple Pecan Yule Log, 66
Honey Hazelnut Roulade, 62
Peach Cream, 60
Sauces
Amaretto Cream, 17
Apricot Purée, 36
Warm Orange, 35
Shortcakes
Blueberry, 40
Classic Strawberry, 40
Peach, 40
Raspberry, 40
Tortes
Chocolate Chestnut, 16
Frozen Hazelnut Cream, 50
Frozen Lemon Meringue, 48
Hazelnut Mocha, 52
Wedding
Carrot, 30
Chocolate, 28

Cantaloupe
Frozen Yogurt, 118

Caramel
Classic Crème Caramel, 104
Gooey Sauce, 112
Orange Custard, 104
Peaches with Mascarpone, 143
Pecan Squares, 175
Pear Pie, 80
Carrot
Wedding Cake, 30
Charlottes
Amaretto Almond, 110
Fruited Ricotta, 108
Cheese. *See also* **Mascarpone**
and **Ricotta**.
Cream Icing, 30
Quark, 107
Strawberry Creamy Hearts, 107
Strudel, 97
Cheesecakes
Baking, 8
Fruity Trifle, 127
Lemon Mousse, 11
Light Cranberry, 10
Mocha Marble, 8
Tiny Tangerine, 10
Warm Rhubarb Cheesecake Pie, 76
Cherries
Clafouti, 132
Prizewinning Sour Cherry Pie, 73
Chestnuts
Chocolate Eclairs, 102
Chocolate Torte, 16
Selecting, 102

CHOCOLATE
Brownie Miniatures, 179
Crêpes with Banana Filling, 151
Dipped Strawberries, 149
Drizzled Cookie Shells, 116
Drizzled Nut Brittle, 178
Fondue, 149
Hot Fudge Soufflé, 141
Icing, 28
Melting, 18
Orange Truffles, 176
Peanut Butter Melts, 179
Storing, 18
Truffle Mice, 169

Truffles, 176
Types, 18
White Chocolate Almond Bark, 179
Cakes
Apricot Mousse, 14
Banana Layer, 20
Cassata, 24
Chestnut Torte, 16
Coffee Toffee Fudge, 22
Cream Meringue, 44
Cupcake Cones, 42
Date and Nut Loaf, 59
Flecked Angel Food, 34
Four-Layer, 17
Fudgy Hanukkah, 26
Icebox, 51
Microwave, 23
No-Regrets Double Chocolate, 19
Wedding, 28
White Chocolate Petits Fours, 41
with Candied Orange and Ginger, 27
Cookies
Best-Ever Chocolate Chip, 158
Dipped Bars, 169
Divine Brownies, 170
Fat Teddies, 165
Layered Wedding Diamonds, 152
Pecan Bars, 171
Peppermint Pinwheels, 160
Reverse Chocolate Chip, 158
Garnishes
Curls, 27
Leaves, 29
Roses, 28
Silhouettes, 123
White Chocolate Hearts, 23
Ice Cream
Bittersweet Orange, 114
Pastry
Berry Cream Tarts, 95
Chestnut Eclairs, 102
Double Whammy Cream Pie, 88
Puddings
Hot, 131
Orange Fudge, with Rum Sauce, 131
Sauces
Dark Chocolate, 112
Fast, 18

Choux Pastry
Chocolate Chestnut Eclairs, 102
Classic Cream Puffs, 100
Cream Puffs, 99
Crème Pâtissière, 101
Frozen Profiteroles, 100
Glazing, 100
Making and Shaping, 99
Paris-Brest, 101
Paris-Brest Ring, 99
Profiteroles, 99

CHRISTMAS
Apple and Mincemeat Crumble, 138
Brandied Mincemeat Ring, 65
Creamy Maple Pecan Yule Log, 66
Ginger Tree Ornaments, 166
Glazed Nutty Fruitcake, 64
Golden Fruit Pound, 59
Meringue Wreaths, 169
Microwave Shortcuts for
Puddings, 135
Mincemeat Strudel, 97
Orange Custard Sauce, 135
Orange Hard Sauce, 136
Pavlova, 46
Plum Pudding, 136
Shortbread, 163
Three-Fruit Pudding, 135

Cobblers
Pear and Raspberry, 133
Coconut
Cream Pie, 84
No-Bake Apricot Balls, 165
Thumbprints, 168
Toasting, 84
Coffee
Cappuccino Cream, 107
Cointreau Custard, 143
Drops with Mocha Glaze, 157
Toffee Fudge Cake, 22
Coffee Cakes
Blueberry Cinnamon, 56
Cranberry, 55
Lightened Lemon-Yogurt, 54
Compotes
Nectarine and Orange, 150

COOKIES

Almond Shells, 116

Chocolate-Drizzled Shells, 116

Honey Spice, 156

Lemon, 164

No-Bake Apricot Coconut Balls, 165

Orange-Blossom Shells, 116

Spicy Orange Ginger, 164

Spritz, 162

Strawberry Meringue Kisses, 155

Sugar Cookie Cutouts, 161

Sweet Table, 155

True Love Hearts, 154

Tulip Shells, 116

Baking

Baking Sheets, 159

Basics, 159

Freezing, 159

Measuring, 65

Storing, 159

Substitutions, 46

Sugar, 60

Bars and Squares

Apricot, 173

Baking, 172

Caramel Pecan, 175

Chocolate Pecan, 171

Classic Nanaimo, 170

Crispy, 175

Divine Chocolate Brownies, 170

Fresh Plum Macaroon, 174

Grand Marnier Nanaimo, 170

Lunchbox Granola, 172

Mocha Shortbread, 163

Pan Shortbread, 163

Peanut Butter, 175

Plenty of Applesauce, 171

Raisin-Date, 172

Rocky Road, 175

Chocolate

Best-Ever Chocolate Chip, 158

Dipped Bars, 169

Fat Teddies, 165

Layered Wedding Diamonds, 152

Peppermint Pinwheels, 160

Reverse Chocolate Chip, 158

Christmas

Chocolate-Dipped Bars, 169

Coconut Thumbprints, 168

Ginger Tree Ornaments, 166

Meringue Wreaths, 169

Shortbread, 163

Drop

Best-Ever Chocolate Chip, 158

Coffee Drops with Mocha Glaze, 157

Florentines, 161

Reverse Chocolate Chip, 155

Spice Crispies, 157

Peanut Butter

Extra-Peanutty Peanut Butter, 158

Fat Teddies, 165

Shortbread

Greek, 154

Mocha Bars, 162

Moulded, 163

Pan Bars, 163

Rolled, 163

Cranberries

Apple Crisp, 139

Coffee Cake, 55

Light Cheesecake, 10

Crème Caramel

Classic, 104

Orange Custard, 104

Crème Fraîche, 144

Crème Pâtissière, 101

Crêpes

Apple Filling, 150

Chocolate, with Banana Filling, 151

Dessert, 150

Storing, 150

Crisps

Cranberry Apple, 139

Mixed Berry, 139

Rhubarb, 139

Crumbles

Apple and Mincemeat, 138

Peach, with Ginger, 138

Cupcakes

Chocolate Cones, 42

Dress-Up, 43

Easter Bunny, 43

Flowerpot, 43

Custard

Cherry Clafouti, 132

Classic Crème Caramel, 104

Cointreau Coffee, 143

Crème Pâtissière, 101

Orange Caramel, 104

Orange Sauce, 135

Raspberry Squares, 111

Strawberry Meringue Pie, 86

D

Dacquoise

Chocolate Cream, 44

Easy Orange, 44

Mocha Cream, 44

Dates

Chocolate Nut Loaf, 59

Raisin Squares, 172

E

Eclairs

Chocolate Chestnut, 102

Eggs

Beating Whites, 140

Storing, 140

What to do with Half an Egg, 140

F

Flans

Summer Fruit, 38

Flowers

Chocolate Roses, 28

Garnishing, 16

Fondue

Chocolate, 149

Frozen Yogurt

Cantaloupe, 118

Fruity, 118

Pan-Freezing, 118

Peach, 118

Raspberry, 118

Strawberry, 118

FRUIT. *See also* Names of Fruit.
Chocolate Fondue, 149
Dried, 144
Gratin of Red Fruits, 148
Margarita Salad, 145
Ricotta Charlotte, 108
Summer Flan, 38
Sweet Table, 155
Winter Fruit Bowl, 144
Sauces
Amaretto Cream, 17
Citrus Curd, 149
Cointreau Coffee Custard, 143
Crème Fraîche, 144
Fruitcakes
Brandied Mincemeat Ring, 65
Glazed Nutty, 64
Golden Pound, 59

G

Garnishes
Candied Lemon, 11
Chocolate Curls, 27
Chocolate Leaves, 29
Chocolate Roses, 28
Chocolate Silhouettes, 123
Flowers, 16
Frosted Grapes, 127
Nuts, 51
Pecan Meringue Mushrooms, 67
Punch Bowls, 32
White Chocolate Hearts, 23
Granola
Lunchbox Bars, 172
Grapes
Frosted, 127

H

Hazelnuts
Frozen Cream Torte, 50
Honey Roulade, 62
Mocha Torte, 52
True Love Hearts, 154
Truffles, 176

Honey
Hazelnut Roulade, 62
Measuring, 56
Pumpkin Pie, 82
Snacking Spice Cake, 56
Spice Cookies, 156

I

Ice Cream and Ices. *See also* **Frozen Yogurt**.
Almond Cookie Shells, 116
Almond Praline Semifreddo, 115
Bittersweet Chocolate Orange, 114
Celebration Cake, 51
Chocolate-Drizzled Cookie
    Shells, 116
Easy Rhubarb and Strawberry, 115
Make-your-own Banana Splits, 42
Make-your-own Sundaes, 112
Making, 114
Orange-Blossom Cookie Shells, 116
Peach, 116
Simply the Best Vanilla, 112
Sundae Pie, 89
Tulip Cookie Shells, 116
Sauces
Dark Chocolate, 112
Fast Chocolate, 18
Gooey Caramel, 112
Raspberry, 112
Icing
Chocolate, 28
Cream Cheese, 30
Decorator, 166
Fluffy, 161
Smoothing, 30

K

Kids
Chocolate Cupcake Cones, 42
Crispy Squares, 175
Dress-Up Cupcakes, 43
Easter Bunny Cupcakes, 43
Fat Teddies, 165

Flowerpot Cupcakes, 43
French Toast Pudding, 134
Ginger Tree Ornaments, 166
Hot Chocolate Pudding, 131
Lunchbox Granola Bars, 172
Make-your-own Banana Splits, 42
Peanut Butter Squares, 175
Rocky Road Squares, 175
Sugar Cookie Cutouts, 161

L

Lemon
Almond Pound Cake, 58
and Lime Soufflé, 122
Bite-Size Tarts, 94
Candied, 11
Citrus Angel Food Cake, 34
Cookies, 164
Floating Islands on Lemon
    Cream, 106
Frozen Meringue Torte, 48
Grating Rind, 122
Juice, 106
Lightened Yogurt Coffee Cake, 54
Meringue Pie, 81
Mousse Cheesecake, 11
Perfect Pie Filling, 81
Raisin Bundt Cake, 54
Lime
and Lemon Soufflé, 122
Citrus Angel Food Cake, 34
Grating Rind, 122
Liqueurs and Fruit Spirits, 119

M

Mandarins
Trifle, 124
Mascarpone
Caramel Peaches, 143
Tiramisu, 123
Meringues
Apple Pudding, 133
Baking, 44, 47
Beating Egg Whites, 140

Chocolate Cream Cake, 44
Christmas Pavlova, 46
Christmas Wreaths, 169
Easy Orange Dacquoise, 44
Floating Islands on Lemon
    Cream, 106
Frozen Hazelnut Cream Torte, 50
Frozen Lemon Torte, 48
Lemon Pie, 81
Making, 48
Mocha Cream Cake, 44
on Apricot Coulis, 47
Pecan Mushrooms, 67
Shaping, 45, 47
Strawberry Custard Pie, 86
Strawberry Kisses, 155
Mincemeat
and Apple Crumble, 138
Brandied Ring, 65
Strudel, 97

Mocha
Bars, 162
Cream Meringue Cake, 44
Hazelnut Torte, 52
Marble Cheesecake, 8
Mousses
Amaretto Almond Charlotte, 110
Black Currant, 120
Black Currant Cake, 13
Fruited Ricotta Charlotte, 108
Chocolate Apricot Cake, 14
Lemon Cheesecake, 11
Peach Parfait with Berries, 119
Raspberry, 120
Raspberry Cake, 13
Raspberry Pie, 85
Rhubarb, 120
Setting and Moulding, 121
Strawberry, 120

Nanaimo Bars
Classic, 170
Grand Marnier, 170

Nectarines
and Orange Compote, 150
Nuts. *See also* **Almonds, Chestnuts,
Coconut, Hazelnuts, Peanuts, Pecans**
and **Walnuts**.
Chocolate Date Loaf, 59
Chocolate-Drizzled Brittle, 178
Liqueurs, 119
Toasting, 51

Oranges
and Nectarine Compote, 150
Bittersweet Chocolate
    Ice Cream, 114
Caramel Custard, 104
Chocolate Truffles, 176
Custard Sauce, 135
Easy Dacquoise, 44
Fudge Pudding with Rum Sauce, 131
Gateau Breton, 58
Liqueur, 119
Orange-Blossom Cookie Shells, 116
Pecan Cake, 57
Spicy Ginger Cookies, 164
Stewed Rhubarb, 149
Warm Sauce, 35

Parfaits
Cappuccino Cream, 107
Peach Mousse, with Berries, 119

PASTRY. *See also* **PIES** and **Tarts**.
Chilling, 72
Finishing Touches, 72
Glazing, 77
Make-Ahead, 72
Making, 70
Perfect Every Time, 71
Perfect Processor, 71
Pre-Baking Pie Shells, 92
Principles, 71
Rolling, 72

Choux
Chocolate Chestnut Eclairs, 102
Classic Cream Puffs, 100
Cream Puffs, 99
Frozen Profiteroles, 100
Glazing, 100
Making and Shaping, 99
Paris-Brest, 101
Paris-Brest Ring, 99
Profiteroles, 99
Phyllo
Apple Pecan Crisps, 98
Apple Strudel, 97
Buying and Using, 97
Cheese Strudel, 97
Easy Rhubarb Strudel, 97
Mincemeat Strudel, 97
Strawberry Cream Layers, 96

Pavlovas
Christmas, 46
Peaches
Buying, 143
Caramel, with Mascarpone, 143
Cream Roll, 60
Crumble with Ginger, 138
Double-Crust Pie, 77
Frozen Yogurt, 118
Ice Cream, 116
Mousse Parfait with Berries, 119
Peeling, 119, 143
Pie with Peach Coulis, 74
Shortcake, 40
Storing, 143
Peanut Butter
Extra-Peanutty Cookies, 158
Fat Teddies, 165
Melts, 179
Squares, 175
Peanuts
Brittle, 178
Pears
and Raspberry Cobbler, 133
Canary Pudding with Pear Sauce, 128
Caramel-Topped Pie, 80
Fruit-Poached, 148
Poached, with Brandied Cheese, 148
Saucy Poached, 146
Types, 146

Pecans

Apple Phyllo Crisps, 98

Brittle, 178

Caramel Squares, 175

Chocolate Bars, 171

Creamy Maple Yule Log, 66

Crunchy Pie, 68

Meringue Mushrooms, 67

Orange Cake, 57

Toasting, 51, 98

Petits Fours

White Chocolate, 41

Phyllo Pastry

Apple Pecan Crisps, 98

Apple Strudel, 97

Buying and Using, 97

Cheese Strudel, 97

Easy Rhubarb Strudel, 97

Mincemeat Strudel, 97

Strawberry Cream Layers, 96

PIES. *See also* **Tarts**.

Almond and Red Currant, 78

Apple, 77

Berry Crisp, 80

Blueberry, 77

Caramel-Topped Pear, 80

Country-Style Apple, 78

Crunchy Pecan, 68

Down-Home Seeded Raisin, 76

Freezing, 77

Ice Cream Sundae, 89

Lemon Meringue, 81

Peach, 77

Peach, with Peach Coulis, 74

Perfect Double-Crust Fruit, 77

Plum, 77

Prizewinning Sour Cherry, 73

Raspberry Mousse, 85

Raspberry, 77

Strawberry Meringue Custard, 86

Strawberry Rhubarb, 74

Warm Rhubarb Cheesecake, 76

Baking

Basics, 72

Making Pastry, 70

Measuring, 65

Pastry Principles, 71

Pie Plates, 88

Pre-Baking Pie Shells, 92

Substitutions, 46

Cream

Banana, 84

Coconut, 84

Double Whammy Chocolate, 88

No-Bake Pumpkin, 84

Pastry

Glazing, 77

Perfect Pastry Every Time, 71

Perfect Processor, 71

Principles, 71

Pumpkin

Harvest, 82

Honey, 82

No-Bake Cream, 84

Plum Puddings

Christmas, 136

Orange Hard Sauce, 136

Plums

Double-Crust Pie, 77

Fresh Macaroon Squares, 174

Selecting, 93

Tart, 93

PUDDINGS. *See also* **Cobblers,**
Crisps, Crumbles and **Soufflés**.

Four-Berry Summer, 110

Hot Chocolate, 131

Baked

Apple Meringue, 133

Cherry Clafouti, 132

Snow, with Tropical Fruit Sauce, 130

Tangerine Sponge, 130

Warm Saskatoon, 132

Bread

French Toast, 134

with Rye Whisky Sauce, 134

Christmas (Steamed)

Make-Ahead, 136

Microwave Shortcuts, 135

Orange Custard Sauce, 135

Orange Hard Sauce, 136

Plum, 136

Three-Fruit, 135

Steamed

Basics, 128

Canary, with Pear Sauce, 128

Orange Fudge, with Rum Sauce, 131

Pumpkin

Harvest Pie, 82

Honey Pie, 82

No-Bake Cream Pie, 84

Purées

Apricot, 36

Strawberry, 107

R

Raisin

Date Squares, 172

Down-Home Seeded Pie, 76

Lemon Bundt Cake, 54

Raspberries

and Pear Cobbler, 133

Berry Cream Chocolate Tarts, 95

Berry Crisp Pie, 80

Custard Squares, 111

Double-Crust Pie, 77

Four-Berry Summer Pudding, 110

Frozen Yogurt, 118

Gratin of Red Fruits, 148

Mousse, 120

Mousse Cake, 13

Mousse Pie, 85

Sauce, 112

Shortcake, 40

Summer Berry Tart, 90

Truffle Trifle, 126

Red Currants

and Almond Pie, 78

Rhubarb

and Strawberry Pie, 74

Crisp, 139

Easy Strawberry Ice, 115

Easy Strudel, 97

Mousse, 120

Orange Stewed, 149

Warm Cheesecake Pie, 76

Ricotta

Fruited Charlotte, 108

Fruity Cheesecake Trifle, 127

Rose Water, 154
Roses
  Chocolate, 28
  Garnishing with Fresh, 16

Saskatoon Berries
  Warm Pudding, 132
Sauces
  Amaretto Cream, 17
  Apricot Purée, 36
  Black Currant Purée, 13
  Citrus Curd, 149
  Cointreau Coffee Custard, 143
  Crème Fraîche, 144
  Dark Chocolate, 112
  Fast Chocolate, 18
  Gooey Caramel, 112
  Orange Custard, 135
  Orange Hard, 136
  Raspberry, 112
  Strawberry Purée, 107
  Warm Orange, 35
Semifreddo
  Almond Praline, 115
Shortbread
  Greek, 154
  Mocha Bars, 162
  Moulded, 163
  Pan Bars, 163
  Rolled, 163
Shortcakes
  Blueberry, 40
  Classic Strawberry, 40
  Peach, 40
  Raspberry, 40
Soufflés
  Hot Fudge, 141
  Lemon and Lime, 122
  Vanilla, with Strawberry Coulis, 140
Soured Milk
  Making, 133
Squares. *See* **Bars and Squares**.
Steamed Puddings
  Canary, with Pear Sauce, 128
  Christmas Plum, 136

  Making, 128
  Orange Fudge, with Rum Sauce, 131
  Three-Fruit, 135
Strawberries
  and Rhubarb Pie, 74
  Berry Cream Chocolate Tarts, 95
  Berry Crisp Pie, 80
  Buttercream Cake, 32
  Chocolate-Dipped, 149
  Classic Shortcake, 40
  Cleaning, 90
  Cream Layers, 96
  Creamy Hearts, 107
  Easy Rhubarb Ice, 115
  Four-Berry Summer Pudding, 110
  Freezing, 90
  Frozen Yogurt, 118
  Gratin of Red Fruits, 148
  Ice Ring, 32
  Meringue Custard Pie, 86
  Meringue Kisses, 155
  Mousse, 120
  Picking, 90
  Purée, 107
  Summer Berry Tart, 90
Strudels
  Apple, 97
  Cheese, 97
  Easy Rhubarb, 97
  Mincemeat, 97
Substitutions, 46
Sweet Table, 155

Tangerines
  Sponge Pudding, 130
  Tiny Cheesecakes, 10
Tarts
  Berry Cream Chocolate, 95
  Bite-Size Lemon, 94
  Old-Time Butter, 95
  Summer Berry, 90
Tarts (Large)
  Fresh Blueberry, 94
  Maple Walnut, 92
  Plum, 93

Tiramisu, 123
Tortes
  Chocolate Chestnut, 16
  Frozen Hazelnut Cream, 50
  Frozen Lemon Meringue, 48
  Hazelnut Mocha, 52
Trifles
  Fruity Cheesecake, 127
  Mandarin, 124
  Raspberry Truffle, 126
  Tiramisu, 123
Truffles
  Chocolate, 176
  Chocolate Orange, 176
  Hazelnut, 176
  Mice, 169
  Peanut Butter Melts, 179

Vanilla
  Ice Cream, 112
  Soufflés with Strawberry Coulis, 140

Walnuts
  Maple Walnut Tart, 92
Weddings
  Carrot Cake, 30
  Chocolate Cake, 28
  Cutting and Serving Cake, 30
  Sweet Table, 155

Yogurt
  Cantaloupe Frozen, 118
  Lightened Lemon Coffee Cake, 54
  Pan-Freezing, 118
  Peach Frozen, 118
  Raspberry Frozen, 118
  Strawberry Frozen, 118

Design, Typography and Art Direction:	Gordon Sibley Design Inc.
Editorial Director:	Hugh Brewster
Project Editor:	Wanda Nowakowska
Editorial Assistance:	Beverley Renahan Catherine Fraccaro
Production Director:	Susan Barrable
Production Assistance:	Donna Chong
Color Separation:	Colour Technologies
Printing and Binding:	Friesen Printers
Canadian Living Advisory Board:	Robert A. Murray Maureen Cavan Bonnie Baker Cowan Elizabeth Baird Anna Hobbs

Canadian Living's Desserts
*was produced by Madison Press Books
under the direction of Albert E. Cummings.*